MODERN BRITISH PLAYWRITING: THE 1970s

VOICES, DOCUMENTS, NEW INTERPRETATIONS

Chris Megson is Senior Lecturer in Drama and Theatre at Royal Holloway, University of London. He has taught and published widely in the field of modern drama, and is co-editor of *Get Real: Documentary Theatre Past and Present* and editor of *The Methuen Drama Book of Naturalist Plays* (Methuen Drama, 2010).

MODERN BRITISH PLAYWRITING: THE 1970s

VOICES, DOCUMENTS, NEW INTERPRETATIONS

Chris Megson

Series Editors: Richard Boon and Philip Roberts

Methuen Drama

Methuen Drama

1 3 5 7 9 10 8 6 4 2

First published in Great Britain in 2012 by Methuen Drama

Methuen Drama, an imprint of Bloomsbury Publishing Plc

Methuen Drama
Bloomsbury Publishing Plc
50 Bedford Square
London WC1B 3DP
www.methuendrama.com

Copyright © 2012 by Chris Megson

General Preface copyright © Richard Boon and Philip Roberts
'Caryl Churchill' copyright © 2012 by Paola Botham
'Howard Brenton' copyright © 2012 by Richard Boon
'David Edgar' copyright © 2012 by Janelle Reinelt

The rights of the authors to be identified as the editors of these works have been asserted
by them in accordance with the Copyright, Design and Patents Act, 1988

Paperback ISBN 978 1 408 12938 8
Hardback ISBN 978 1 408 18132 4

Available in the USA from Bloomsbury Academic & Professional, 175 Fifth Avenue /3rd
Floor, New York, NY 10010. www.BloomsburyAcademicUSA.com

A CIP catalogue record for this book is available from the British Library

Typeset by Mark Heslington Ltd, Scarborough, North Yorkshire
Printed and bound in the UK by MPG Books Ltd, Bodmin, Cornwall

CONTENTS

GENERAL PREFACE

This book is one of a series of six volumes which seek to characterise the nature of modern British playwriting from the 1950s to the end of the first decade of this new century. The work of these six decades is comparable in its range, experimentation and achievement only to the drama of the Elizabethan and Jacobean dramatists. The series chronicles its flowering and development.

Each volume addresses the work of four representative dramatists (five in the *2000–2009* volume) by focusing on key works and by placing that work in a detailed contextual account of the theatrical, social, political and cultural climate of the era.

The series revisits each decade from the perspective of the twenty-first century. We recognise that there is an inevitable danger of imposing a spurious neatness on its subject. So while each book focuses squarely on the particular decade and its representative authors, we have been careful to ensure that some account is given of relevant material from earlier years and, where relevant, of subsequent developments. And while the intentions and organisation of each volume are essentially the same, we have also allowed for flexibility, the better to allow both for the particular demands of the subject and the particular approach of our author/editors.

It is also the case, of course, that differences of historical perspective across the series influence the nature of the books. For student readers, the difference at its most extreme is between a present they daily inhabit and feel they know intimately and a decade (the 1950s) in which their parents or even grandparents might have been born; between a time of seemingly unlimited consumer choice and one which began with post-war food rationing still in place. Further, a playwright who began work in the late 1960s (David Hare, say) has a far bigger body of work and associated scholarship than one whose emergence has come within the last decade or so (debbie tucker green, for example). A glance at the Bibliographies for the earliest and latest volumes quickly reveals huge differences in the range of secondary material available to our authors and to our readers. This inevitably means that the later volumes allow a greater space to their contributing essayists for original research and scholarship, but we have also actively encouraged revisionist perspectives – new looks – on the 'older guard' in earlier books.

So while each book can and does stand alone, the series as a whole offers as coherent and comprehensive a view of the whole era as possible.

Throughout, we have had in mind two chief objectives. We have made accessible information and ideas that will enable today's students of theatre to acquaint themselves with the nature of the world inhabited by the playwrights of the last sixty years; and we offer new, original and often surprising perspectives on both established and developing dramatists.

Richard Boon and Philip Roberts
Series Editors
September 2011

Richard Boon is Professor of Drama and Director of Research at the University of Hull.

Philip Roberts is Emeritus Professor of Drama and Theatre Studies at the University of Leeds.

ACKNOWLEDGEMENTS

I am grateful to my three academic colleagues who have contributed their excellent essays to this volume: Paola Botham, Richard Boon and Janelle Reinelt. I'm deeply appreciative of their enthusiasm, expertise and critical rigour. I'd also like to thank Richard (once again) and Philip Roberts for their invitation to write for the Modern British Playwriting series and their invaluable help and guidance as series editors throughout the project. I'm indebted to Mark Dudgeon, Ross Fulton, Chris Parker and Neil Dowden at Methuen Drama, who have ensured a smooth and efficient publication process.

I would like to extend sincere thanks to Howard Barker, Ian Blower, Howard Brenton, David Edgar, David Gant, Tim Hardy, Barry Kyle, Peter McEnery, Ian McNeice, Ann Mitchell, Di Seymour, Mary Sheen and Kit Surrey for their time and generosity in contributing original material to this book. They are representatives of a theatrical generation of inspiring vitality and acumen. I'd also like to acknowledge with appreciation the late James Aubrey.

Thank you to the following for their practical assistance and/or conversation in the course of my research for this book: Steve Barfield, Colin Chambers, Susan Croft, Sir Richard Eyre, Lynette Goddard, Jennifer Megson, Vivi Mellegard, Kaori Nakayama, Helen Nicholson, Dan Rebellato and Graham Saunders. I am grateful to Royal Holloway College for granting me a term of sabbatical leave to write this book and to the Drama departmental research fund for help with costs.

I was born at the start of the 1970s and some of my earliest memories are of power cuts and candlelight, the heat wave of 1976 and the voice of Karen Carpenter, the theme tune from *The Wombles* and staying up late to watch *Starsky and Hutch* . . . the list goes on. This book is dedicated to my mum, dad and sister Nicola with whom I shared that great first decade.

INTRODUCTION: LIVING IN THE 1970s[1]

1. Domestic life

Things we bought

Pocket calculators, digital watches, Polaroid cameras, microwave ovens, lava lamps, trim phones, home-brew kits, fondue sets, Ford Cortinas, Mateus Rosé and Blue Nun wine, shag rugs, Portmeirion pottery, pet rocks, candy cigarettes, Space Hoppers, Matchbox toy cars, Sindy and Action Man dolls, Raleigh Chopper bicycles, Lego. Board games launched in the 1970s: Connect Four, Mastermind.

What things cost

In the early 1970s:

Loaf of bread: 9p	Two cinema tickets: 90p
Mini: £600	Range Rover (launched 1970): £2,000
Pint of lager: 20p	Pack of twenty cigarettes: 20p
Bottle of wine: £1	Bottle of whisky: £2.69
Average house price (1975): c. £10,500	Average weekly pocket money: 9p

Family life

People are living longer and more people are choosing to live alone. Life expectancy in 1970: 68.7 years for men and 75 years for women (by 2008, it is 77.8 years for men and 81.9 years for women). In 1970, there are 340,000 first marriages in England and Wales (143,000 in 2007). Average household size is 2.9 people, with one-person households comprising 18 per cent of the total (by 2009: average household size is 2.4 people, one-person households comprising 29 per cent of the total). In 1971, the proportion of babies born to women aged under twenty-five in England and Wales is 47 per cent (by 2008: 25 per cent).

In 1970, nearly half of all households in Britain have no regular use of a car. Food and non-alcoholic drinks form the largest category of household expenditure (by 2008: housing, water and fuel are the largest categories). In 1970, 55 per cent of men and 44 per cent of women smoke cigarettes and smoking is permitted in all public spaces from train carriages to offices. Health warnings appear on packets from 1973 as smoking begins its historic decline.

Work life

Average weekly wage in the early 1970s: £32. In 1979, the typical weekly wage for a manual worker is £90 in industry, £54 in the public sector. Median monthly disposable income falls from £202 in 1974 to £187 in 1977 due to the economic crisis.

In 1968, 43 per cent of British workers are trade union members; by 1979, the figure is 55 per cent. The number of shop stewards (workplace union organisers) quadruples in the decade: there are around 300,000 by 1975. By the mid-1970s, the Transport and General Workers' Union (TGWU), Britain's largest trade union, has two million members. In 1976, more than half of Britons regard Jack Jones, then leader of the TGWU, as the country's most powerful man.

2. Society

Crime

> The terrorist activity is worldwide and most of it is carried out by a new type in the history of political warfare: the urban guerrilla.
>
> – *Time* magazine, November 1970

Early in the decade, there is an explosion of left-wing terror groups, many of them comprising disaffected young radicals from the 1960s counterculture: the Weather Underground (US), the Palestinian 'Black September' group, the Tupamaros (Uruguay), the Baader-

Meinhof/Red Army Faction (West Germany), the Revolutionary Cells (West Germany), the Gauche Prolétarienne (France), the Red Army (Japan), the Red Brigades (Italy) and in the UK . . .

The Angry Brigade

A group of young anarchists launches a year-long bombing campaign from 1970. Targets include banks, embassies, army recruitment offices, the Imperial War Museum, the Biba boutique in Kensington and the residences of Conservative politicians including the Minister for Employment, Robert Carr. Following arrests, there is a lengthy trial at the Old Bailey and a massive police crackdown on the counterculture. Most members of the Brigade are middle class and university educated. One of those imprisoned, Jake Prescott, commented many years later: 'As the only working-class member, I was not surprised to be the first in and last out of prison. When I look back on it, I was the one who was angry and the people I met were more like the Slightly Cross Brigade.'

The heist of the decade: in 1971, robbers dig a tunnel into Lloyds Bank in London's Baker Street, clearing three million pounds of cash and valuables from deposit boxes.

John Poulson, a Yorkshire architect, businessman and Freemason, is convicted of large-scale corruption and bribery in 1974. His web of contacts stretches across Britain's political and civic establishment. The stink of corruption reaches the highest levels of government: Reginald Maudling, the Home Secretary (and former director of a Poulson company), resigns in 1972.

Serial killer Peter Sutcliffe, the 'Yorkshire Ripper', commits his first murder in 1975 and kills twelve more women before his arrest in 1981.

Feminism

In 1961, 42 per cent of women aged between twenty and sixty-four are in paid employment; by 1971, the figure is 52 per cent. During the 1970s, the decline in manufacturing, the rise of service industries, and the expansion of the public sector presents new opportunities for women but there is gender inequality in pay and opportunity.

1970: The first National Women's Liberation Conference is held at

Ruskin College, Oxford, with over 500 attendees. A number of pioneering feminist texts are published: Eva Figes's *Patriarchal Attitudes*, Germaine Greer's *The Female Eunuch* and Kate Millett's *Sexual Politics*. The Equal Pay Act is passed. In November, feminists invade the 'Miss World' contest presented by Bob Hope at the Royal Albert Hall in front of a mass television audience. The women throw bags of flour and scatter leaflets: 'We're not beautiful, we're not ugly. We're angry.' Annie Nightingale becomes the first female DJ on BBC Radio 1.

1971: International Women's Day provides a focus for burgeoning women's activism. The first women's refuge is established in Chiswick. The Wimpy burger chain lifts its ban on women entering its premises alone after midnight.

1972: Feminist magazines *Spare Rib* and *Red Rag* begin circulation; Gloria Steinem publishes the influential *Ms* in the US. Five Oxford colleges and the Jockey Club admit women for the first time. Nawal El Saadawi publishes *Women and Sex*, a ground-breaking critique of attitudes to women in Arab cultures.

1973: Stella Brummel, the manager of a concrete mixing company, is voted Britain's first Businesswoman of the Year. Women are allowed on to the floor of London's Stock Exchange for the first time. The US Supreme Court legalises women's right to abortion in the landmark *Roe v. Wade* case. Erica Jong's inspiring feminist novel *Fear of Flying* is published.

1974: Contraception becomes free on prescription to British women. Virago Press, the feminist publishers, is launched. The Working Women's Charter is published by the trade union movement.

1975: The United Nations (UN) declares 1975 'International Women's Year'. The Sex Discrimination Act, the Social Security Pensions Act and the Employment Protection Act are passed. The Equal Opportunities Commission (EOC) is founded. Jacqueline Tabbick becomes Britain's first woman rabbi.

1976: The Domestic Violence Act is passed. Anita Roddick opens the first Body Shop in Brighton.

1977: The first Rape Crisis Centre opens in London. Marilyn French publishes her novel *The Women's Room*.

1978: Women's self-help takes off with the publication of Susie Orbach's *Fat is a Feminist Issue*.

1979: Britain elects its first woman Prime Minister, Margaret Thatcher. An unprecedented number of women leaders take power in the 1970s including Sirimavo Bandaranaike (Sri Lanka, 1970), Isabel Martínez de Perón (Argentina, 1974) and Maria de Lourdes Pintasilgo (Portugal, 1979). Indira Gandhi is Prime Minister of India 1966–77.

Lesbian and gay liberation

Following the Stonewall Riots in 1969, the world's first Gay Pride march takes place in New York City in June 1970. In October, inspired by these events, the Gay Liberation Front (GLF) is founded at the London School of Economics (LSE). In November, Britain's first gay protest demonstration (against police harassment) is held by the GLF in Highbury Fields in London.

In 1971, GLF publishes its manifesto urging gay people to 'come out'. Members of GLF include Peter Tatchell and *Monty Python* star Graham Chapman: Chapman is one of the few British celebrities to 'come out' publicly in the 1970s (others include the Olympic ice skater John Curry and the singers Tom Robinson and Freddie Mercury); the only openly gay MP during the decade is Labour's Maureen Colquhoun.

The invasion of the 'Festival of Light'

In September 1971, GLF disrupts an evangelical rally organised by moral campaigner Mary Whitehouse at Westminster Central Hall. The 'Festival of Light' is a Christian movement that denounces the so-called 'permissive' society of the 1960s. GLF activists infiltrate the event (some of them disguised as nuns in costumes paid for by Chapman). Once inside, they release mice, clap hysterically at inopportune moments, brandish bananas and perform a conga down the central aisle.

GLF eventually splinters into smaller groups from 1972 and off-shoot organisations include the London Lesbian and Gay Switchboard (founded in 1974). *Gay News*, billed as the 'national homosexual newspaper', publishes its first issue to coincide with Britain's first official Gay Pride march in London on 1 July 1972.

In 1971, E. M. Forster's 'homosexual novel' *Maurice*, written in 1913–14, is published for the first time. In 1975, the TV adaptation of Quentin Crisp's autobiography *The Naked Civil Servant* wins a BAFTA for the actor John Hurt and his performance is the television highlight of the year. In 1976, Mary Whitehouse launches a private prosecution against *Gay News* and its editor Denis Lemon. She objects to the publication of a poem about a Roman centurion's love for Christ ('The Love That Dares to Speak Its Name', by Professor James Kirkup). At the Old Bailey, the judge invokes the 1697 Blasphemy Act, Lemon is given a suspended jail sentence and the paper is charged thousands of pounds in fines and costs. After the verdict, two socialist papers publish the poem in protest against censorship.

In 1976, the leader of the Liberal Party, Jeremy Thorpe, becomes embroiled in the decade's most sensational sex scandal and is eventually forced to resign. He stands trial for the attempted murder of Norman Scott, his alleged ex-lover. Thorpe is acquitted but the case is criticised for its pro-establishment bias.

Jeffrey Weeks publishes his pioneering history of homosexuality, *Coming Out*, in 1977. That year, Harvey Milk is elected the first openly gay city-council Supervisor in San Francisco – an inspiration for emerging gay communities around the world. He is assassinated, with Mayor George Moscone, in 1978.

Racism and the National Front (NF)

In 1967, the NF is founded by A. K. Chesterton, a former leading figure in the British Union of Fascists. Membership reaches 17,500 by 1972. In 1973, the NF wins nearly 5,000 votes in the West Bromwich by-election and contests enough parliamentary seats to be permitted a political broadcast on television in both general elections of 1974.

In east London, the trades council reports over one hundred racist incidents, including two murders, in an eighteen-month period from January 1976. In 1975–7, racially motivated crime increases by one-third across Britain and there are thirty-one racist murders of non-whites from 1976–81. In 1977, the NF begins recruiting in schools and lowers its minimum age of membership to fourteen. The anti-fascist magazine *Searchlight* is formed in 1975, the Anti-Nazi League (ANL) in 1977. The 1976 Notting Hill Carnival ends in riots with police and there are violent clashes with fascists in Lewisham and Birmingham. In 1979, riots erupt in Southall and Blair Peach, an ANL member, is killed after being assaulted by a police officer: 10,000 people flock to his funeral.

In 1971, Dilip Hiro publishes the first historical account of British race relations, *Black British, White British*. The controversial Immigration Act of that year ends primary immigration to Britain from the Commonwealth. However, levels of immigration follow a downward trend throughout the late 1970s: 55,000 in 1976, 44,000 in 1977, with further reductions each year (most immigrants are, in fact, relatives of British citizens). In 1976, one child in fourteen born in Britain has an immigrant mother (one in three in London).

Asian women are in the vanguard of industrial struggle throughout the decade. In 1972, staff at Mansfield Hosiery Mills in Loughborough protest at their treatment in relation to white workers. Two years later, workers at Imperial Typewriters in Leicester strike against poor treatment but win only small concessions. In 1976–8, the strike at Grunwick brings into focus the exploitation of migrant labour in Britain. The Race Relations Act (1976) builds on anti-discrimination legislation of the 1960s and establishes the Commission for Racial Equality (CRE). Institutional racism is endemic: in 1976, there are only seventy black officers in a police force of 22,000. Camden Council becomes one of the first local authorities in Britain to introduce practices of positive discrimination in 1978.

In January 1978, Conservative leader Margaret Thatcher makes an inflammatory remark on ITV's *World in Action*: 'People are really rather afraid that this country might be rather swamped by people with a different culture.' Her comments are widely condemned but the Conservatives attract voters away from the NF. In the general election of 1979, the NF vote drops by more than half from 1974 and the party is nearly bankrupted.

The 'blacking up' of white actors remains a staple feature of TV comedy during the 1970s, most notoriously in *The Black and White Minstrel Show* (which attracts primetime audiences of eighteen million viewers but finally ends its twenty-year run in 1978). The sitcoms *Mind Your Language* and *Love Thy Neighbour* trade in racial stereotypes in ways that would be unthinkable today. *Crossroads* becomes the first British soap to include a black family in 1974 and Lenny Henry stars in the first black British sitcom – *The Fosters* – in 1976. Few drama series address multicultural realities with some exceptions such as the BBC's *Gangsters* (1976) and *Empire Road* (1978). Beverly Johnson becomes the first black woman to feature on the cover of *Vogue* in 1974, Arthur Ashe is the first black man to win Wimbledon in 1975 and Viv Anderson becomes the first black footballer to play for England at international level in 1978. Hot Chocolate is the biggest-selling black British pop group of the decade.

'Rock Against Racism'

In April 1978, the 'Rock Against Racism' rally is held in Trafalgar Square followed by a concert in Victoria Park. Its purpose is to support anti-fascist activism, condemn the singer David Bowie's flirtation with fascist iconography and protest against remarks reportedly made by British rock star Eric Clapton during a concert in 1976 when he drunkenly endorsed the racist views of the politician Enoch Powell: 'Keep Britain white!' Up to 100,000 people attend 'Rock Against Racism' and the event sows the seeds for the emergence of protest pop and Live Aid seven years later.

The environment

The decade is marked by increasing environmental activism as well as eco-paranoia.

The year 1970 is designated European Conservation Year and Earth Day is marked for the first time. The Environmental Protection Agency and the Department of the Environment are formed in the US and Britain, respectively. In 1972, the world's first UN Environment Summit takes place in Stockholm and the United Nations Environment Programme (UNEP) is set up to address growing concerns about overpopulation and food. Greenpeace and the British wing of Friends of the Earth are established in 1971;

the PEOPLE Party, Britain's first green political party, is founded in 1973.

Hal Lindsey and Carole C. Carlson's apocalyptic *Late, Great Planet Earth*, Gordon Rattray Taylor's *The Doomsday Book* (which predicts global warming) and Britain's first environmental magazine, *The Ecologist*, appear in 1970. Spinoffs from *The Ecologist – Can Britain Survive?* (1971) and *A Blueprint for Survival* (1972) – become best-sellers while a 1972 report from the high-powered Club of Rome, *The Limits to Growth*, sells four million copies.

E. F. Schumacher's *Small is Beautiful* (1973) advocates a return to a simpler, more natural life (it carries the wry subtitle: *Economics as if People Mattered*). The back-to-basics Campaign for Real Ale is founded in 1971 and John Seymour's *Complete Book of Self-Sufficiency* (1975) sells over one million copies. The popular BBC drama *Doomwatch*, about a government agency dealing with eco-crises, runs during 1970–2 while the eco-friendly sitcom *The Good Life* begins in 1975. Richard Adams's poignant *Watership Down* is published in 1972.

Natural and human-made disasters bring environmental issues to the fore throughout the 1970s. The century's worst cyclone disaster, in the Ganges delta region, kills an estimated 500,000 people in 1970 with a subsequent famine in Bangladesh claiming up to one million lives by 1974. In 1976, the Tangshan earthquake in China kills in excess of 250,000 people: the highest death toll for an earthquake in the twentieth century. In the same year, a herbicide plant explodes near Milan in Italy, releasing a toxic cloud. In 1979, the near-meltdown of the nuclear reactor at Three Mile Island, in Pennsylvania, prompts panic evacuation and media frenzy. In the 1970s, mass protests against industrial logging, desertification and deforestation gather in force across the world from Kenya to the Himalayas.

By 1975, more than one-third of the world's population live in cities (up from one-seventh in 1900). Bucking this trend, East Anglia and the South West are the only two areas of Britain to show signifi-cant population growth as more Britons migrate to rural areas. The sweltering heat wave of 1976, causing the worst drought for 250 years, enters British folk memory.

Education

Modernising legislation is passed early in the decade: the classification of disabled children as 'unfit for education at school' is discontinued and the school-leaving age is raised to sixteen in 1972. Conservative minister Margaret Thatcher, then Education Secretary, axes the universal provision of milk in schools earning her the infamous nickname 'Thatcher, milk snatcher'. During Heath's premiership, there are more pupils in comprehensive than selective schools for the first time.

Education becomes a key battleground for hard-line Conservatives. During 1974–6, an unprecedented media storm about teaching methods is triggered by a staff dispute at William Tyndale primary school in London. During 1969–77, a series of right-wing thinkers publish five so-called 'Black Papers' on education that attack 'progressive teaching'. In a 1977 article in the *News of the World*, the right-wing Conservative MP Rhodes Boyson writes of a teacher 'who actually refused to teach decimals because it was used in the form of accounting which accompanied the capitalist system'. The tabloid pillorying of the so-called 'loony left', characteristic of the 1980s, has its origins in the bitter education debates of the 1970s.

Labour's Education Act (1976) endorses the 'general principle' that education should not be 'based (wholly or partly)' on selection but contains so many loopholes that its effect is negligible. Prime Minister Callaghan calls for a 'Great Debate' about education in a major speech at Ruskin College: he advocates a more utilitarian emphasis in maths and science, and an end to liberal teaching methods. In 1977, the government urges schools to 'restore the rigour without damaging the real benefits of the child-centred developments'. There is an ideological turn against the perceived liberalism and 'softness' of 1960s education policy.

More children stay on at school post-sixteen, especially those from higher-income families. There are 621,000 higher-education students in 1970, increasing to 827,000 by 1981 (by 2007–8, the figure is 2.5 million).

3. Culture

Music

The launch of FM stereo radio in the late 1960s enables static-free listening while the ubiquity of cassette tapes heralds an era of bootlegging and home taping. In club culture, the festival scene expands and the rise of the DJ begins.

Festival culture

The first intentionally free festival is held outside Worthing in 1970: the free festival movement, often associated with drugs, anarchism and 'free love', prompts a media backlash and occasional standoffs with the police throughout the early 1970s. A mind-boggling 600,000 people attend the Isle of Wight Festival in August 1970 – the largest music event of its time – featuring the Doors, the Who and Jimi Hendrix.

The first embryonic Glastonbury Festival is held in September 1970, the day after Hendrix's death, attracting 1,500 people. The number of attendees leaps to 12,000 in 1972, when the event moves to summertime, becomes free of charge and adapts the name 'Glastonbury Fayre'. By 1979, Glastonbury has become a three-day event.

A triumvirate of iconic rock stars die suddenly at the start of the decade, all of them twenty-seven years old: Hendrix (1970), Janis Joplin (1970) and Jim Morrison (1971). Elvis Presley's death in 1977 triggers a global media sensation.

At the start of the decade, retro-groups like Mud and Showaddywaddy revive high-school pop of the 1960s while the tartan-clad boy band the Bay City Rollers scores massive chart success. However, it is David Bowie's concept album *The Rise and Fall of Ziggy Stardust and the Spiders from Mars* (1972) and Pink Floyd's astonishing *The Dark Side of the Moon* (1973) that encapsulate musical innovation in the decade. Rock music embraces gender and sexual ambiguity, particularly in its various 'glam' incarnations (Roxy Music, Marc Bolan, Gary Glitter). Elton John, Fleetwood Mac and the Carpenters set the mood music of the decade and 'rock opera' is honed to perfection by Queen ('Bohemian Rhapsody', 1975). 'God Rock' musicals – *Godspell* (1971) and Tim Rice and Andrew

Lloyd-Webber's *Jesus Christ Superstar* (1971) – become huge commercial hits.

Heavy metal bands like Led Zeppelin, Black Sabbath and Deep Purple reach their zenith in the early 1970s. Northern Soul also peaks in legendary venues such as Blackpool Mecca and Wigan Casino. Singer-songwriters Bob Dylan, Bob Marley, Joni Mitchell and, later, Bruce Springsteen and Elvis Costello exert huge influence across the decade.

In the world of pop, the US record industry introduces a new platinum award in 1976 to keep up with rocketing album sales as new synthesiser technology produces increasing diversification. ABBA wins the Eurovision Song Contest in 1974 with the classic 'Waterloo'. Disco becomes the soundtrack to gay liberation as the Bee Gees, Village People and Donna Summer set the charts on fire. The Strawbs' 'Part of the Union' (1973), an ideologically ambiguous song about trade union solidarity, becomes *the* talismanic political lyric of the decade.

The Sex Pistols form in 1975 and punk explodes on to the music scene with the controversial 'God Save the Queen' (released in Silver Jubilee year, 1977). Sid Vicious, Poly Styrene, the Ramones, Blondie and the Clash revolutionise the look and pugnacity of youth culture.

By the end of the 1970s, reggae bands (Aswad, Misty in Roots), rap and hip-hop are becoming increasingly popular.

Books

England, sliding, sinking, shabby, dirty, lazy, inefficient, dangerous, in its death throes, worn out, clapped out, occasionally lashing out.

– Margaret Drabble, *The Ice Age*, 1977

British fiction is dominated by themes of decline and crisis. Paul Theroux's *The Family Arsenal* (1976) deals with the Irish Republican Army (IRA) and a commune of radical actors in Deptford while Muriel Spark's *The Takeover* (1976) is set during the 1973 oil crisis. Doris Lessing's *The Summer Before the Dark* (1973), J. G. Ballard's *Concrete Island* (1974), John Fowles's *Daniel Martin* (1977) and

Margaret Drabble's *The Ice Age* (1977) all place anxiety and paranoia at the emotional centre of storytelling. James Herbert's *The Rats* (1974) reinvigorates British horror fiction with its underlying critique of urban decay. Conspiracies, assassins and gangsters dominate men's popular fiction, exemplified in Mario Puzo's *The Godfather* (1969), Frederick Forsyth's *The Day of the Jackal* (1971) and the bestselling paperbacks of Robert Ludlum and Dick Francis. George Shipway's *The Chilian Club* (1971) focuses on retired army officers who take the law into their own hands to reverse Britain's perceived decline.

In 1970, Alvin Toffler's influential *Future Shock* claims that technological change is creating what he calls 'information overload'. Typical of the left's (misplaced) confidence early in the decade, Tariq Ali's *The Coming British Revolution* (1972) proclaims that 'we shall once again see [workers'] Soviets in Europe in the Seventies'. The siege mentality prompted by the economic and industrial crisis is captured in a tranche of doom-laden mid-decade publications including Correlli Barnett's *The Collapse of British Power* (1972), Robert Moss's *The Collapse of Democracy* (1975), *Why is Britain Becoming Harder to Govern?*, edited by Anthony King (1976), Stephen Haseler's *The Death of British Democracy* (1976) and Tom Nairn's seminal *The Break-Up of Britain* (1977). Jeremy Seabrook's *What Went Wrong? Working People and the Ideals of the Labour Movement* (1978) paints a dystopian picture of Britain's impersonal shopping malls and dispossessed youth. However, there is a more upbeat emphasis in Bernard D. Nossiter's prescient *Britain: A Future that Works* (1978): 'Britons [. . .] appear to be the first citizens of the post-industrial age [. . .] They are choosing leisure over goods.'

Intellectual activity on the left is nourished by New Left Books (now Verso) founded in 1970. In critical theory, Edward Said's *Orientalism* (1978) sets the parameters of post-colonial discourse and Hayden White's *Tropics of Discourse* (1978) argues that the writing of history has 'more in common' with literature than science. At the end of the decade, the philosopher Jean-François Lyotard publishes his seismic *The Postmodern Condition* (1979), a foundational text of postmodernism.

Art

Richard Serra's huge steel sculptures – *Strike* (1969–71) – and Andy Warhol's *Skulls* (1976) represent the best of 1970s iconic art. David Hockney paints his most famous naturalistic portrait *Mr and Mrs Clark and Percy* (1970–1) and Gilbert & George become notorious for *The Singing Sculpture* (1970) in which they appear gold-painted while miming to a Flanagan and Allen song. During the decade, modern art becomes the target of conservative moral backlash. In 1976, COUM Transmissions, an artists' collective, creates an art work called *Prostitution* at the Institute of Contemporary Arts (ICA) using pornographic images and sanitary towels. There is a media storm and the Conservative MP Nicholas Fairbairn labels COUM 'wreckers of civilisation'. In the same year, a sculpture of bricks, titled *Equivalent VIII*, by American Carl Andre, is vandalised at the Tate.

Sport

The New York Marathon is launched in 1970 as running, squash and 'fitness culture' become increasingly popular.

In 1971, sixty-six people are killed, many of them children, at the Ibrox Stadium disaster in Glasgow when crowds surge to the exits at the end of a Celtic–Rangers football match.

At the 1972 Summer Olympics in Munich, the US swimmer Mark Spitz wins seven gold medals, the Russian Olga Korbut wins three golds for gymnastics and Britain's Mary Peters takes gold for the women's pentathlon. Alex 'Hurricane' Higgins wins the world snooker title at his first attempt in 1972: his popularity is responsible for the success of the sport on television from this point on. The Romanian Nadia Comăneci wins the first perfect score in gymnastics at the 1976 Summer Olympics in Montreal.

In 1973, Billie Jean King wins the 'Battle of the Sexes' tennis match against Bobby Riggs: a major turning point for women in athletics at the height of the feminist surge. Björn Borg reigns as undisputed men's champion at Wimbledon during 1976–80. In Jubilee year (1977), Virginia Wade wins the ladies' singles finals for Britain and the much-loved racehorse Red Rum wins his third Grand National.

In 1974, Muhammad Ali beats George Foreman in the historic

'Rumble in the Jungle' heavyweight boxing match in Zaire. Sugar Ray Leonard and Britain's John Conteh also win major boxing bouts during the decade. At the showbiz end of sport, the wrestlers Big Daddy and Giant Haystacks win huge fan followings, especially among grandmothers, on tea-time television.

Liverpool becomes Britain's most successful football team. Brazil (1970), Germany (1974) and Argentina (1978) win the World Cup during the decade but England fails disastrously to qualify for the competition in both 1974 and 1978. The outspoken manager Brian Clough dominates the game during the 1970s.

Travel

Britons make six million holiday trips abroad in 1970, climbing to nine million by 1973 (in 2008, the figure is 45.5 million). The Inter-rail travel pass is launched in 1972, enabling young people to travel cheaply around Europe. In 1975, the Union Travel Club is established by the TGWU and Pickford's Travel: as a result, many working-class families take holidays overseas for the first time. In 1977, Freddie Laker begins inexpensive 'Skytrain' flights to the US: young people descend on airports brandishing 'We Love You Freddie' placards. Laker is awarded a knighthood as the era of cheap flights and package holidays begins: Spain is the most popular destination followed by (in order) Ireland, France and Italy.

In 1976, Concorde, the supersonic transatlantic passenger airliner, flies for the first time. Flying on Concorde becomes the status symbol of the decade.

Leisure

In 1970, full-time manual workers receive, on average, two to three weeks' paid holiday annually; by 1980, this has increased to four or five. There are twenty-seven sports centres in England in 1970; by 1974, there are 167 with plans for a further 612. A 1975 conference ('Building for Leisure') recognises leisure as key to modern urban development. Stanley Parker's prescient *The Sociology of Leisure* (1976) predicts shorter working weeks and longer weekends in future.

Chain stores take over the high street and 'hypermarkets' open out of town: in 1972, there are sixty planning applications for superstores in Lancashire alone. Brent Cross shopping centre opens in 1976 and Manchester's Arndale Centre in 1979.

Health foods like muesli and yogurts move from margins to mainstream on the menu and, in homes and pubs, games such as Pong and Space Invaders reach heights of popularity.

Architecture

Architecture in the 1970s is defined by its reach for the skies. The World Trade Center in Manhattan opens to global acclaim as the world's tallest building in 1972–3. The Sears Tower in Chicago, completed in 1973, holds the 'tallest' record until the CN Tower in Toronto becomes the world's tallest freestanding structure in 1976. Dazzling architectural achievements of the 1970s include the Sydney Opera House (1973), the Pompidou Centre in Paris (1977) and Lloyds of London (from 1978). Riverside development begins with the 'gentrification' of St Katharine Docks in London.

4. Media

Television and radio

Colour TV becomes standard in Britain but there are more black-and-white sets than colour up to 1977 (colour TVs are a status symbol in the first half of the decade). There are only three channels: BBC1, BBC2 and ITV.

Police and detective series remain popular but the 1970s format is grittier. The long-running *Dixon of Dock Green*, *Softly Softly* and *Z-Cars* are replaced by the machismo realism of *The Sweeney* and *The Professionals*. Charismatic US cop shows like *Kojak* and *Starsky and Hutch* become firm fixtures of weekend schedules.

Many popular shows appeal to nostalgia: there is a ten-year waiting list to be in the audience for the BBC's music hall extravaganza *The Good Old Days*, while *Upstairs, Downstairs* and *All Creatures Great and Small* are 'period' hits.

Television becomes a site of serious and engaged play production.

The golden age of children's television

Serials for younger children include the stop-frame animation classics *The Wombles* (1973) and *Bagpuss* (1974), both of which are premised on themes of environmental recycling. For older children, the in-yer-face *Tiswas* is launched in 1974 followed by the BBC's *Multi-Coloured Swap Shop* (1976). With their phone-ins, pop videos and outside broadcasts, these shows set new benchmarks for live broadcasting and interactivity across television culture. Popular series reflect changing times: the patrician Jon Pertwee is replaced by the anarchic Tom Baker in the title role of *Doctor Who* while *Blake's 7* focuses on a gang of outlaws fighting a fascistic 'Federation'. Following the success of *Star Wars* in the cinema, television begins to emulate film in US series such as *Battlestar Galactica*.

The landmark series *Play for Today* runs from 1970 to 1984, including Mike Leigh's *Nuts in May* (1976) and the adaptation of his stage play *Abigail's Party* (1977). Dennis Potter writes his extraordinary *Brimstone and Treacle* (censored by the BBC in 1976 and not transmitted until 1987) and *Pennies from Heaven* (1978). Trevor Griffiths's landmark *Bill Brand* runs for eleven episodes on peak-time ITV in 1976. Innovative 1970s drama series include the apocalyptic *Survivors*, *Rock Follies* (with its style influenced by fringe theatre), the wartime drama *Colditz* and the BBC's brilliant adaptation of Robert Graves's *I, Claudius*.

Commercial radio is launched in 1973 with the opening of London's LBC. Radio phone-ins become very popular in the 1970s, blazing the trail for more interactive broadcasting across media.

Film

Oscar-winning films of the 1970s include *The Godfather* (1972), *One Flew Over the Cuckoo's Nest* (1975) and *Annie Hall* (1977). Jack Nicholson becomes an international star in *Five Easy Pieces* (1970) and *Chinatown* (1974) as does Robert De Niro in *Mean Streets* (1973). Jane Fonda and British actress Glenda Jackson become double Oscar winners during the decade. Key directors include Steven Spielberg, Martin Scorsese, George Lucas, Francis Ford Coppola and Nicolas Roeg.

In the early 1970s, disaster movies such as *The Poseidon Adventure*

(1972), *Earthquake* (1974) and *The Towering Inferno* (1974) are perfectly attuned to an age of anxiety. In the aftermath of Watergate, themes of government conspiracy and paranoia surface in *The Parallax View* (1974) and *All the President's Men* (1976) while *The Deer Hunter* (1978), *Coming Home* (1978) and the legendary *Apocalypse Now* (1979) evoke the terrible cost of the Vietnam War.

The violence in *Dirty Harry* (1971), *Straw Dogs* (1971) and, most notoriously, Stanley Kubrick's *A Clockwork Orange* (1971) provokes heated debate. The latter generates a spate of copycat violence leading Kubrick to withdraw his film from circulation in Britain in 1974. *Last Tango in Paris, Don't Look Now* (both 1973) and the first 'mainstream' pornographic film *Deep Throat* (1972) trigger media furore for their explicit treatment of sex.

The Exorcist (1973), *The Omen* (1976) and *Carrie* (1976) are classic examples of the 1970s vogue for slash-and-hack horror, while *Taxi Driver* (1976) and *Marathon Man* (1976) quickly become nail-biting cult classics. Spielberg's magnificent *Jaws* (1975) triggers the era of the epic blockbuster: Lucas's *Star Wars* – the highest-grossing film of the decade – and Spielberg's *Close Encounters of the Third Kind* are both released in 1977. At the end of the 1970s, there is a turn to buffed-up all-American fantasy in *Superman* (1978) and tear-jerking sentimentality in *Kramer versus Kramer* (1979).

The gender-bending *Rocky Horror Picture Show* (1975) and stylish camp of *La Cage aux Folles* (1978) reflect an era of new sexual possibility. There's a wave of innovative musicals such as *Cabaret* (1972), *Bugsy Malone* (1976) and *Grease* (1978) while John Travolta in *Saturday Night Fever* (1977) disco-dances his way into film history.

British films

Get Carter (1971) and *The Wicker Man* (1973) attract huge notoriety for their violent content. *Private Road* (1971), about a novelist forced into a day job in advertising, marks the end of 1960s idealism. By mid-decade, toxic Britain comes to the fore in Lindsay Anderson's epic *O Lucky Man!* (1973) and Derek Jarman's punk-fest *Jubilee* (1977). Christopher Petit's *Radio On* (1979) offers a melancholy end-of-decade meditation on a decaying Britain redeemed by its vibrant music scene.

Newspapers

In 1969, Rupert Murdoch relaunches the *Sun* to appeal to the skilled working class in Britain's 'new towns'; it grows in popularity, becomes tabloid in format, and switches its support from Labour to Conservative. During 1970–5, the cost of newsprint doubles and the industry suffers from high inflation and poor industrial relations. Strip cartoons like *Peanuts* (with its very 1970s catchphrase: 'Good Grief!') and *Doonesbury* help sell newspapers: the dog Snoopy, from *Peanuts*, becomes a global emblem of 1970s 'cool'.

The satirical magazine *Oz* is the focus of an infamous obscenity trial in 1971 for publishing a sexualised Rupert Bear parody in an edition compiled by teenagers. The defendants are convicted but this is overturned on appeal: the case becomes a countercultural *cause célèbre* in the increasingly polarised debates about sexual permissiveness.

In 1977, *2000AD* is launched marking a more violent turn in boys' comics. *Jackie* is the bestselling teen magazine of the 1970s, with sales increasing to over 500,000 by 1976. The music magazine *Smash Hits*, founded in 1978, is a runaway success and soon switches from monthly to fortnightly publication. In 1979, *Viz* is launched as a scatological pastiche of the ascendant tabloid style.

Fashion

Early 1970s fashion is typified by hippie chic, endless polyester, the ubiquitous platform shoes, loon pants and bell-bottomed or hipster jeans. For men: turtle-necked shirts, polo-neck jumpers, kipper ties, Afghan coats, neckties, sideburns, Bryan Ferry quiffs. For women: floral, Asian and 'ethnic' prints, cheesecloth dresses, chiffon head-scarves, Dr Scholl's shoes. At the start of the decade, Laura Ashley's turnover is less than one million pounds; by the end, it is twenty-five million pounds.

Malcolm McLaren and Vivienne Westwood's SEX shop opens in 1974. The punk look comprises safety pins, Doc Marten's boots, silk-screen T-shirts, studs, ripped jackets, piercings, Mohican hair.

By the end of the decade, 'boob tubes' (tops without sleeves and shoulder-straps) are popular with women. The craze for designer jeans begins in 1978 with the launch of Calvin Klein's. The long, straight hair favoured at the start of the decade gives way to perms (on both men and women), flicked fringes and the 'feathered' style of *Charlie's Angels* star Farrah Fawcett. The large round Afro becomes a 1970s icon.

Comedy

World leaders have been meeting in Washington over the past week to consider the ever worsening problems of inflation, overpopulation, racism, pollution – you name it, they've considered it. [. . .] It is their unanimous decision that at twelve o'clock tonight, in a final act of unprecedented international military cooperation, the world will be blown up.

– *The Goodies*, 'Earthanasia' sketch, BBC TV, Christmas 1977

Ground-breaking television comedy in the early 1970s is anchored in a very British surrealism. *Monty Python's Flying Circus* (1969–74) revolutionises TV satire: during the decade, the Pythons tour a stage show and release classic films including *The Holy Grail* (1974) and *Life of Brian* (1979). The Pythons' influence is clearly discernible in *Saturday Night Live* (1975) and *Not the Nine O'Clock News* (1979). *The Goodies* (1970) also focuses on the surreal debunking of national stereotypes.

The seventies is the golden age of television sitcom. *George and Mildred, The Good Life, Terry and June, Porridge, Whatever Happened to the Likely Lads?* and *Are You Being Served?* are all launched in the decade. *Fawlty Towers, Rising Damp* and *The Fall and Rise of Reginald Perrin* are classic encapsulations of worn-out, run-down Britain. *Citizen Smith*, about a young Communist planning the revolution from Tooting, pastiches the youth politics of the time ('Power to the people!'). *Robin's Nest* (1977) is the first British sitcom to focus on an unmarried couple.

The undisputed kings of TV comedy are *The Two Ronnies* and *Morecambe and Wise* (whose Christmas show in 1977 is watched by half the country's population: twenty-eight million people). Stars from variety backgrounds, such as Bruce Forsyth, Des O'Connor and impressionist Mike Yarwood, win huge family audiences.

5. Science, technology and industry

Science

The horizons of medical science are expanded with the appearance of computerised axial tomography (CAT) and magnetic resonance imaging (MRI) for health scanning in 1971 and 1977, respectively. Louise Brown, the world's first 'test tube' baby conceived through in vitro fertilisation (IVF), is born in Oldham in 1978. The last Moon landing to date, Apollo 17, takes place in 1972. China and Japan join the space race and the European Space Agency is established.

Technology

Bar codes for consumer products are launched in the US in 1970. The world's first microprocessor goes on sale and International Business Machines (IBM) introduces the eight-inch floppy disk in 1971. The first primitive email network goes online in 1972 and the first call from a hand-held mobile phone – which is the size of a large brick – is made in 1973. The first home computer, Altair, is launched in 1975, laying the foundations of the seismic communications revolution to come: the Microsoft Corporation is founded in 1975 and Apple in 1976. Catalytic converters, which reduce emissions from cars, are produced from 1973. Video cassette recorders and electronic type-writers sell in increasingly large numbers throughout the decade. The Sony Walkman, a 1980s icon, is marketed from 1979.

Industry

> I had a strong sense that the traditional industries were all contracting simultaneously in the seventies. The mills in my constituency in Stockport were just melting away.
>
> – Tom McNally, adviser to Prime Minister
> James Callaghan, quoted in 2009

During 1950–70, Britain's share of world manufacturing exports shrinks from over a quarter to a tenth. Productivity grows at an annual average of 2.8 per cent in Britain (in West Germany: 5.8 per cent; Japan: 7.5 per cent). Foreign investment in British businesses reduces by nearly 50 per cent from 1969 to 1981. The Heath government embarks on vast building schemes to try and stimulate growth, including the Channel Tunnel, Thames Barrier and the construction of 'new towns' like Milton Keynes.

British Leyland is nationalised in 1975 in order to save thousands of jobs. By 1977, 250,000 cars are lost through industrial disputes at the firm. The Secretary of State for Industry, Tony Benn, puts forward a radical Industry Bill that promotes nationalisation of industry and state planning of the economy. It causes major consternation among the business community and Harold Wilson demotes Benn in 1975. This is widely regarded as a major defeat for the left and a symbolic capitulation of socialist principle to big business.

North Sea oil

In 1969, British Petroleum (BP) strikes oil in the North Sea, creating an upsurge in optimism at a time of economic malaise. In 1975, the first North Sea oil pipeline to Britain is opened by the Queen in a barrage of publicity. Between 1976 and 1979, a staggering 25 per cent of all British manufacturing investment is related to the North Sea. However, oil production is sluggish, and inflation and capital investment lead to soaring production costs: BP spends £800 million on the Forties oilfield, far in excess of its forecast £300–500 million. It is not until 1985 that British oilfields begin to reap economic dividends: in 1978–9, oil production contributes only 1 per cent to government income; by 1985, the figure is 10 per cent.

In 1976, the Organisation for Economic Co-operation and Development (OECD) publishes *Guidelines for Multinational Enterprises*, reflecting concern about the escalating power of global corporations. There is accelerated economic growth and industrialisation in the export-driven 'tiger' economies of Singapore, Japan, Hong Kong and Taiwan. Japan exceeds the US as the world's foremost industrial power in 1979.

6. Political events

British politics

Goodbye, Great Britain. It was nice knowing you.

– *Wall Street Journal*, April 1975

1970: In June, the Conservatives unexpectedly win the general election with a majority of thirty-one and Edward Heath becomes Prime Minister. Weeks later, he declares a state of emergency (the first of five in his premiership) as dockworkers go on strike. In the autumn, refuse and sewerage workers take industrial action (the 'dirty jobs strike') resulting in untreated sewage pouring into the Thames while Leicester Square becomes deluged with uncollected rubbish. Electricians also begin strike action, leading to power cuts.

> **Europe**
>
> Negotiations for British entry into the European Economic Community (EEC), or 'Common Market', are renewed in 1970. Britain is admitted as a member of the EEC on 1 January 1973 and an official national festival, 'A Fanfare for Europe', commemorates the momentous event. However, when food prices increase in 1973, the Common Market is widely blamed although British exports to the EEC increase substantially from £4.1 billion in 1973 to £6.4 billion by 1975. In 1975, the newly elected Labour government conducts a referendum on British entry into Europe: 67 per cent of Britons support the decision but the political parties are split on the issue and remain so into the next century. A spate of novels about the killer disease rabies appears in 1976–7 (e.g. Walter Harris's *Saliva*, Jack Ramsay's *The Rage*): cultural scare-mongering about the 'importing' of rabies from Europe in the mid-1970s suggests a deep-seated Euro-anxiety.

1971: On 15 February, British currency is decimalised. The Trades Union Congress (TUC) refuses to support Heath's Industrial Relations Bill, which places heavy regulations on union conduct: 250,000 demonstrators march to 'Kill the Bill' but it passes into law in August. The government refuses economic support to the ship-builders of the Upper Clyde and they begin a 'work-in', led by

Communist shop steward Jimmy Reid, to assert the viability of their industry. During 1971, the price of fresh food increases by an average of 12 per cent and oil overtakes coal as the leading fuel consumed in Britain. The National Union of Mineworkers (NUM) begins an over-time ban in November.

1972

The lights all went out and everybody said that the country would disintegrate in a week. All the civil servants rushed around saying, 'Perhaps we ought to activate the nuclear underground shelters and the centres of regional government, because there'll be no electricity and there'll be riots on the streets. The sewage will overflow and there'll be epidemics.'

– Brendon Sewill, special adviser in Whitehall,
reflecting on 1972

Unemployment exceeds one million and inflation hits 14 per cent. In January, miners begin strike action over pay supported by railway workers, who refuse to drive coal trains. Heath establishes the secret Civil Contingencies Unit (CCU) to maintain supplies should the country fall into chaos. There is a major confrontation with police as miners force the closure of Saltley Gates depot in Birmingham and national reserves of coal fall to ten days' supply. In February, the strike ends in total victory for the miners. In July, five shop stewards are imprisoned for picketing against containerisation of the ports in east London: this contravenes the new Industrial Relations Act and a national dock strike begins (the men are released shortly afterwards). Nearly twenty-four million working days are lost to strike action in 1972.

1973

Absolute chaos tonight: official
– headline in the London *Evening Standard*, March 1973

On 1 May, 1.6 million public-sector workers go on strike. As the economy nosedives, spending cuts are imposed and interest rates are raised to their highest levels since 1914. The result is 'stagflation' – a

Northern Ireland

In 1970, the British army launches a counter-insurgency campaign as Republican snipers begin to target British soldiers. In January 1971, sixteen IRA bomb attacks take place in Ulster, increasing to thirty-eight the following month. In August, internment without trial is introduced in Northern Ireland prompting a wave of violence. The Ulster Defence Association (UDA) is formed and paramilitary violence increases.

On 30 January 1972, thirteen unarmed people are killed by the British army in Derry on 'Bloody Sunday' (another man dies later). In the aftermath, the Independent Ulster MP Bernadette Devlin slaps Reginald Maudling, Home Secretary, in the face in the House of Commons. Lord Widgery leads an inquiry into Bloody Sunday: his report, which is widely condemned as a whitewash, exonerates the British army. Civilian deaths escalate from sixteen in 1970 to over two hundred by 1972. In March 1972, the Stormont Parliament is suspended and Direct Rule from Westminster is imposed. By late 1972, there are four bomb explosions and thirty shootings per day in Northern Ireland. The IRA adopts a new strategy and takes its campaign of terror to England.

On 1 January 1974, a 'power-sharing Executive' is sworn in in Ulster but is fiercely opposed by the Ulster Workers' Council who organise a general strike in the province in protest. The executive is dissolved by Harold Wilson in May. In November 1974, two pubs in Birmingham are bombed by the IRA, killing twenty-one people. Four days later, the Prevention of Terrorism Act allows for detention of suspects without charge for up to seven days and the expulsion of suspects from Britain. There are terror attacks on the Tower of London, the Old Bailey, London's Hilton hotel, Euston Station, pubs in Guildford, and on Heath's private residence. A four-man IRA unit, the Balcombe Street Gang, conducts shootings and bombings in the capital each week. In 1979, Conservative politician Airey Neave is killed by the Irish National Liberal Army (INLA) in a car bomb and Lord Mountbatten, a member of the Royal Family, is blown up by the IRA.

joint rise in 'inflation' and 'stagnation' (unemployment, no growth) leading to high interest rates. In October, the Yom Kippur War prompts the Organization of Petroleum Exporting Countries (OPEC) to impose oil embargoes and the era of cheap energy imports comes to an end. Within months, a barrel of oil costs over $11 – a fivefold increase in two years. The NUM begins another overtime ban in November (it demands a 40 per cent pay rise) reducing coal production by one-third. As the energy crisis bites, European countries begin imposing car-free days and weekends. In December, Cabinet minutes acknowledge the '[g]ravest economic crisis since the Second World War' and the government announces the three-day week.

1974

The 'three-day week'

From New Year's Eve 1973, all non-essential shops and businesses receive electricity on only three days of the week to conserve coal supplies. Street lighting is dimmed, TV output shuts down at 10.30 p.m., offices, factories and schools close early, petrol rationing coupons are circulated. A government poster advises the public: 'SOS – Switch Off Something now.' The Minister for Energy, Patrick Jenkin, urges people to clean their teeth in the dark to save energy. By February, there is a shortage of bread and other food, Britain's national income is down between 10 and 15 per cent, and nearly one million people have lost jobs. However, some people write to newspapers saying they appreciate the reduction in traffic and the sense of life slowing down. Articles on reading and gardening appear in newspapers, and the pleasures of leisure begin to take hold.

During 1974, birth rates fall and emigration levels climb steeply: 269,000 Britons leave the country, primarily for South Africa and Australia. In February, the NUM votes to strike once again, prompting Heath to call a general election on 28 February focused on the key question: 'Who governs Britain?' The outcome is the first hung parliament since 1929: Labour wins by only four seats but has no overall majority. On 4 March, Heath resigns and Harold Wilson returns as Labour prime minister. The miners' strike is avoided and the three-day week comes to an end. Wilson increases his majority to three in a second general election in October.

The Conservative politician Keith Joseph, disgusted with Heath's economic policy and perceived subjugation by the miners, establishes the right-wing Centre for Policy Studies: the ideology of Thatcherism emerges from Joseph's think tank and begins its ascendancy.

Princess Anne, the Queen's daughter, escapes a kidnap attempt when a man ambushes her car near Buckingham Palace. November is a month of disappearances: Lord Lucan vanishes after the murder of his children's nanny (his whereabouts still remain a mystery) and Labour MP John Stonehouse drowns himself in Miami, leaving his clothes on a beach: or so it is thought. He is later discovered living in Australia under a false name and is jailed for faking his death. Stonehouse blames his bizarre actions on disillusionment with politics.

1975

'The social contract'

The 'social contract' brings Wilson's new Labour government closer to trade union influence and in return unions agree to pay restraint. The government adopts a series of union-friendly policies: increases in the state pension, a freeze on council house rents and the passing of the Health and Safety at Work Act (1974). The Advisory, Conciliation and Arbitration Service (ACAS) is founded in 1975 to mediate industrial disputes and Heath's reviled Industrial Relations Act is repealed. To pay for this, the top rate of income tax is increased to 83 per cent. In 1974, wages rise by nearly 30 per cent, leading to fewer strikes; however, prices also increase by 26 per cent in roughly the same period.

In February, Margaret Thatcher replaces Heath as leader of the Conservative Party, Britain's first woman leader of a major political party. As the economic crisis worsens, Denis Healey, Chancellor of the Exchequer, slashes public spending. Inflation in Britain peaks at its highest level in the twentieth century: nearly 27 per cent. The value of earnings and personal savings plunges and house prices fall by 13 per cent in 1974 and 16 per cent in 1975. Share dividends are reduced or are left unpaid, unemployment doubles and there is more 'stagflation'. Betting on the pools increases by 80 per cent in four years; alcohol consumption rises sharply. A number of right-wing organisations are founded at this time, including the National Association for Freedom (NAFF), the Middle Class Association, GB75 and Civil Assistance – some of these groups are connected to the security services and military, and are actively mobilising for a coup.

1976

> For the last three years, ever since the miners brought down Ted Heath, there have been long and passionate discussions in all the rooms of Westminster except the chamber of the House of Commons, in the bars, in the restaurants, even in the splendid marble halls of the toilets, about the possibility of revolution in this country. I am by no means the only MP who thinks that it is not only possible, but, in fact, quite likely *if* the present situation is allowed to continue.
>
> – Cyril Smith, Liberal MP, 1976

On 8 March, the pound drops five cents in one hour. Between February and April, Bank of England reserves fall by one-third in an attempt to prop up sterling. On 16 March, an exhausted Wilson resigns as prime minister and James Callaghan replaces him on 5 April. Healey arranges a five-billion-dollar credit agreement from the US and other central banks, and cuts public spending further. On 27 September, the pound hits a record low of $1.68. The following day, Healey turns back his car at Heathrow Airport in order to deal with the crisis. Callaghan gives his maiden speech as prime minister to the Labour Party conference in Blackpool: 'The cosy world we were told would go on for ever, where full employment would be guaranteed by a stroke of the chancellor's pen, cutting taxes, deficit spending – that cosy world is gone . . .' Britain applies for a £2.3 billion loan from the International Monetary Fund (IMF), the biggest loan in IMF history up to that point. The IMF demands eye-watering cuts of £2.5 billion in spending over two years. The Cabinet is bitterly divided about cutting spending during a recession but the loans are eventually approved. Union leader Alan Fisher: 'In meeting the conditions made by the IMF, the Government have accepted a cheque that may bounce at the next general election.' In August, a strike begins at the Grunwick factory in London over workers' rights to union representation. After she attacks the USSR in a speech, the Russian press label Thatcher 'the Iron Lady'.

1977: With the government reduced to a majority of one, Callaghan and Liberal Party leader David Steel announce the Lib–Lab pact: in exchange for parliamentary support of Labour, the Liberals are consulted on legislation. In June, there are mass pickets at Grunwick: a boycott of postal services brings strikers to the edge of victory but NAFF begins secretly collecting mail in an attempt to smash the Grunwick strike. In November, the Fire Brigades Union takes unprecedented industrial action.

However, by late 1977, average disposable income starts to grow and income inequality reaches its lowest recorded levels. The pound climbs in value and the IMF loan is paid back ahead of schedule. A poll reveals Britons regard themselves among the happiest people on the planet. The Queen celebrates her Silver Jubilee.

1978: In January, inflation drops below 10 per cent for the first time since 1973. Unemployment and working days lost to industrial action begin to fall, the number of people below the poverty line reaches its lowest recorded levels, and – in the twelve months from August 1977 – earnings increase by nearly double the rate of inflation. Social mobility in modern Britain peaks during Callaghan's administration. Labour leads the polls in the autumn and increases its majority in an October by-election.

In July, the Lib–Lab pact is ended, removing Labour's majority. The Grunwick strikers concede defeat as the tide begins to turn against trade unions. In August, the advertising firm Saatchi and Saatchi launches its election campaign for the Conservatives: the poster shows a snaking dole queue beneath the slogan 'Labour Isn't Working'. Only twenty posters are put up across Britain but their impact is enormous. In the autumn, the 'social contract' is terminated. Union leaders warn of a 'Winter of Discontent' if the government attempts to restrain public-sector pay. Callaghan makes a fatal error and decides to wait until the spring before calling a general election.

1979

Devolution for Scotland and Wales is rejected in a major constitutional referendum on 1 March 1979: poor campaigning by an

---

The 'Winter of Discontent': January–February 1979

The largest industrial action since the General Strike of 1926. Nearly thirty million working days are lost: the equivalent of every working person in the country taking a day's strike action. There are strikes by lorry drivers, rail workers, pilots, ambulance workers, dinner ladies, bin men, nurses, riggers, civil servants and gravediggers. Some strikers demand up to 40 per cent pay increases (the government insists on 5 per cent). Fuel prices are sent soaring by inflation, ports are sealed off by pickets, supermarkets ration basic foods, rubbish piles up in public spaces, schools are forced to close and newspapers shrink because of shortages in newsprint. The fact that strikes impact on services as well as traditional industry sets very emotive terms for public debate and the press claims the vulnerable are being hit hardest. It coincides with the coldest winter since 1962–3.

On 22 January, 1.5 million public-sector workers take strike action. The city of Hull is blockaded by road hauliers; due to severe rationing, Hull is nicknamed 'Stalingrad'. Meanwhile, Callaghan is photographed sunbathing at a summit on the island of Guadeloupe. His complacent remarks to the media provoke the infamous headline: 'Crisis? What Crisis?' On TV, Thatcher calls for trade union reform: 'Someone's got to grasp this nettle.' Industrial action ends in February with many workers attaining increased pay deals. By this point, the Conservatives have reversed Labour's poll lead and are nineteen points ahead.

---

embattled Labour government is blamed for the defeat. On 28 March, Callaghan loses a no-confidence motion by one vote in Parliament and calls a general election. Thatcher describes the free market as 'an idea whose time has come'. On 3 May, she is elected Britain's first woman prime minister and the Conservatives win an overall majority of forty-three: the first viable majority for a government since 1970.

World politics

1970: In 'Black September', the Jordanian army moves against Palestinian guerrillas as violence destabilises the Middle East. The Baader-Meinhof Gang unleashes a campaign of terror in West Germany that causes mayhem throughout the decade. Four students are killed by US National Guardsmen during anti-war protests at Kent State University, Ohio. Mortgage-backed securities are sold for the first time in the US, a key foundation of the emerging global economy.

1971: East Bengal (Bangladesh) secedes from Pakistan amid violent conflict.

1972: Ferdinand Marcos declares martial law in the Philippines and establishes autocratic rule. The dictator of Uganda, Idi Amin, expels thousands of Asians in a brutal policy of 'Africanisation': around 28,000 settle in the UK. US President Richard Nixon's diplomacy in China and the USSR thaws relations with the West; he is elected for a second term in a landslide vote. The Palestinian 'Black September' group massacres Israeli athletes at the Munich Olympics causing worldwide revulsion. The Strategic Arms Limitation Talks (SALT) result in Presidents Nixon and Brezhnev (of the USSR) signing the Anti-Ballistic Missile Treaty in Moscow. Five men are arrested breaking into the Democratic Party National Committee HQ at the Watergate hotel complex in Washington.

1973: The Paris Peace Accords end US involvement in Vietnam. Nixon's closest aides, Bob Haldeman and John Ehrlichman, resign (and are later sent to prison) as the investigation of the Watergate break-in points to the complicity of the White House. The fascist General Augusto Pinochet overthrows and murders the democratically elected President Salvador Allende in Chile with CIA support. The Yom Kippur War is triggered in October: Egypt and Syria declare war on Israel and invade the Sinai Peninsula. The oil crisis sends the global economy into free-fall.

1974: The US is thrown into national trauma as President Nixon resigns when faced with impeachment for covering up his involvement in 'Watergate': he is incriminated on the basis of his own tape-recorded conversations. Gerald Ford becomes the new president. Fascist dictatorships are toppled in Greece and Portugal. Patty Hearst, granddaughter of newspaper magnate William Randolph Hearst, is kidnapped and brainwashed by a left-wing guerrilla group called the Symbionese Liberation Army in California: she helps them to rob a bank before her arrest in 1975.

1975: The Vietnam War comes to an end with the fall of Saigon. The fascist dictator Francisco Franco dies and Spain begins its transition to democracy. In the aftermath of US bombing of Kampuchea (Cambodia), Pol Pot's Khmer Rouge takes power and begins a murderous programme of starvation and genocide that kills around 20 per cent of the population (over 1,000,000 people) by 1979. The first multilateral G6 summit is held in France.

1976: The Soweto Uprising escalates the anti-apartheid struggle in South Africa. Chairman Mao Zedong dies and China begins its long march towards market economics. The military junta in Argentina intensifies its 'Dirty War' against civilians, leading to the murder of thousands of people. Milton Friedman, intellectual guru of Margaret Thatcher, wins the Nobel Prize for Economics. Jimmy Carter, a Democrat, wins the US presidential election. Writer Tom Wolfe coins the term 'Me decade' in *New York* magazine.

1977: Steve Biko, anti-apartheid activist, dies in police custody in South Africa after an interrogation lasting twenty-two hours. Dissidents in Soviet-controlled Czechoslovakia, including the playwright Václav Havel, set up Charter 77 to advocate human rights.

1978: In Italy, the Red Brigades kidnap and execute the former prime minister Aldo Moro. The Camp David Accords are signed by Egypt and Israel in a boost for peace in the Middle East. John Paul II is inaugurated as the youngest pope in over one hundred years. Over nine hundred members of an apocalyptic cult, led by Reverend Jim Jones, commit suicide in Jonestown, Guyana: the largest death toll of US civilians in a non-natural disaster in American history (until 9/11). The evangelical lobby Moral Majority gathers force in the US.

1979: The Iranian Revolution topples the ruling Pahlavi dynasty, the Shah is exiled and Iran declares itself an Islamic Republic – the era of the Ayatollahs begins. In November, Iranian revolutionary guards storm the US embassy in Tehran: the resulting siege lasts for over a year and damages President Carter in his election campaign against

Ronald Reagan. The SALT II treaty is signed between the US and USSR, raising the prospect of arms reductions. Saddam Hussein becomes President of Iraq. The USSR invades Afghanistan, escalating Cold War hostilities. The World Health Organization (WHO) declares the global eradication of the killer disease, smallpox. By the end of the decade, eleven heads of state have been assassinated – a record in modern history.

CHAPTER 1
THEATRE IN THE 1970S

If the Sixties were a wild weekend and the Eighties a hectic day at the office, the Seventies were a long Sunday evening in winter, with cold leftovers for supper and a power cut expected at any moment.[1]

The political context

Francis Wheen's view of the 1970s as a rude awakening from the reveries of sixties idealism into a harder and more anxious world reinforces the dominant perception of the decade as a kind of unrelenting hangover. The grounds for this interpretation are easily discernible from the Introduction to this book, where the lexicon of key events – from Bloody Sunday to Watergate, the three-day week to the Winter of Discontent, Jonestown to Soweto – reads like a roll-call of crisis. It is, indeed, the theme of crisis that brings the 1970s into close proximity with the present, as evidenced in the tranche of recent publications offering retrospectives on the decade.[2] At the time of writing, in summer 2011, Britain is in the throes of a formidable economic downturn; unemployment and inflation are increasing; a coalition government is in power; public-sector strikes are erupting across the country; Britain is on high alert for terrorist attacks; racial tensions have escalated into rioting across English cities; there has been global concern about the meltdown of nuclear reactors overseas; energy security and unwinnable wars dominate the news – and, amid all this, the Queen is preparing for a right royal Jubilee. Each of these social phenomena, of course, has a direct equivalent in the 1970s. As Andy Beckett observes, with what may be understatement, 'a very seventies unease has seeped back into how we see the world'.[3]

Popular culture has been in the vanguard of 1970s revivalism. In 2008, three major films were released inspired by political crises of the decade: *The Baader-Meinhof Complex*, *Milk* and *Frost/Nixon*. The musical nostalgia-fest based on the back catalogue of ABBA, *Mamma Mia!*, was also released that year. In theatre, there have been major revivals of 1970s plays including David Hare's *Plenty* (Sheffield Crucible, 2011) and Simon Gray's *Butley* (Duchess Theatre, London, 2011). On television, the BBC drama *Life on Mars*, in which a police officer from 2006 wakes up, inexplicably, in 1973, ran for two successful series from 2006–7, and there are plans to reboot flagship 1970s series such as *Charlie's Angels* (a big-screen version of which was released in 2000) and the soap opera *Dallas*. Meanwhile, flares, tank-tops and retro-glasses are back in fashion while, on the home front, even the sale of fondue sets is rocketing.[4]

Yet, irrespective of the nostalgia boom and the parallels between past and present, it is crucial to preserve a sense of the historical specificity of the 1970s. In his recent study of the decade, Alwyn W. Turner draws attention 'to an incipient crisis of national self-confidence, an underlying loss of certainty, a sometimes inchoate belief that things could not continue on the same path and that consensus was not the answer'.[5] The word 'consensus' carries important freight in this sentence: it is a shorthand term denoting the broad attachment of the British political class in the mid-twentieth century, irrespective of party allegiance, to the 'mixed economy' as theorised by the influential J. M. Keynes. Keynes's economic model was 'mixed' because, alongside private enterprise, he advocated the nationalisation of tracts of industry, and a large role for government and the public sector in stimulating growth. Edward Heath, British prime minister from 1970 to 1974, made an infamous 'U-turn' in 1971 in which he steered the direction of Conservative economic policy towards Keynes when he had previously indicated he would do the opposite: for example, he increased public spending on housing and nationalised the aircraft division of Rolls-Royce which, at that time, was facing bankruptcy. However, as a consequence of the bitter industrial disputes that plagued his premiership, and especially after the miners' victorious strike in 1972, 'consensus politics' began to be attacked from all sides of the ideological spectrum. To many on the left, 'consensus' was a compromised notion that blocked the full efflorescence of a socialist society. To those on the right, it was inefficient and suspiciously interventionist. Appalled by Heath's 'U-turn' towards Keynes, the right wing of the Conservative Party began to advocate the philosophy of monetarism, which sought to reduce the government's role, reduce taxes and release the much-vaunted 'energies' of competition, from this point on. In the second half of the decade, the resurgent Conservative Party upheld an almost messianic commitment to the pursuit of growth through free market enterprise and, ironically, after Margaret Thatcher's general election victory in 1979, the left began to defend the 'mixed economy' as the last best hope of a redistributive economic policy. The upending of the post-war settlement, as exemplified in the jettisoning of 'consensus politics', triggered eddies and occasional tsunamis of despair and revolutionary verve throughout a decade marked by fierce ideological polarisation and economic turbulence not seen in Britain since the 1930s. In addition, unprecedented levels of violence in Northern Ireland, the IRA's campaign of terror on the British mainland, the vexed question of devolution for Scotland and Wales, the issue of sovereignty over North Sea oil, and Britain's accession to the European Community in 1973 all raised pressing questions about the prospects, mandate and identity of post-imperial Britain.

It would be misguided, however, to cast the 1970s as a period of unremitting gloom. During the decade, new forms of political identification garnered visibility and agency. As Beckett argues, '[f]or many political people in Britain in the seventies, the time was dominated not by Heath and Thatcher and Callaghan but by the rise of environmentalism, or feminism, or the Gay Liberation Front, or Rock Against Racism, and other new forms of politics with their own rhythms and preoccupations, only sometimes connected to those of the House of Commons'.[6] While trade union membership increased dramatically during the decade, and industrial struggle strengthened the traditional institutions of the working class, the 1970s saw the emergence of 'identity politics' – feminism, anti-racism and gay rights – premised on the notion that 'the personal is political'.

This chapter offers an overview of British theatre during this remarkable decade, drawing on a selection of examples to illustrate broader transformations and developments. As we shall see, theatre artists engaged with, and sought to shape, these new political and social realities in myriad ways.

Alternative theatre

For many of us, the fringe was where our theatrical hearts lay. It was our laboratory, our playground; it was where we made our statement, where our voices were heard. It was experimental by definition, in production, writing and acting. You had an idea for a play or for a production and you simply put it on.[7]

The words 'underground' and 'fringe' have been deployed to describe the multiple forms of theatrical performance that emerged from the 1960s counterculture. Such categories are invariably problematic because they tend to codify a set of fixed oppositions ('fringe' versus 'mainstream') and give the misleading impression of homogenisation. In this chapter, I have elected to use the term 'alternative' because it was deployed by many theatre people at the time to designate a broad set of working and creative practices that challenged those predominant in the commercial and subsidised sectors.

There were two events in the late 1960s that contributed to the exponential growth in alternative theatre at the start of the new decade. First, the Theatres Act (1968) abolished the state censorship of theatre and removed the powers invested in the Lord Chamberlain to license plays for performance. This legislation expedited the process of making theatre and removed certain restrictions on stage representation that had in the past inhibited theatre's engagement with topical and satirical content. Second, there was a large expansion in public subsidy for theatre at the end of the 1960s, the impact of which is considered later in this chapter. There were additional, perhaps less immediately apparent, factors that enabled the growth of alternative theatre at this time. For example, the Ford Transit van – the veritable domicile of the 1970s touring company – was launched in Britain in 1965, and *Time Out* magazine, which supported alternative theatre with free listings and serious reviewing, began in 1968.[8]

The groups that emerged in the early 1970s were usually democratic or cooperative in structure, committed to reaching new audiences outside conventional theatre spaces, and often constituted for a specific purpose. As the director Chris Parr reflects: 'I remember at the time being very conscious that on the theatre level they were very like pop groups. They started like pop groups, coming out of nowhere, and they finished like pop groups, often acrimoniously.'[9] Some companies focused on the staging of new plays (such as Portable Theatre, 7:84 and Joint Stock) whereas others tapped into the performance art traditions coming out of art schools and colleges (such as the Bradford College of Art Theatre Group and Welfare State) but these groupings were not mutually exclusive. Throughout the seventies, there was an immense cross-pollination of personnel as the large number of conferences, festivals, marches and campaigns led to the emergence of yet more groups with varying political creeds and aesthetic practices. Individuals migrated from universities or Theatre in Education (TIE) companies to touring and fringe theatres. There was a regional focus to some groups, national touring for others; some were building-based, others were determinedly not. The playwright and director John McGrath's assertion that alternative theatre demanded a 'different' and greater level of personal involvement suggests that the key mantra of identity politics – 'the personal is political' – translated into a close identification between worker and product across the vast spectrum of alternative theatre practices.[10]

Early influences

A seminal influence on the British counterculture was Jim Haynes, an expatriate American who opened the Arts Lab in London's Drury Lane in November 1967. Haynes had previously founded an Edinburgh bookshop which included a theatre space as well as the Traverse Theatre, which he ran from 1962 to 1965 as a centre for new, and especially Scottish, playwriting. The Arts Lab was created from the conversion of two adjoining warehouses and included a cinema, an exhibition gallery and a theatre/restaurant. In its brief year of existence, the Arts Lab hosted work by new groups such as Portable, Freehold, Pip Simmons, the People Show and the Brighton Combination, and Steven Berkoff staged his first professional production there.[11] 'It was part coffee bar, part arts centre, part flop house [. . .],' recalls Tony Bicât of Portable. 'Jim's artistic policy was – "Sure, go ahead".'[12] The critic J. W. Lambert, writing in 1974, is rather less amenable: for him, the Lab was 'an uncovenanted and bankrupt doss-house'.[13] Irrespective of Lambert's reservations, the influence of this multi-purpose, inclusive and experimental space was enormous: Arts Labs opened in Birmingham, Manchester and many other cities, and there were more than 140 arts centres in Britain by the end of the 1970s.[14]

Following a similar model, the Brighton Combination was established in the late 1960s by Noël Greig, Jenny Harris and Ruth Marks. It occupied a converted Victorian schoolhouse in Brighton and included one of the first 'black box' theatres in the country.[15] Among its early members were the future International Director of the Royal Court Theatre, Elyse Dodgson, and Howard Brenton. In the words of the latter:

> I did a collective show, and included a local painter who painted us – the actors and the whole theatre – for it. There was that kind of variety. Mixed film shows – it was all there, done very ignorantly and very quickly, and in terrible poverty. They also ran a restaurant, they tried to repair the roof. They had to get over difficulties, small difficulties like the box-office telephone being cut off, because they didn't have the money to pay the bill. There were candlelight shows – always full – because there was no electricity [. . .][16]

In 1971, the Combination moved to the Albany Theatre in Deptford, where it became one of the first building-based companies, post-1968, to forge strong links with its local audience through community initiatives. Over in south London, meanwhile, an equivalent venture was the Oval House run by Peter Oliver from 1961 to

1974. This key venue provided touring companies with rehearsal and photocopying facilities as well as opportunities to share work. The People Show performed early pieces at the Oval House, the comedy troupe Low Moan Spectacular was based there and it hosted an annual 'Gay Times' festival of theatre, cabaret and music.

Another extraordinary initiative was Inter-Action, founded in 1968 by Ed Berman who, like Haynes, was American. It operated out of various venues including the Ambiance Lunch Hour Theatre, which, in 1968, was situated in the basement of the Ambiance restaurant in Queensway, west London. The director Roland Rees staged Ed Bullins's *The Electronic Nigger* in the venue: 'We used to rehearse in an atmosphere that was still steamed up from the previous evening [. . .] at 11 a.m. [. . .] the guy who ran the Ambiance, from Trinidad, I think, used to sleep in the toilets and would wander out in a turban with his girlfriend in the middle of rehearsals. Extraordinarily difficult circumstances. We were all mad.'[17] Later, the Ambiance-in-Exile Lunchtime Theatre operated from the Green Banana restaurant in Soho, run by the Guyanese actor Norman Beaton (who was later active in the Black Theatre of Brixton). In 1972, Inter-Action moved to the Almost Free Theatre in Rupert Street, Piccadilly. The Almost Free operated a 'pay what you can' policy (hence its name) and was in the vanguard of the popular lunchtime theatre movement in the early 1970s. Lunchtime productions broke the conventions of established theatregoing, extended opportunities for emerging talent (the Almost Free premiered plays by Tom Stoppard, among many others) and supported the local economy of pubs and restaurants.

Berman was a visionary of organisation and programming. In 1970, a 'Black and White Power' season was held at the Ambiance, giving valuable impetus to emerging black playwrights; a Women's Theatre season was organised in 1973 at the Almost Free, leading to the formation of the Women's Theatre Group; a season called 'Homosexual Acts' was produced in 1975, triggering the creation of Gay Sweatshop; and a 'Rights and Campaigns' season, in 1978, focused on Jewish issues. As Sandy Craig put it in 1980, '[t]he Almost Free, almost single-handedly, has transformed the idea of community from that of a geographical area to that of a minority grouping with a community of interests within society'.[18] In other words, the Almost Free became the principal site for the theatrical mobilisation and expression of identity politics in London at this time.

Inter-Action settled in Kentish Town in 1977 as a cooperative arts resource centre and city farm. By 1978, thirty city farms around the country had been established, inspired by its example. A large number of Inter-Action activity groups were running each week employing around one hundred people (some of them hired for individual projects). At various points during the 1970s, Inter-Action ran youth and playground activities, a theatre group for children called Dogg's Troupe (which averaged nearly 600 performances each year) and a brightly-painted Routemaster bus – the 'Fun Art Bus', with a converted upper deck for theatre and a cinema downstairs – which toured Britain and Europe from 1972 to 1974. There was also The Other Company (TOC), an exploratory theatre group led by Naftali Yavin, and the British American Repertory Company founded in 1979 (with the support of the actors' trade union Equity) to encourage Anglo-American collaboration. By 1978, a report from the Council of Europe cited Inter-Action as 'the most exciting community arts group in Europe'.[19]

Another important venue, the Open Space, was founded in 1968 by Thelma Holt and US director and critic Charles Marowitz in a basement in London's Tottenham Court Road. Marowitz had worked with the director Peter Brook in the 1960s on the RSC/LAMDA 'Theatre of Cruelty' season and also with Haynes in developing a Traverse Season in London in 1966. The Open Space performed early work by Howard Barker, who became Resident Dramatist, and Trevor Griffiths. Property development eventually forced the company into temporary premises in the Euston Road in 1976 and it folded in 1980; Holt became the director of the vibrant Roundhouse in Camden from 1977.

A range of other spaces for alternative theatre, many of them still in existence, opened in London in the early 1970s: the King's Head (1970), the Orange Tree (1971), the Bush and Soho Poly (both 1972), and the Riverside Studios (1975). The Half Moon opened in a disused synagogue in Aldgate in 1972 but moved, in 1979, to an old

Methodist chapel in Stepney. The Institute of Contemporary Arts (ICA) on the Mall was run by the producer Michael Kustow from 1967 to 1971 and became a major centre of avant-garde performance.

By mid-decade, the explosion of small-scale theatre was beginning to attract wider attention, including from literary satirists. David Nobbs's 1975 novel *The Death of Reginald Perrin* (which was the inspiration for the 1970s television comedy *The Fall and Rise of Reginald Perrin*) includes a character called Mark, Reggie's son, who is a struggling actor. At one point, we learn that Mark has appeared as a hat stand in a twelve-minute play, *Can Egbert Poltergeist Defeat the Great Plague of Walking Sticks and Reach True Maturity?* Needless to say, the venue for this extravaganza is 'a new experimental tea-time theatre in Kentish Town'.[20]

Case study: Bradford

Born in Manchester, Alan's unofficial acting diploma lists occupations ranging from bricklayer to antique dealer, via hospital-porter, printer and computer technician, trainee accountant & mail order clerk. After leaving school at 16 Alan had a shot at all these, as well as a brief spell as an Art Student – before being thrown out as a 'disruptive element'. Then in 1970 he got the job of information officer for the Bradford Festival, and as a result was appointed Administrator for the 1971 Arts Festival. He initiated various projects for children's theatre, and appeared in a few local productions. Chris Parr [. . .] invited him to take parts in a couple of plays he was directing for the Edinburgh Festival in February 1971, as a result of which he joined the General Will.[21]

Outside of the metropolitan south east, there were regional hubs of alternative theatre, including in Bradford, West Yorkshire. The city hosted two cultural festivals in 1970 and 1971 which gave a strong profile to the new alternative theatre companies and performance groups. The quotation above comprises the short biography of the actor Alan Hulse which was included in the programme for the production of David Edgar's *Rent or Caught in the Act*, written for the socialist theatre company, the General Will, in 1972. If Mark in *The Death of Reginald Perrin* is the fictional cliché of bit-part-actor-as-hat-stand, Hulse's potted biography gives two insights into the actualities of alternative theatre at this time. First, note the flexibility that was possible outside of 'professionalised' theatre structures (Hulse's trajectory into acting seems to have been via art school, administration and theatre-related project management). Second, Hulse acquired his experience from the spread of interconnected theatrical opportunities opening up in Bradford at this juncture (including the festivals, the theatre initiatives of Chris Parr and the General Will).

Much of the creative energy in Bradford derived from the expertise and commitment of Albert Hunt. Hunt taught complementary studies at Bradford College of Art from 1965 and established a theatre group there in 1968. He had worked with Peter Brook on the RSC's controversial production of *US* (1966) and he was also inspired by the work of the socialist theatre director Joan Littlewood at the Theatre Royal Stratford East. In Bradford, Hunt designed two-week intensive projects for his students focused on the creation of large-scale, research-driven art events. These included *The Russian Revolution in Bradford* (1967), which was performed on the city's streets by 300 students to mark the fiftieth anniversary of the Soviet revolution; *The God Show* (1968), in which students invented a religion; *Looking Forward to 1942* (1970), which explored questions of faith and history; and *John Ford's Cuban Missile Crisis* (1971), which cast the Cuban Missile Crisis of 1962 as a Hollywood Western.

Chris Parr, a director of new writing, was also a lightning conductor for countercultural energies in the city. In 1969, he was appointed a Fellow in Theatre at Bradford University, where he commissioned young writers, including Brenton, Edgar, Richard Crane and John Grillo, to produce work for his students at the university. Some of these took the form of what would now be called 'site-specific' performances on a huge scale: Brenton's *Wesley* (1970) was staged in the Methodist Hall and his *Scott of the Antarctic* (1971) at the ice rink, Edgar's *The End* (1972) in the university's Great Hall and Crane's *David, King of the Jews* (1973) in Bradford Cathedral.[22]

In 1971, the General Will was formed out of Parr's Bradford University group in order to tour Edgar's agitprop play *The National Interest*. 'Agitprop' – a conflation of the words 'agitation' and 'propaganda' – is a form of touring left-wing theatre intended to mobilise working-class audiences, especially at times of industrial struggle. With deep historical roots in the workers' theatre movements of revolutionary Russia and the 1930s, agitprop is characterised by archetypal characters, direct address, and topical content built around bold and often humorous visual metaphors. The General Will was one of the most active and important of the agitprop companies to emerge in the early 1970s. Discussion and research fed into the development of the plays and material was updated regularly: for Edgar, the achievement of the company was 'the sophistication with which it treated economic history'.[23]

However, by the mid-1970s, tensions opened up in the company between those who endorsed the classic Marxist analysis and those involved in the new identity politics ascendant at the time. Noël Greig, formerly of the Brighton Combination, had by this point come to Bradford and was a member of both the General Will and the Gay Liberation Front (GLF). During a benefit performance of Edgar's *The Dunkirk Spirit* (1974) in front of an audience of International Socialists, Greig halted the performance and went on strike to protest at the company's neglect of sexual politics. Edgar recounts this episode as a symbolic moment of fissure and fragmentation within the alternative theatre movement:

There were huge arguments about feminism and its importance or lack of importance, and gay rights, but the crucial thing for me was the General Will falling apart, which resulted from a conflict between the heterosexual men in the group and the one gay man in the group, Noël Greig. That was the moment when I realised that a kind of fragile unity had been broken.[24]

Socialist theatre

The varying aesthetics of socialist theatre in the 1970s reflects, as John McGrath puts it, 'a fusion of many past traditions and experiences

– like those of Joan Littlewood, the Unity theatres, the Workers' Theatre Movement of the 30s, the political theatre of Brecht, Piscator, O'Casey, Odets and many others'.[25] The pioneering socialist groups CAST (Cartoon Archetypical Slogan Theatre) and Red Ladder emerged in the late 1960s but the appearance of many others in the new decade coincided with an upsurge in industrial militancy: Bruce Birchall's West London Theatre Workshop (originally called the Notting Hill Theatre Workshop) was established in 1970; the General Will, 7:84 and North West Spanner in 1971; Foco Novo in 1972; Belt and Braces and 7:84 (Scotland) in 1973; Broadside Mobile Workers' Theatre in 1974. By the late 1970s, Edgar counted 'at least 18 full-time subsidized socialist groups' in Britain.[26]

The diversity of approach is exemplified in the work of the leading companies. CAST, founded in 1965 by Roland and Claire Muldoon, was renowned for its rapid-fire narrative, satirical take on contemporary politics and direct address to the audience. The Manchester-based North West Spanner developed from a children's theatre group but staged plays focused on local industrial disputes with a surreal edge to its agitprop caricatures. Foco Novo, founded by Roland Rees with David Aukin and Bernard Pomerance, toured to non-traditional venues such as miners' welfare and youth clubs, produced translations of Brecht and Büchner, and gave an early platform to the black playwrights Mustapha Matura, Tunde Ikoli and Alfred Fagon. Meanwhile, throughout the decade, the Leeds-based Red Ladder sought to strengthen relationships with local and trade union audiences. The group evolved out of the London-based Agitprop Street Players in 1968 and its early pieces included *The Big Con* (1970), performed for the Institute for Workers' Control in Nottingham, and *The Cake Play* (1971), written in opposition to the Conservative government's much-loathed Industrial Relations Act. The latter was performed eight times at the huge rally against the Industrial Relations Bill that took place in Hyde Park in February 1971, and the group also performed outside Pentonville Prison the following year during the national strike of dockworkers. In 1971, the company changed its name to Red Ladder (after a much-used prop) and applied for an Arts Council grant in 1973. At this point, the plays produced by the company became longer and more complex. For example, *Strike While the Iron is Hot* (also known as *A Woman's Work is Never Done*) is a key feminist text of the period influenced by Brecht's *The Mother*. It was staged in 1974 in the aftermath of the Equal Pay Act of 1970 (which came into force in 1975) and toured until 1976. The ebbing of working-class militancy in the mid-1970s, and trade union compliance in the new Labour government's 'social contract', led one section of Red Ladder to form the Broadside Mobile Workers' Theatre to perform bespoke touring plays to specific labour and trade union audiences. Red Ladder moved north to Leeds in 1976 and developed shows for broad-based working-class audiences in the region.

John McGrath was an established writer who changed the direction of his career to work in socialist theatre. He studied at Oxford University in the 1950s, worked briefly at the Royal Court, and wrote and directed early episodes of the BBC's police drama *Z-Cars*. Inspired by the revolutionary events of 1968, McGrath contributed to the underground newspaper *Black Dwarf* and, after a spell at the Liverpool Everyman Theatre, he founded 7:84 in 1971. The work of the company, according to Nadine Holdsworth, represents 'a determined rejection of metropolitan-centred, bourgeois and universal concepts of culture'.[27] The name '7:84' was culled from a statistic in a 1966 edition of *The Economist*: 7 per cent of the population own 84 per cent of the wealth. Most of its plays early on were written by McGrath but the company also staged Trevor Griffiths's *Occupations* and John Arden and Margaretta D'Arcy's *The Ballygombeen Bequest* (both 1972). Another landmark production was Arden's *Serjeant Musgrave Dances On* (1972), directed by Richard Eyre, which was an adaptation of Arden's 1959 play reset in the context of the Bloody Sunday massacre. In 1973, McGrath founded a Scottish 7:84 with Ferelith Lean and David and Elizabeth MacLennan; its production of *The Cheviot, the Stag and the Black, Black Oil* (1973) adopted the popular form of the ceilidh and intermixed agitprop caricatures with documentary material to tell the story of the Highland clearances and the squandering of North Sea oil. It toured the entirety of the Highlands and is widely regarded as one of the seminal theatre pieces of the decade.

The Belt and Braces Roadshow was established by Gavin Richards, who had worked with McGrath at the Liverpool Everyman in the early 1970s and 7:84 (England). Roadshow productions were distinctive for their blend of rock music and variety, combined with established acting techniques: the Belt and Braces Band formed links with external groups such as Music for Socialism, Rock Against Racism and the anti-Nazi campaigns. This company also staged the British premiere of Dario Fo's *Accidental Death of an Anarchist* in 1979, resulting in a West End transfer.

During the 1970s, many actors became involved in socialist groups and wider campaigns reflecting theatre's increasing participation in broader coalitions of left activism. The actress Vanessa Redgrave, for example, appeared in a 'Pageant of Labour History' as part of a rally at Wembley in March 1973 organised by the Socialist Labour League. Peter Plouviez, the general secretary of Equity, tried to account for the revolutionary tendencies of his members with a piece of breezy psychoanalysis: 'The proportion of our members involved in ultra-left activities is greater than in most unions. I think it appeals psychologically to some of them. There is an air of drama to a life based on a belief in imminent revolution.'[28]

Physical theatre and performance groups

The first edition of the academic journal *Theatre Quarterly*, published at the start of 1971, includes a 'Guide to Underground Theatre'. This is an important document, one of the first attempts to catalogue the burgeoning alternative or 'underground' theatre scene. Among the listings is an entry for a theatre group called Platform which is billed as follows: 'Platform is a fluid group of people who tackle anything that particularly interests them at any one time.'[29] This statement might seem non-committal to the point of vacuous but the word 'fluid' catches the eye, designating a refusal to be boxed in by genre or fixed through definition. In this respect, it captures an important impulse in the early 1970s towards openness of content and interdisciplinary method in the creation of performance. A number of key groups in the British counterculture translated 'fluidity' into aesthetic terms by incorporating, variously, improvisation, dance, music and ritual into their work, and by exploring the physical expressivity of the performer. Often, the intent was to produce sites of encounter, removed from conventional theatre spaces, which subverted or dissolved the traditional 'fourth wall' separating performer and spectator.

The hugely influential People Show, founded in 1966, created performances based on improvisation and bold choreography inspired by Dada and 1960s 'Happenings'. The Pip Simmons Theatre Group, established in 1968 and strongly inspired by the work of US companies such as LaMaMa and the Living Theatre, drew on an eclectic range of source material, from *Alice in Wonderland* to Superman. Its major piece of the decade, *An Die Musik* (1975), is a powerful meditation on the Holocaust and memory. The long-running performance group Welfare State was founded in 1968 by John Fox and Sue Gill. Fox worked at Bradford College of Art with Albert Hunt and the work of Welfare State was inspired by the large-scale, 'site-specific' spectacles that were a vital component of the Bradford Festivals. When the company was resident in Burnley, for example, it staged *Parliament in Flames* (1976) on 5 November ('Bonfire Night'), which involved the immolation of a mock Houses of Parliament. Other groups, such as John Bull's Puncture Repair Kit (founded in 1969) and Lumière and Son (1973), produced environmental pieces of immense visual orchestration and resonance. The street theatre troupe the Natural Theatre Company (founded in 1970 in Bath) and Medium Fair (1973, Devon) further exemplify the breadth of community-based theatrical activity at this time.

Two important companies, both founded in 1968, used physical theatre to deconstruct and reimagine canonical texts. Nancy Meckler (later the Artistic Director of Shared Experience) and Beth Porter of Freehold used collage-style techniques to perform the work of Sophocles and John Webster, while Steven Berkoff's London Theatre Group focused on adaptations of Kafka in *The Trial* (1970) and Edgar Allan Poe in *The Fall of the House of Usher* (1974). Berkoff's landmark play of the 1970s is *East* (1975), a visceral 'elegy' to London's East End that fuses verbal dexterity with punchy physicality.

Feminist theatre

The Women's Street Theatre Group (WSTG) was formed in the summer of 1970 as part of the rising feminist movement. Its founding members included Buzz Goodbody and Lily Susan Todd, both major theatre directors of the decade. On International Women's Day, 6 March 1971, the WSTG joined the march in London brandishing giant sanitary towels and a huge fake penis decorated in the colours of the Union Jack; they also picketed the Miss World Contest and the religious Festival of Light rally in 1971. Their performances cohered around striking visual parodies exemplified in *The Flashing Nipple Show* and an agitprop piece in which Todd represented the church, Goodbody played capitalism and Michèle Roberts (now a distinguished writer) appeared as a downtrodden woman chained between the two.[30] The WSTG also participated in an 'auction' of women on the London Underground and commandeered the Ladies lavatory in the Miss Selfridges store on Oxford Street.

The WSTG changed its name to Punching Judies and devised, in 1972, *The Amazing Equal Pay Show*. Based on a women's strike for equal pay at the Ford factory in 1968 (an event documented in the 2010 film *Made in Dagenham*), this was a piece of cartoon agitprop emphasising the connections between personal and workplace politics. Barbara Castle, the former Labour Minister for Employment, is satirised throughout: 'Bubble bubble toil and trouble/In Barbara's cauldron turn to rubble;/Crouch round while I make my spell/To give the women workers hell.'[31]

A landmark event was held in summer 1973: the Women's Theatre Festival at the Almost Free. It attracted more than one hundred women and included discussions, readings, workshops and a ten-week programme of lunchtime plays. Goodbody acted in the festival, Todd was one of the directors, and the playwrights Pam Gems and Michelene Wandor had their work presented. Afterwards, two groups were formed: the Women's Company and the Women's Theatre Group (WTG). The former comprised professional theatre women interested in promoting equal opportunities. It produced two shows: Pam Gems's *Go West, Young Woman* (1974), directed by Todd, and, in 1976, *My Name is Rosa Luxemburg*, translated by Gems from

Marianne Auricoste's play. However, the group lacked coherent identity, failed to get Arts Council funding and members dispersed to take on freelance work.

The WTG was, as its publicity stated, 'directed towards exploration of the female situation from a feminist viewpoint'.[32] Its first piece was *Fantasia* (1974), a collectively devised exploration of two women's fantasies, which toured a number of London venues. WTG policy was focused on making work for teenagers and building up new audiences; also central to its identity was its status as an all-women company and its use of post-show discussions to generate debate. The plays were didactic, socialist-feminist in orientation, and drew on pastiche and song mixed with naturalist plotting: *My Mother Says I Never Should* (1975) is a group-devised play on the theme of contraception; *Work to Role* (1976) traces the school-leaving experience of a young woman; and *Out on the Costa del Trico* (1977), staged at the time of the women-led strike at Grunwick, focuses on equal pay. From 1978, as the company became increasingly professionalised, it commissioned writers for the first time: *Hot Spot* (1978) by Eileen Fairweather and Melissa Murray, *Soap Opera* (1979) by US writer Donna Franceschild and Bryony Lavery's *The Wild Bunch* (1979). The WTG was one of the most enduring of the alternative theatre companies; it changed its name to Sphinx in 1990 and was honoured with an exhibition in 2005 at the National Theatre marking its thirtieth anniversary.

In October 1975, another Women's Theatre Festival was held at the Haymarket Theatre in Leicester. Jill Posener's *Any Woman Can* was performed along with pieces by Gems, Wandor, Caryl Churchill and Olwen Wymark. Monstrous Regiment, co-founded by Gillian Hanna (formerly of Belt and Braces) and Mary McCusker, was formed from this event. Monstrous Regiment aimed for high artistic standards, commissioned established writers from outside the group, and the company also included men, although they remained in a minority. Its first show was *Scum: Death, Destruction and Dirty Washing* (1976), by Claire Luckham and Chris Bond, a musical set in a laundry during the 1870 Paris Commune, which was directed by Todd. Subsequent productions included Churchill's *Vinegar Tom* (1976); *Kiss and Kill*

(1977), written and directed by Todd and the actress/director Ann Mitchell, which focuses on violence in various arenas of private and public life; Lavery's *Time Gentlemen Please* (1978), a controversial cabaret about sex; and David Edgar and Todd's *Teendreams* (1979) about political disillusionment in the aftermath of 1968.

In November and December 1977, Nancy Diuguid and Kate Crutchley, both experienced practitioners with Gay Sweatshop, organised the landmark Women's Festival 77 at Action Space (now the Drill Hall) in London. This was a life-changing event for many of the women who attended and it attracted participants from all over the world. Susan Griffin's *Voices* was performed, which Diuguid directed, and the schedule included concerts, workshops, art exhibitions and photography. Following from this, the Women's Project performed two plays in 1978: Michelene Wandor's *AID Thy Neighbour* at the New End Theatre in London, a comedy focused on artificial insemination by donor, and Kate Phelps's and Diuguid's *Confinement* at the Oval House, focused on women in prison. By the end of the decade, in a measure of the impact of feminism in theatre, smaller venues such as the Young Vic and Battersea Arts Centre (BAC) were holding women's festivals while the increasing level of women's activism was flagged in an article published in *Time Out* in 1977 headlined 'The Theatre's (Somewhat) Angry Young Women'.[33]

Feminist theatre groups sprang up throughout the decade, from the Bristol-based Sistershow in the early 1970s to the comedy trio Clapperclaw in 1977. Sidewalk Theatre Company toured *How the Vote was Won*, a compilation of songs and sketches to celebrate fifty years of female suffrage, in 1978. In that year, the feminist revue Bloomers and the theatre troupe Beryl and the Perils were established, and the punk-inspired Sadista Sisters re-formed. In 1979, Cunning Stunts and Hormone Imbalance were founded; Clean Break began work with women in the criminal justice system; the radical feminist troupe Siren was established in Brighton; Spare Tyre devised a play called *Baring the Weight* (based on Susie Orbach's recently published *Fat is a Feminist Issue*); and Winged Horse in Scotland was set up to promote female playwrights. Mrs Worthington's Daughters also produced its first season in early 1979. A mixed group founded by

Anne Engel, Stacey Charlesworth, Maggie Wilkinson, Steve Ley and director Julie Holledge, its focus was the historical recovery of 'lost' or neglected plays by women such as Susanna Cibber and Margaret Wynne Nevinson.

Major women playwrights of the 1970s include Caryl Churchill (whose work is considered in detail in Chapter 3), Olwen Wymark, who explored female subjectivity in plays such as *Find Me* (1977) and *Loved* (1978), and Michelene Wandor, whose prodigious writing for theatre in the 1970s included her fascinating adaptation of Elizabeth Barrett Browning's verse novel *Aurora Leigh* (1979). Pam Gems's breakthrough play, *Dusa, Fish, Stas and Vi*, was first performed as *Dead Fish* at the Edinburgh Festival in 1976, before transferring to Hampstead Theatre and then the West End in the following year. Her major play of the decade, however, is *Queen Christina* (1977). A biographical drama that places women's experience centre stage, the play was rejected by the male management of the Royal Court on the spurious grounds that it would 'appeal more' to women.[34] In fact, *Queen Christina* became the first play by a woman to be staged at the RSC's the Other Place. Gems consolidated her success with another inventive biographical text that crossed over into musical drama, *Piaf* (1978), which was staged by the RSC before transferring to the West End and Broadway.

The most commercially successful play by a woman in the 1970s was Mary O'Malley's convent comedy *Once a Catholic* (1977). This was staged by the Royal Court and transferred to the West End for two years. Another promising writer won early success before turning her career in a rather different direction: Tina Brown's award-winning first play *Under the Bamboo Tree* (1973) was produced at the Edinburgh Festival and this was followed by *Happy Yellow* (1977) at the Bush; in later decades, Brown resurfaced as the high-profile editor of *Vanity Fair* and the *New Yorker*. Louise Page, a graduate of David Edgar's playwriting course at Birmingham University, had her first plays produced at the end of the 1970s: *Tissue* (1978), about breast cancer, *Lucy* (1979), about euthanasia, and *Hearing* (1979), about the exploitation of workers and deaf people. Successful comedy writers of the 1980s also began to make an impact in theatre towards the end of the decade in the guise of Sue Townsend's *Womberang* (1979) and Victoria Wood's *Talent* (1978).

The women's theatre movement of the 1970s fostered an outstanding range of directors including Lily Susan Todd, Nancy Meckler, Nancy Diuguid and Buzz Goodbody. Jane Howell ran the Northcott Theatre in Exeter; there was also Verity Bargate at the Soho Poly, Thelma Holt at the Roundhouse, and Clare Venables at the Manchester Library Theatre and, later, the Theatre Royal Stratford East. Kate Crutchley became theatre programmer at the Oval House in 1980. Julie Parker performed with Gay Sweatshop, co-organised the Women's Festival in 1977 and was later appointed Artistic Director of the Drill Hall. The designers Andrea Montag and Di Seymour created the look and texture of many iconic theatre productions of the 1970s. Margaret (Peggy) Ramsay, the legendary theatrical agent, represented and inspired a generation of writers who came to prominence in the decade.

The sense of women's optimism that stretched across the 1970s is captured by Gillian Hanna: 'in the late seventies, feminism was the most exciting thing going, especially for people interested in politics. It was in the air, the most radical thing that had hit anybody since 1968, and for some of us since a long time before that'.[35] Activism by women theatre workers produced significant gains. From 1976, a Feminist Theatre Study Group campaigned for the foundation of a Women's Sub-Committee in Equity (and achieved this by 1978). The group picketed West End shows to protest about the roles and working conditions of actresses, in October 1978, and initiated events that resulted in two major conferences: 'Women and Creativity' (1980) and 'Women Writers Talking – Is There a Women's Culture?' (1982).

Looking back on the 1970s, Wandor notes how the bold images, direct address and campaigning orientation of early agitprop gave way to the formation of professional companies.[36] With increases in subsidy, these groups began to employ directors, designers and writers and moved away from collective authorship and class-based activism. The end of the decade saw a rise in women performers questioning genres, popular forms and established representations of gender (some of this critique fed into the alternative comedy of the early 1980s). At the same time, reductions in funding limited the opportunities for collaborative work and pushed the emphasis towards individually authored plays.

In spite of feminist achievement in the decade, in 1980 the *British Alternative Theatre Directory* listed 327 playwrights, of whom thirty-eight were women. In the same year, Methuen's list of forty modern British playwrights included only one woman (plus one as co-author) while Faber's list of thirty-five published playwrights included one woman.[37] In respect of theatre directing, Clare Venables, in an article also published in 1980, observed that: '[n]o woman has ever directed a major production at the National, and since Jane Howell left the Royal Court ten years ago no woman has directed a major production there'.[38] The gains of feminism, in other words, were far from secured. Hanna, commenting in interview in 1989 after a decade of feminist backlash, picks up this point: 'In 1978, you could see a future for alternative theatre and imagine a place for yourself in it. You thought you could have an influence. It was like being on a trampoline. But we've stopped bouncing. None of us, even in our worst nightmares, saw what was coming in the next ten years.'[39]

Gay and lesbian theatre

In summer 1974, Ed Berman invited gay theatre workers to organise a festival at the Almost Free along the lines of the Women's Festival held the year before. The ensuing season, 'Homosexual Acts', had an extended run over lunchtimes from March into the summer of 1975. The programme included Laurence Collinson's *Thinking Straight*, two pieces from Robert Patrick – *One Person* and *Fred and Harold* – and Martin Sherman's *Passing By*. Stewart Trotter, Gerald Chapman and Drew Griffiths were among the directors, and Antony Sher and Simon Callow were in the acting company. Aside from its lack of any historical precedent, the season was distinctive for two reasons: it gave a high profile to US writers (Patrick and Sherman are American) and it focused exclusively on men.

The liberationist politics of the 1970s is exemplified in the work of the company formed out of this season: Gay Sweatshop. It was established by Chapman and Griffiths in 1975 as a touring group focused on new writing. Its first production was Roger Baker and Griffiths's *Mister X*, a play notorious for its impassioned 'coming out' speech at the end. The piece was performed at the Campaign for Homosexual Equality (CHE) conference in Sheffield in 1975 and toured around Britain. Alan Sinfield gives a memorable summation of its impact:

> The audience at Sheffield stood and cheered, many of them in tears [. . .]. Around the country, nothing remotely like this had been seen before. Local bigots raised various kinds of furore, but the effect was to incite gay people to attend – a brave thing to do in their home town. The discussions between the cast and the audience after the show disclosed isolation, distress, courage and exhilaration.[40]

Fortified by this experience, Gay Sweatshop organised a second season of plays at the ICA which ran from February to July 1976. Lesbians became involved at this point with the production of Jill Posener's *Any Woman Can*, which had premièred as a rehearsed reading the previous autumn at the Leicester Women's Theatre Festival, with Miriam Margolyes in the central role. The season also included Edward Bond's allegorical play *Stone*, written at the request of the company, Baker and Griffiths's *Indiscreet*, and Andrew Davies's *Randy Robinson's Unsuitable Relationship*. After the ICA season, *Any Woman Can* went on a national tour often billed with *Mister X*.

Although the male and female members of Gay Sweatshop worked together on Christmas pantomimes and on projects such as *Age of Consent* (1977), which was staged at the Royal Court as part of its Young People's Theatre Programme, the men and women quite quickly divided into single-sex companies under the same organisational structure. This split, while cordial, reflected the different political priorities and experiences of oppression of each gender. The divergence was also linked to aesthetic strategy, with the men embracing camp and drag, and the women agitprop and documentary. In 1977, the men toured Noël Greig and Griffiths's *As Time Goes*

By, which framed homophobia within a broad historical canvas, while the women produced *Care and Control*, written by Michelene Wandor, about the state's interference in women's reproductive rights.

Throughout the decade, members of Gay Sweatshop were subjected to homophobic violence, threats and pickets, and they were turned away from accommodation while on tour.[41] A performance of *Iceberg* (1978), jointly staged by the men and women, took place at Queen's University in Belfast, where the Democratic Unionist Party (DUP) responded to the company's presence with an intimidating torch-lit parade and hymn-singing at the venue. This was in the context of DUP leader Ian Paisley's so-called 'Save Ulster from Sodomy' campaign to prevent the decriminalisation of homosexual acts in Northern Ireland (his campaign ultimately failed: decriminalisation took place in 1982).

Aside from the pioneering work of Gay Sweatshop, the possibilities of sexual and gender identity were figured onstage in a variety of ways in a number of extraordinary productions during the decade. Richard O'Brien's *The Rocky Horror Show* (1973) – a transsexual stockings-and-stilettoes extravaganza that perhaps marks the apotheosis of the 1970s aspiration for participatory theatre – began its global ascent in the somewhat subdued environs of the Royal Court Theatre Upstairs. In 1976, the Oval House hosted a visit from the New York gay cabaret troupe Hot Peaches: one of the group's British admirers, a young actor called Peter Bourne, insinuated himself into their European tour, transformed himself into the drag artist Bette Bourne and founded the radical drag collective Bloolips, which ran for the next two decades.[42] The lesbian company Hormone Imbalance created an original piece from Melissa Murray's deconstructive verse play *Ophelia* in 1979. And, at the end of the decade, Martin Sherman's *Bent* (1979) at the Royal Court, starring Ian McKellen, was a major turning point that signalled, as Dominic Shellard puts it, 'the first step for gay theatre from fringe venues to the mainstream of subsidised theatre'.[43]

Black and Asian theatre

In 1970, Inter-Action hosted an Ambiance Lunch Hour 'Black and White Power' season at the ICA. This event launched the playwriting career of the Trinidadian-born Mustapha Matura, while two of the actors involved, Alfred Fagon and T-Bone Wilson, were themselves inspired to become writers as a result of their participation in the season. In the early 1970s, the Royal Court promoted the work of Matura, and his colleague Michael Abbensetts, and its production of the former's *Play Mas* (1974) was the first transfer of a play by a Caribbean playwright into the West End. In 1979, Matura established the Black Theatre Co-Operative, later called Nitro, to create more opportunities for black theatre artists.

Dark and Light, in the words of Colin Chambers, was 'the first British theatre company with any continuous presence and its own base to be shaped and defined by black talent'.[44] Established by the Jamaican actor Frank Cousins in 1969 in south London, its first production was a revival of Athol Fugard's *Blood Knot* in 1971. Dark and Light became the Black Theatre of Brixton in 1975 and the emphasis moved to building strong community links. Over the following three years, before its closure in 1978, it produced work by Jamal Ali, Jimi Rand and Steve Wilmer, among others, and convened a festival, 'Black Explosion', at the Roundhouse in 1975.

There was an 'extraordinary mushrooming' of black and Asian theatre groups during the 1970s, from Acacia and African Dawn to Wall Theatre and the West Indian Drama Group of Bristol.[45] Many theatre initiatives were tied to community action such as the vibrant Theatre Workshop that operated under the auspices of the Keskidee arts resource in north London from 1971. In 1974, Cy Grant and John Mapondera began their attempt to establish a national black arts resource, the Drum Arts Centre: they organised a two-week season of Caribbean plays at the ICA ('Mas in the Mall', 1975) and an ambitious workshop collaboration with Morley College in Lambeth.

One of the major companies of the decade was Temba, founded in 1972 by the actors Oscar James (who had appeared in the Ambiance season) and Alton Kumalo, to create a platform for black writers from Britain and South Africa. It performed the work of Matura, Fugard,

Leroi Jones, David Halliwell, John Kani and Winston Ntshona, among others, and was the first black British theatre company to receive an Arts Council subsidy. The influential Asian company Tara Arts was established in 1977 by Jatinder Verma in the aftermath of the racist murder of the Sikh schoolboy Gurdip Singh Chaggar the year before; its early pieces, such as *Fuse* (1978), carried an anti-racist message.

In 1976, Naseem Khan published a ground-breaking study, *The Arts Britain Ignores*: the first in-depth analysis of arts and ethnic minorities in Britain. She identified a devastating lack of opportunity in funding, training and institutional infrastructure. In his discussion of Khan's report, Chambers notes the hard realities faced by black actors in the mid-seventies: '[i]n spring 1975, there were only ten British-born/-raised/-based black drama students in eight London drama schools of a total of 675 students. [. . .] no black actor was a permanent member of a repertory company.'[46] In consequence, the Minorities' Arts and Advisory Service (MAAS) was established, which began to coordinate publications, campaigns and conferences.

While black and Asian playwriting in Britain gathered momentum and visibility in the 1970s, it remained largely dominated by men until the 1980s. However, in October 1979, the performance at the Royalty Theatre in London of Ntozake Shange's stirring 'choreopoem', *for colored girls who have considered suicide/when the rainbow is enuf*, broke new ground in experimental black women's theatre.

Playwriting and politics

Towards the middle of the decade, with inflation nearing 30 per cent, trade unions compliant with the Labour government's pay policy and socialists defeated in the referendum on Britain's entry into Europe, there was disillusionment and increasing bitterness on the left. These divisions triggered debate among socialist theatre practitioners about their political and aesthetic priorities. These discussions coincided with a period in which the new generation of playwrights were attempting, for both ideological and career reasons, to break onto the established stages and write new kinds of plays that were responsive to changing circumstances.

Reflecting in 1979 on his departure from the General Will, Edgar comments: 'I was increasingly thinking that the politics you could get across [in agitprop plays] were very crude, whereas the world about us was getting more complicated. Or perhaps we were getting more complicated, and just noticing that that's the way the world had always been.'[47] Edgar elaborates his argument in an article published in *Socialist Review* in 1978, which was reprinted as 'Ten Years of Political Theatre' in the winter 1979 edition of *Theatre Quarterly*.[48] The ideas in the essay were first articulated at a weekend drama conference at King's College, Cambridge, in March 1978. This event was organised by the academics Peter Holland and Stephen Copley, and attended by Edgar, John McGrath and David Hare amongst others: all three playwrights made speeches on the status and viability of socialist theatre in the new context and, for this reason alone, the conference stands as a landmark event in the history of British alternative theatre.

Edgar contests, in particular, the view of socialist theatre put forward in an anonymous article published in the left-wing *Wedge* magazine in summer 1977. Its author was later revealed to be the playwright and Artistic Director of West London Theatre Workshop, Bruce Birchall. In his article, Birchall argues: 'the post-1968 breakaway movement became absorbed into the theatrical mainstream by state funding, and [. . .] what had begun as a piece of political practice ended up as a job, with the result that cultural workers began to see themselves as "left-wing artists", rather than as socialists who used artforms for political ends'.[49] Birchall's concern was that the 'professionalisation' of alternative theatre that followed on the heels of increases in state subsidy had neutered the terms of theatre's ideological intervention, leading it to forsake socialist activism for commercial prerogative. He argued, for example, that what he perceived to be the increasing prevalence of naturalism in alternative theatre actually reflected a reactionary shift on the part of theatre directors to win grants.

Edgar took a different view: for him, the theatrical techniques and propagandising impetus of agitprop, while apposite for a period of industrial militancy, were 'not suited to the tasks of a period of class retreat'.[50] In addition, Edgar suggested that the focus of Marxist critique had moved from the point of production to the point of consumption: the obligation of socialist theatre practice, therefore, was to attend not only to the fact of exploitation in class society but also to the sense of alienation in the consumer cornucopia. As he puts it: 'Revolutionary politics was seen as being much less about the organization of the working class at the point of production, and much more about the disruption of bourgeois ideology at the point of consumption. The centre of the revolution had shifted from the factory-floor to the supermarket.'[51] Edgar also notes that, in the early 1970s, the General Will attracted some working-class audiences but principally its shows were attended by what he describes as the 'local polytechnic and local government left'.[52] His playwriting, therefore, turned increasingly towards addressing this constituency, most emphatically in his play *Destiny* (1976). The issue was not merely that agitprop was unsuited to the new political climate but there was also a fundamental lack of cultural connection between some alternative theatre companies and the working class they sought to engage. Clive Barker, a leading figure in British socialist theatre at this time, makes an identical point: 'The Alternative Theatre in England during the early 1970s had too many examples of groups of students explaining to car-workers how the car-workers were being exploited, a subject on which the car-workers were experts and the students were not.'[53]

Similar concerns were inflected in different ways by other playwrights. As I describe in Chapter 3 of this book, David Hare's lecture to the conference enacted a scorched-earth critique of Marxist theatre. Howard Barker, too, was frustrated by his perception of British theatre's – and especially the Royal Court's – delusionary and parasitical relationship with the working class. In an interview given in 2010, he comments: 'I experienced this nausea in the sheer amount of propaganda that that place was issuing out, in the name of the working class, with whom the directors had no relationship whatsoever.'[54] Indeed, by the middle of the decade, the playwright Trevor Griffiths had abandoned theatre altogether. These are his words from 1972: 'I don't see [theatre] as in any way a major form of communicating descriptions or analyses or modifying attitudes [. . .]. It's in television that I think, as a political writer, I want to be, because very large numbers of people, who are not accessible any other way, *are* accessible in television.'[55]

While Griffiths relinquished theatre for television, John McGrath moved in the other direction. Like Edgar and Hare, McGrath also spoke at the 1978 conference and published an important article based on his paper 'The Theory and Practice of Political Theatre' in *Theatre Quarterly* in 1979; the ideas in this article set the foundation for his subsequent series of talks at Cambridge University, later collated in his barnstorming book *A Good Night Out* in 1981.[56] In the afterword to his article, McGrath accuses Edgar of 'indifference to the development of working-class culture', and of giving theatre workers 'a "socialist" reason for deserting the working class and settling down to experimenting with "the upending of received forms" for the cosmopolitan cultural elite'.[57] McGrath asserts the ongoing utility of popular forms which were not, as he aims to demonstrate in *A Good Night Out*, 'dying a lingering death in the Celtic twilight'.[58] No doubt drawing from his own early professional experiences in screen media, McGrath rejects entirely Griffiths's view: 'I finally came to the conclusion that the mass media, at the moment, are so penetrated by the ruling class ideology, that to try to dedicate your whole life – as distinct from occasional forays and skirmishes – to fighting within them is going to drive you mad.'[59]

Writers like Hare and Edgar – having completed a significant body of work by the mid-1970s – were increasingly concerned to address complex subject matter and prise open the relationship between politics and individual psychology. In an interview published in 1979, Edgar recalls his determination to write about 'public subjects which did not take place in rooms but in *areas* [. . .]. Because streets are larger than houses, and battlefields are larger than bedrooms.'[60] Howard Brenton, in a book published in 1980, makes a similar point when discussing his decision to accept the National Theatre's commission for his 1976 play *Weapons of Happiness*: 'You just can't write a play that describes social action with under ten actors. With fifteen you can describe whole countries, whole classes, centuries [. . .]'[61] In the endeavour to break out from fringe spaces on to the larger subsidised stages, Brenton made advances with his adaptation of *Measure for Measure*, which was produced at the Northcott Theatre in Exeter in 1972, but this experience was dogged by controversy and lack of support from the theatre's board. Brenton fought hard the following year to solicit a main stage production for *Magnificence* at the Royal Court, but audiences were poor. The first successful inroad into main stage performance of a play from fringe writers was Brenton and Hare's *Brassneck* at Nottingham Playhouse in 1973: as Peter Ansorge comments, '[i]t was the hit of the season, won national praise from the critics, and established the fringe as a powerful potential force in the traditional theatre'.[62] In the year that *Brassneck* was staged, Edgar began writing *Destiny* and it proved to be an enormous challenge to find a theatre that would agree to produce the play.[63] The televising of *Destiny* in 1978 – five years after he began work on the play – was 'an event regarded by many as one emphatic vindication of the political theatre movement'.[64] This 'vindication' would not have been possible without the new director–playwright partnerships – Richard Eyre and Howard Brenton/Trevor Griffiths, Max Stafford-Clark and Caryl Churchill, Ron Daniels and David Edgar – that facilitated the performance of new writing in larger theatres.

By the mid-1970s, the divisions between alternative and mainstream were becoming more porous: Griffiths had written for 7:84 and the RSC, Hare for Portable and the Hampstead Theatre, Barker for the Open Space and the Royal Court.[65] It is striking that Ansorge ends the final chapter of his 1975 book with a plea to managements of larger theatres to commission work from the 'alternative' generation: 'The idea of having Brenton adapt a modern version of *Measure for Measure* for the Royal Shakespeare Company, or Pip Simmons directing *The Bacchae* at the National, should seem like stimulating ideas to the powers that be.'[66]

'State of the nation' is a term often used to designate the form of playwriting produced by these writers for the large subsidised theatres, which included, of course, the newly opened National Theatre on the South Bank. Commensurate with the fractious mid-decade political context described earlier, state of the nation dramaturgy arbitrates the sense of alienation and disillusionment, especially with (and from within) the left. In terms of the rejection of agitprop, it is disposed towards social realism in place of broad-stroke caricature.[67] Edgar, in particular, was influenced by his reading of John Berger's *Art and Revolution* (1969) and the writings of the Marxist literary critic Georg Lukács. The following description of the style of his play *Destiny*, by the drama critic Anthony Everitt, is taken from the programme note for the RSC production in 1976:

> The *thesis* is 'bourgeois' drama, which describes human behaviour but does not explain it. The *antithesis* is agitprop drama which portrays men and women as being totally determined by social and economic conditions.
>
> Edgar is now attempting a *synthesis* which explores the dynamic between individual motives and external conditions. [. . .] The mass media have powerfully encouraged a view of drama which emphasises a psychological approach to character. The writer who ignores this may isolate himself [*sic*] from the audiences he seeks.[68]

Brenton describes the 'synthesis' achieved in the state of the nation play as '"British epic theatre"', arguing that 'characters, like William Blake's poems, go from innocence to experience'.[69]

Aside from social realism on an 'epic' scale, playwrights throughout the 1970s conjured a broad range of styles and image repertoires to negotiate contemporary concerns. Edward Bond produced an extraordinary canon during the decade: *Lear* (1971), *The Sea* (1973) and *The Fool* (1975) were all staged by the Royal Court, *Bingo* (1976) and *The Bundle* (1978) by the RSC, and *The Woman* (1978) by the National Theatre. Barker's series of 'state of England' plays – including *Claw* (1975), *Stripwell* (1975) and *The Hang of the Gaol* (1978) – excavate the subaltern desires that suffuse public and private action while David Rudkin's *The Sons of Light* (1974) is premised on a fantastical and compelling image of class society.[70] A tranche of major plays re-envision history and historical processes: Arden's *The Non-Stop Connolly Show* (1975) and *Vandaleur's Folly* (1978), McGrath's *The*

Cheviot, the Stag and the Black Black Oil (1973), Hare's *Fanshen* (1975), Churchill's *Light Shining in Buckinghamshire* (1976), Gems's *Queen Christina* (1977) and Peter Whelan's *Captain Swing* (1978). On a more intimate scale, Simon Gray's *Butley* (1971), Stephen Poliakoff's *City Sugar* (1975) and *Strawberry Fields* (1976), and Barrie Keeffe's *A Mad World, My Masters* (1977) evoke the flattened aspirations and new socioeconomic pressures of mid-1970s Britain. This is also, of course, the territory of Mike Leigh's bleakly comical *Abigail's Party* (1977) – for many, the iconic play of the decade.

In 1977, the publisher John Calder hailed 'an incredible flowering of outstanding political plays' but observed, too, that the idealism of the 1960s was finished: 'The strength of our political theatre lies in its negative attitude. It does not posit any ideal or even reasonable society, but criticises the societies we have, exposing their weaknesses, dangers and inhumanities.'[71] This pervading sense of negativity was criticised by some socialist practitioners, including McGrath, who saw it as a modish form of ideological retreat served up by a group of writers too eager to infiltrate the established citadels of British theatre.

Funding

The Arts Council received its Royal Charter in 1967 as an independent subsidising organisation and entered its so-called 'golden age' under Jennie Lee, Labour's Arts Minister (1964–70), and its Chairman, Arnold Goodman (1965–70). However, from the outset, the council's attitude towards alternative theatre was distinctly patrician, as is demonstrated in Goodman's introduction to his Annual Report of 1969–70: 'we had, rightly or wrongly, heard that a group of youngsters around the country had some new ideas and the rumour grew with disturbing persistence. Reverberations came from arts laboratories in London and nearby seaside resorts, from towns rarely associated with artistic explosions [. . .] there was something astir [. . .]'[72] The council set up a subcommittee (later called the New Activities Committee) to support alternative theatre in the late 1960s. From 1971 to 1978, Arts Council money for alternative theatre increased from around £7,000 to £1.5million.[73] Maria DiCenzo observes that grants increased exponentially in the first half of the decade: between 1972–3 and 1975–6, for example, Red Ladder's funding increased from £1,105 to £18,950, and 7:84 (England)'s from £1,296 to £29,950.[74]

Increased subsidy enabled companies to become stable and held out the prospect of secure and diverse career pathways for alternative theatre workers. However, as grants increased, they came with strings. A new administrative structure was created comprising management boards and top-down hierarchy. The Arts Council refused the collective management which many alternative companies, such as 7:84 and Hull Truck, had implemented. In a sign of the times, Monstrous Regiment appointed a full-time administrator in 1976 but, within a few years, the administrator was the only full-time employee.[75] The need for forward planning militated against the staging of theatre focused on topical content and, to ensure bookings, socialist groups relied increasingly on organisations within the Labour movement and these were not always predisposed towards plays critical of the Labour government from 1974. When savings needed to be made, touring was often an early casualty and this skewed resources, once again, towards London.

There were also concerns about the kinds of appropriation that reliance on subsidy might engender. Clive Barker argues that 'Alternative Theatre became gradually absorbed into the Establishment by subsidy', Charles Marowitz dismissed it as 'hush money', while John McGrath felt that subsidy rendered alternative theatre a 'vast recruiting-ground for the RSC and the National and the bigger reps'.[76] During the decade, there was heated debate about how the money was spent, how much was available and how unequally it was distributed. Catherine Itzin notes that, in 1973, alternative theatre received only 4 per cent of the total £3.2 million allocated to drama; by 1973–4, it received £250,000 – one half of the budget of the National Theatre – to be shared by sixty companies.[77] From 1970–1 to 1980–1, as Baz Kershaw explains, the percentage of the entire Arts Council budget for theatre spent on the National Theatre and RSC increased from 30 to 43 per cent.[78]

A pressure group called the Association of Lunchtime Theatres was formed in 1972, which led to the founding of The Association of Community Theatre (TACT). It held its first conference in 1974 to put pressure on the Arts Council to increase subsidy so that companies could pay the Equity minimum wage. When this was eventually achieved, grants had to be based on union-agreed minimum wages matching those in other parts of subsidised theatre. This made subsidy more expensive and the extra money had to be factored into budgets at a time when more companies were appearing. In 1975, for the first time in ten years, there was no increase in money from the Arts Council. A conference at the Oval House in October 1975 attracted fifty theatre groups and thirty writers to protest against cuts and policy changes.[79] The Theatre Writers' Group, later the Theatre Writers' Union (TWU), emerged from this event. Amid increasing signs of the 'professionalisation' of alternative theatre, TACT merged with the Independent Theatres Council (ITC) and related professional associations, such as the Society for British Theatre Designers, were constituted.

There was also controversy about a perceived lack of accountability in the Arts Council. In 1975–6, in his first report as Secretary General, Roy Shaw made a revealing gaffe when waxing lyrical about 'roses for the few' and 'dandelions for the many' in his statements on the relative value of the arts.[80] His words carried the implication that alternative theatre was an unweeded garden overrun with sub-quality work. In his report the following year, Shaw added insult to injury by making crude distinctions between high art ('often complex and demanding') and popular forms ('less demanding').[81] Malcolm Griffiths, the director, writer, academic and member of the Arts Council from 1971 to 1976, wrote a stinging assault on council policy in the spring 1977 edition of *Theatre Quarterly*. It was titled, caustically, 'The Drama Panel Game': '[the Arts Council uses] its internal structure directly to affect the work of a company it disapproves of by shunting it around inside itself'.[82] Even Hugh Jenkins, Labour's Arts Minister from 1974 to 1976, despaired of the council's conservatism and opacity in his book *The Culture Gap: An Experience of Government and the Arts*, published in 1979. The Labour Party launched discussion and policy documents on the arts in 1974 and 1975, and the Trades Union Congress (TUC) also produced a consultative paper from its Working Party on the arts, but theatre workers felt that these were 'simply [. . .] exercises in structural shell-making'.[83]

The distribution of money through local authorities and Regional Arts Associations (RAAs) became increasingly important as part of the wider movement towards devolution in Scotland, Wales and the English regions. In 1978, there were fifteen RAAs already in existence and it seemed logical to distribute money through them. RAAs became more involved in organising tours in partnership with theatre companies: while this helped to ensure access to theatre across a region, the focus tended to be on studio theatres and arts centres leading to a neglect of working-class cultural spaces. The new funding mechanism also produced flagrant instances of censorship. In 1977, the North West Arts Association cut its grant to North West Spanner because of the latter's Marxist politics. This move was initiated by a Conservative councillor who was a member of the new right-wing National Association for Freedom (NAFF). The incident provoked an outcry, even from Shaw – '[i]f devolution puts clients at the mercy of political pressures, we shall have to reconsider the whole question' – and the funding cut was eventually overturned by a well-organised local campaign.[84]

There was an earlier flashpoint that further illuminated the link between funding and censorship. This pertained to 7:84's production of *The Ballygombeen Bequest* by John Arden and Margaretta D'Arcy in 1972. Their play attacked British actions in Northern Ireland and accused the British Army of using torture. The production was halted after legal advice in the final week of its run at the Bush Theatre. The controversy related to a programme note about a real absentee English landlord who was in the process of evicting a tenant and whose contact details were listed in the programme. The landlord issued a writ on the writers in a civil action and the military also complained about the play's content. The case was eventually settled out of court but the company's annual grant was removed, forcing it to rely on project funding (where a funding application has to be made for each new show). In similar vein, in 1976, Foco Novo staged *The Nine Days and Saltley Gates*, a play which supported industrial unrest, only to have its grant reduced the next year. As Maria DiCenzo points out, '[t]he upshot of actions like these was to foster a greater degree of self-censorship on the part of companies seeking or trying to maintain funding'.[85] Self-censorship was to become a staple conundrum for theatre workers in the 1980s.

As the economic climate worsened, the Association for Business Sponsorship of the Arts (ABSA) was established in 1976 and grew in influence. Under the new Conservative government in 1980, the Arts Council announced the suspension of programme grants, withdrew funding from forty companies and moved the emphasis to project grants. This was a devastating and indeed terminal blow for many alternative theatre companies at the start of the Thatcherite decade.

Flagship theatres

The RSC

In 1968, Trevor Nunn succeeded Peter Hall as Artistic Director of the RSC. There were four key figures who shaped institutional policy during the 1970s: Nunn, David Jones, John Barton and Terry Hands (the latter joined the company from the Liverpool Everyman and became joint Artistic Director in 1978). The achievements of the RSC during the 1970s include its opening of a smaller 'studio' space at Stratford (the Other Place in 1974) and a venue for new writing in London (the Warehouse, 1977). The company also nurtured a remarkable generation of actors (including Ben Kingsley, Peter McEnery, Helen Mirren, Patrick Stewart and Janet Suzman) and undertook an ambitious range of programming and support for new writers.

Three productions of the decade are among the most highly regarded in the RSC's history. Peter Brook's direction of *A Midsummer Night's Dream* in 1970, set within a white cube, eschewed conventional saccharine treatments of the play by focusing on the actors' physical and circus skills to mesmerising effect. *Macbeth*, directed by Nunn, was staged in the Other Place in 1976, and starred Ian McKellen as Macbeth and Judi Dench as his wife. The action was performed within a simple black circle on the floor, an image of desolate intensity. In 1977, Terry Hands directed the *Henry VI* trilogy at the Royal Shakespeare Theatre, with Alan Howard as the eponymous king. The cycle was performed in its entirety from mid-morning to late evening – an astonishing feat of logistics and stamina that foreshadowed the RSC's gravitation towards large-scale 'event' theatre in the 1980s. The RSC's commitment to new writing, enhanced by director Howard Davies's programming at the Warehouse, was evidenced in memorable productions of Tom Stoppard's *Travesties* (1974), Edward Bond's *Bingo* (1976), David Edgar's *Destiny* (1976), Peter Nichols's *Privates on Parade* (1977) and Howard Barker's *That Good Between Us* (1977).

However, the RSC was not immune from the highly charged politics of the early 1970s. In 1972, John Arden and Margaretta D'Arcy picketed the production of their play *The Island of the Mighty* at the Aldwych Theatre, the RSC's London venue, claiming that the company had distorted its anti-imperial message. The authors eventually 'disowned the production entirely' and William Gaskill records them '[climbing on to] the stage to pull down the scenery in protest'.[86] In 1972, the RSC refused to produce a play commissioned from Arnold Wesker, *The Journalists*, after a revolt by the cast over the representation of Conservative politicians in the play: Wesker claimed that the actors were dominated by the influence of the Workers' Revolutionary Party and sued for breach of contract.

In 1974, the Other Place, a small converted 'tin hut' that reflected the intimate spaces occupied by many alternative companies, opened at Stratford. Its founder and first Artistic Director, Buzz Goodbody, staged two inspired productions of Shakespeare in the new venue, *King Lear* (1974) and *Hamlet* (1975). Her suicide in 1975, aged twenty-eight, was a terrible blow to the company and the wider theatre community. By the end of the decade, the Other Place had made an enormous impact: '[f]ive shows had transferred to larger auditoria, two had been televised, and one, *Piaf*, had gone into the West End'.[87]

The RSC intensified its commitment to small-scale touring during the 1970s and hosted seasons in Newcastle; some of its productions were also adapted for television. In 1978, with chilly economic winds blowing, the company agreed a sponsorship deal with Hallmark cards to fund a regional tour: worth £12,000 in 1978, the sum had increased to £45,000 by 1980.[88]

The National Theatre

In 1969, construction began on the new National Theatre complex, designed by Denys Lasdun, on London's South Bank. The National Theatre Company was, at this time, based around the corner at the Old Vic Theatre under the stewardship of Laurence Olivier, its first Artistic Director from 1963. By 1971–2, average audience attendance had declined from 97 per cent to 79 per cent and Olivier, who suffered a thrombosis on his leg in August 1970, began to resemble 'a latter-day theatrical Moses, destined never to lead his people into the promised land'.[89] In 1973, Peter Hall, the founding director of the RSC in 1961 and former director of Glyndebourne, succeeded Olivier as Artistic Director.

During this period of uncertainty and transition, Olivier gave two of the defining stage performances of his career in the early 1970s: in Eugene O'Neill's *Long Day's Journey into Night* at the New Theatre (1971) and as the communist John Tagg in Trevor Griffiths's *The Party*, directed by John Dexter (1973). Griffiths's play provoked consternation amongst members of the National's board, including the Labour-supporting Victor Mishcon, who were unhappy with its politics: should the National, Mishcon asked, 'deal with subjects which are critical of politics and of the British way of life and in some sense are revolutionary, even anarchist?'[90] Tynan disagreed and, in a rhetorical flourish reflective of its time, described the play as 'the most inspiring call to revolution ever heard on the English stage'.[91] *The Party* opened in December, less than a fortnight before the onset of the three-day week, and won praise for its interrogative approach to democracy. This was Olivier's final stage performance: 'I'll never forget,' recalled Griffiths later, 'three or four times when I saw Olivier snap the theatre with his performance.'[92]

After Olivier's departure in March 1974, there was a change of direction: Hall's first major success was his 1975 production of Ralph Richardson in Ibsen's *John Gabriel Borkman*. On 16 March 1976, the

Lyttelton Theatre opened with Albert Finney in *Hamlet*, while in July, Howard Brenton's *Weapons of Happiness* became the first new play to be staged there; on 4 October, the Olivier Theatre opened with a staging of *Tamburlaine*; and the smaller Cottesloe Theatre opened the following year. After considerable delay and spiralling costs, the South Bank complex was inaugurated on 4 March 1977. By this point, the National had a new home on the South Bank, it was led by an experienced director and Hall's strategy of recruiting star actors, such as Finney, Richardson, John Gielgud and Peggy Ashcroft, increased the profile of the company. However, there were also severe challenges: the South Bank opened three years late, the directors John Dexter and Jonathan Miller had departed, Hall's administration was plagued by industrial disputes, financial constraints and bad publicity, and his team struggled to cope with running three new spaces.

The National was forever ensnared in debates about its funding and purpose. In October 1974, fourteen directors wrote to *The Times* to criticise the amount of subsidy allocated to the National at the expense of regional theatre (the National's share of the Arts Council drama budget increased from 12.5 per cent in 1972–3 to 25 per cent in 1975–6). By the mid-1970s, the National was £500,000 in deficit and its projected costs were £1 million per year. The government stepped in with a one-off grant but the press labelled the venue a 'white elephant'. In 1976, there was a stage management strike; in May 1977, one hundred backstage staff walked out over the sacking of a plumber; in 1978, there was an overtime ban and, in March 1979, an unofficial strike closed all three theatres for two months. In the ensuing climate of exhaustion and bitterness, 'there was', as Alwyn W. Turner observes wryly, 'an element of pot luck when buying a ticket for a performance'.[93]

Notable productions of the 1970s included Tom Stoppard's *Jumpers* (1972), Robert Bolt's *State of Revolution* (1977), Alan Ayckbourn's *Bedroom Farce* (which was also a strategic money-spinner, 1978) and David Hare's resounding state of the nation play *Plenty* (1978). The production of two of Peter Shaffer's plays book-ended the decade with success: John Dexter directed *Equus* in 1973 while Hall directed *Amadeus* in 1979, with Simon Callow as Mozart. The latter production sold out and transferred to the West End, presaging the vogue for spectacle in the 1980s.

In March 1978, Julia Pascal devised and directed *Men Seldom Make Passes*, a compilation of the work of Dorothy Parker, as a 'platform' performance. In so doing, she became the first woman to direct at the South Bank complex. During the 1970s, women at the National began to agitate for better roles and conditions: the actress Maggie Ford recounts how, in 1978, a male colleague at the National responded as follows to an announcement about a women's meeting: '[w]hat are you going to discuss – knitting patterns and period pains?'[94] The first woman director of a major production was Nancy Meckler, who staged Edward Albee's *Who's Afraid of Virginia Woolf?* in 1981.

In spite of the deluge of challenges, Hall's achievements during the decade were considerable. In addition to some major productions, the National organised music performances and art exhibitions around the complex. Hall hosted visiting practitioners – in 1977: Maximilian Schell directed Ödön von Horváth's *Tales from the Vienna Woods*, Peter Stein directed Maxim Gorky's *Summerfolk* and Victor Garcia directed Ramón del Valle Inclán's *Divinas Palabras* – and invited companies such as the Birmingham Rep and the Library Theatre Manchester. Hall's tenure was also marked by fresh revivals, including his own production of Ben Jonson's *Volpone* with Paul Scofield at the Olivier (1977) and Bill Bryden's staging of *The Passion* (1977) and *Lark Rise/Candleford* (1978–9) at the more intimate Cottesloe.

Royal Court Theatre

At the start of the 1970s, the Royal Court was run by a triumvirate of men – the Artistic Director, Bill Gaskill, and his Associate Directors, Lindsay Anderson and Anthony Page – all of whom were mentored by the founder of the English Stage Company, George Devine. There were long-established partnerships between directors and playwrights – Edward Bond and Gaskill, David Storey and Anderson, Christopher Hampton and Robert Kidd – and these continued into the early 1970s: from 1970 to 1974, Osborne had two productions and one adaptation staged at the Court, Bond two, Hampton three and one adaptation, Storey four. From April 1969 to June 1970, the Court staged no fewer than three new plays by Storey (*In Celebration, The Contractor* and *Home*).

Gaskill, however, was keen to associate the Court with the alternative theatre movement although he recognised that much of this work eschewed the Court's historic emphasis on playwriting:

> The work coming from America was disturbing, demanding social change but not through political action in the left-wing tradition of Arnold Wesker. Pot began to be smoked in the lighting box. It was clear that the Living Theater, La Mama, the Open Theater and the Bread and Puppet Theater, all of whom visited London [. . .] were pushing towards anarchy, to a breakdown of structure and towards a form of theatre that was non-verbal or at least non-literary.[95]

As a step towards embracing the climate of experimentalism, Gaskill opened the Theatre Upstairs in 1969 as a full-time space for new writers. In its first eighteen months, the Theatre Upstairs staged twenty productions that each ran for over a week. However, there was also the problem of 'ghettoisation', as Philip Roberts observes:

> The ghetto [Theatre Upstairs . . .] produced in 1970 work by Brenton, Halliwell, Beckett, Heathcote Williams, Jellicoe, Hampton, Ionesco, Hare and Barker. That they were excluded from the main bill meant that they were not ultimately Court writers. Gaskill's vision in erecting a small auditorium, which set the model for other theatres, also effectively disinherited a generation of writers.[96]

In October and November 1970, the Court made another strong overture to the counterculture in the form of the 'Come Together' Festival. This event was organised by Gaskill (with Bill Bryden, then a staff director at the theatre) and was paid for, ironically, by the West End transfer of Hampton's *The Philanthropist*. It aimed to showcase regional work, encourage cross-fertilisation, and – above all – bring together two traditions: the generation of 1968 and the older generation of the Court. In respect of its broad and inclusive focus, the 'Come Together' Festival mirrors precisely the interdisciplinary emphasis of the Bradford Festivals which were running at this time.

As part of the 'Come Together' programme, there were usually two shows per night in the main theatre and one Upstairs, and spectators could see a number of shows at a cheap price. The design of the theatre was also transformed for the occasion:

> The seats in the stalls were removed, the stage was raised and extended to form a large projecting apron, and there was a pit or promenade in which people could sit or walk about [. . .] There was also tiered seating on the stage to allow for the productions in the round. The Theatre Upstairs was also used, as was Sloane Square itself and even the phone box in the Underground station.[97]

With seats placed on the stage, the removal of the stalls and the effacement of the hierarchies bedded into the proscenium design, the Court embarked on a symbolic democratisation of its spatial infrastructure. Di Seymour painted the theatre in primary colours, the circle bar was soundproofed to allow for an increased volume of noise and food was served dyed in suitably psychedelic colours.[98]

Twenty groups took part in the festival, including Portable, CAST, Ken Campbell's Road Show and Freehold. The People Show opened proceedings by filling the theatre with smoke: their performance featured 'a live rabbit tethered to a chair panicking and knocking over a pot of red paint on the new stage cloth' and ended with loud music, the hurling of oranges at critics, and the herding of the audience – another symbolic moment – out of the theatre and into the street.[99] Peter Dockley performed a bizarre installation piece – *Foul Fowl* – using chickens and a soundscape of clucking that resonated throughout the theatre. The performance artist Stuart Brisley ate bread and water to the background music of 'God Save the Queen' before climbing a scaffolding tower and vomiting. The poet Carlyle Reedy hung a large cod from a hook hanging from the ceiling and raised the eyebrows of theatre personnel by using the same cod for both of her shows. The Royal Court contributed a staging of Heathcote Williams's *AC/DC* (the first play to be transferred from the Theatre Upstairs to the main stage) and a series of Beckett plays directed by Gaskill.

While 'Come Together' represents the single most significant disruption to the conventions of theatregoing undertaken by the Royal Court in its history, some in the hierarchy stood glacially aloof from this rumbustious new intake. According to Gaskill: 'Lindsay [Anderson] had watched this counter-culture sweep through the Court, unmoved. He probably knew it would not seriously change the work of the Court, and indeed it didn't.'[100] This remark needs qualification. Countercultural practices and personnel did impact on the Court in various ways even if they did not fundamentally disturb its pre-eminence as a literary theatre. In 1973, the Young Playwrights' Competition was held for the first time and Gerald Chapman, co-founder of Gay Sweatshop, was appointed Director of the Court's Young People's Theatre Programme and Young Writers' Festival. This was a successful example of talent crossing over from alternative theatre.

The start of the decade was a relatively optimistic time for the Court and there was even discussion about the theatre taking over the Old Vic once the National company had vacated the building. The departure of Lord Harewood from the council and the death of Neville Blond, Chairman of the English Stage Company, in 1970 also led to a weakening of the administrative grip on the directors. The confidence of the theatre at this time is exemplified in an incident that took place in April 1970. The Arts Council threatened to withhold its grant from the Court after the management refused to send free tickets – as is the norm – to the theatre critic of the *Spectator* magazine, Hilary Spurling. The Court justified its decision as follows: '[w]e do not find Mrs Spurling's attitude to our work illuminating, and we do not believe that it furthers our relationship with the public'.[101] In the end, the theatre backed down under Arts Council pressure but the riposte to Spurling suggests a level of confidence and combativeness.

The new generation of writers at the Court were different in background from those associated with the theatre hitherto. David Hare had run Portable by the time he reached Sloane Square and Howard Brenton had worked at the Brighton Combination. They represented what Gaskill calls 'the rootless writer of today'.[102] During the 1970s, there was a loosening of attachment between individual writers and theatres, and the so-called 'Royal Court writer' of yesteryear seemed an increasingly antiquated notion. A negative consequence of this was that the new writers lacked directors to advocate their plays leading to the emergence of collective writer-led projects at the Court, such as *Lay By* (1971), which, to Gaskill's consternation, exacerbated existing tensions between writers and directors. 'There was a generational and professional dust up between us and them,' recalls Howard Brenton, 'with them saying you are not going to get your hands on our theatre.'[103] Gaskill's aspiration for a permanent company conflicted with his awareness that this would place limits on the repertoire and undermine the box-office reliance on star vehicles. At this time, the Court was attempting to build its regular audience while opening itself to a new constituency characterised by Brenton – via Tom Stoppard – as 'denim':

> People who went to the Royal Court would not, at that time, readily go to the National Theatre. The National was associated with Olivier and camp style, whereas the Court was carrying, however briefly, a more youthful, out-of-the-bedsit, rock and roll public. Denim. [. . .] When we went to see a play of mine at the National, Tom Stoppard said to me, 'You've got a lot of denim in tonight.'[104]

The successes of the early 1970s were hardly 'denim' productions. They included David Storey's *Home* directed by Anderson with John Gielgud and Ralph Richardson, and Edward Bond's monumental reimagining of Shakespeare's *Lear*, directed by Gaskill, which the latter has since described as 'perhaps the last of the Court's epic productions in all senses of the word'.[105]

In 1972, after seven years at the helm, Gaskill stepped down as

Artistic Director and was replaced by Oscar Lewenstein, the former General Manager and latterly Chair of the Board. In 1974, under Lewenstein's aegis, there was an innovative South African season featuring two major pieces – *The Island* and *Sizwe Bansi is Dead* – by Athol Fugard, John Kani and Winston Ntshona. In 1975, Nicholas Wright (who had run the Theatre Upstairs) and Robert Kidd became joint Artistic Directors. This was a fraught period at a time of economic crisis but productions in 1975 included Hare's *Teeth 'N' Smiles*, Bond's *The Fool*, Hampton's *Treats* and a production of *Waiting for Godot* directed by Samuel Beckett (in German).

The theatre nearly imploded under the strain of a massive funding crisis in the mid-1970s. The grant from the Arts Council increased annually, reaching £100,000 in 1967–8, but had declined to £89,000 by 1971.[106] Income was generated by a large number of West End transfers in the first half of the decade – including Richard O'Brien's *The Rocky Horror Show* (1973) – and by a raft of plays that produced healthy box-office returns: Osborne's *West of Suez* (1971), Storey's *The Changing Room* (1971) and Hampton's *Savages* (1973). As Gaskill observes, '[t]he theatre had reverted to a pattern of transferring its successes to pay for its experiments'.[107] However, the recession made West End producers more hesitant, and commercial money dried up by mid-decade: income from transfers, rights and other sources was £55,937 in 1973; by the year ending April 1977, it had slumped to £16,773.[108]

Under Wright and Kidd, the Royal Court entered a deficit. In August 1975, the Theatre Upstairs was closed to make economies but reopened in May 1976. During his turbulent tenure as Artistic Director from 1977 to 1979, Stuart Burge even considered closing the theatre for six months but this drastic step would have put the annual grant in jeopardy. 'Those threatening the existence of the Court', he recalled, 'were like ghouls around the place.'[109] The West End transfer of Mary O'Malley's *Once a Catholic* in 1977 provided a welcome financial windfall and supporters also helped reduce the deficit. In 1979, at the end of a challenging decade for the theatre, Max Stafford-Clark took over as Artistic Director, where he remained until 1993.

West End and regional theatre

In 1973, the death of two men in the same week, both titanic figures in London's West End, marked the end of an era: Binkie Beaumont, the theatrical impresario, died on 22 March, and the playwright Noël Coward on 26 March.

The West End of the 1970s was an anaemic shadow of its mid-century heyday. By 1975, nineteen out of thirty-four West End productions were direct transfers from the subsidised theatre.[110] The critic Michael Billington, who in 1971 began his more than forty-year stint as theatre critic for the *Guardian* newspaper, offered the following prescient remarks in October 1979:

> the salvation of the West End theatre does not lie in simply grabbing whatever is available from other quarters. It also lies in recapturing a touch of the sheer showbiz instinct and creative flair that for the moment seems to have passed from the so-called tycoons to the ex-University graduates who run our subsidised theatres up and down the land.[111]

Alan Ayckbourn's ascendancy as the country's most commercially successful West End playwright began in earnest in the 1970s. Based at the Stephen Joseph Theatre in Scarborough, his cavalcade of transfers included *Absurd Person Singular* (1972), *The Norman Conquests* (1973) and *Joking Apart* (1978); his singular flop was the musical collaborative project with Andrew Lloyd-Webber, *Jeeves* (1975).

Ayckbourn's main commercial rival took the form of the American musical in productions of *Godspell* (1971), *Company* (1972), *Grease* (1972) and *A Chorus Line* (1972). Over the course of the decade, Lloyd-Webber and his musical partner, the lyricist Tim Rice, honed their technical virtuosity in the popular hits *Joseph and the Amazing Technicolor Dreamcoat* (1968 but revived during the 1970s), *Jesus Christ Superstar* (1972) and the spellbinding *Evita* (1978).

The commercial West End was vitalised by regional production and the confidence of the latter is evident in the impressive new theatre buildings that appeared during the decade: the Crucible in Sheffield opened in 1971 and Manchester's Royal Exchange in 1976.

Birmingham Rep moved to its new space in Centenary Square in 1971 – Peter Ansorge speculated about its 'rumoured [. . .] annual window cleaning budget of £10,000!' – and, in 1972, a new theatre complex opened at the Bristol Old Vic.[112] However, not all theatres survived the economic challenges of the decade: the Theatre Royal in Lincoln and the Lyceum, Crewe, were forced to close. In 1978, the Albany Empire in Deptford, a key player in Rock Against Racism, was gutted by an unexplained fire.

Many producing theatres, such as Peter Cheeseman's redoubtable Victoria Theatre in Stoke, built up loyal working-class audiences and staged plays with socialist content on local issues. Theatres such as the Bolton Octagon and Coventry Belgrade maintained active Theatre in Education companies and built strong links with schools and youth organisations. Hull Truck was founded by the actor Mike Bradwell in 1971. Over in Nottingham, Richard Eyre replaced Stuart Burge at the helm of the Playhouse from 1973 to 1978 and developed a new writing policy with David Hare as Resident Dramatist. Under Eyre's leadership, Nottingham became a powerhouse of large-scale regional production with a talented company of actors that included Jonathan Pryce, Alison Steadman, Zoë Wanamaker and Tom Wilkinson. Eyre premiered Brenton and Hare's *Brassneck* (1973), Brenton's *The Churchill Play* (1974) and Griffiths's *Comedians* (1975), all of them emblematic state of the nation plays. 'No need to sing sad songs over the inert body of regional drama [. . .],' as one reviewer of *Brassneck* commented, 'the patient has leapt up to cock a snook at those gathered mournfully around the bedside.'[113]

At the Northcott Theatre in Exeter, Jane Howell was Artistic Director from 1971 to 1974. During this period, the designer Andrea Montag learned her craft under Hayden Griffin, the acting company included Bob Peck, Robert Lindsay, Bob Hoskins and Roy Marsden, and key premieres included Bond's *Bingo* (1973) and Brenton's topical and controversial adaptation of *Measure for Measure* (1972).

Another seminal regional company was the Liverpool Everyman, run by Alan Dossor from 1969. Dossor began his directing career at Nottingham Playhouse under John Neville in the 1960s and he was also inspired by the example of Joan Littlewood and Peter Cheeseman.

In the early 1970s, Dossor assembled an outstanding company of actors and writers in Liverpool many of whom became international stars: Julie Walters, Pete Postlethwaite, Bill Nighy, Nicholas Le Prevost and the playwright Willy Russell. John McGrath worked at the Everyman from 1970 to 1972 before setting up 7:84: 'here was someone trying to reach an audience that I knew and loved: the ordinary people of Merseyside'.[114]

Aside from the regional producing houses, the 1970s saw a significant increase in theatre on college and university campuses. In 1975, the Gulbenkian Foundation published a report into professional training for drama called *Going on the Stage*, which led to the establishment of the National Council for Drama Training (NCDT) the following year. This heralded a new period of rationalisation and cultural proximity of drama schools, teacher training and higher education. In 1976, Rose Bruford College in Kent launched the UK's first degree-level programme of actor training ('Theatre Arts') and its initiative was soon followed by other drama schools, colleges and, later, universities. The construction of new arts centres and campus 'black box' studios attended these developments, which were in themselves expressive of the political contradictions of the 1970s. As David Wiles, in his commentary on theatre architecture of this period, remarks: 'The dream was of free and infinite space controlled by the dimmer switch, involving intellectual and moral liberation from the spatial constraints of the past. The reality was a space in which every configuration proved a compromise.'[115]

National and international contexts

Northern Ireland, Scotland, Wales
The Lyric Theatre in Belfast opened in 1968 and famously stayed open throughout the traumatic events of the 1970s. Brian Friel wrote *Freedom of the City* (1973) and *Volunteers* (1975), both of which deal explicitly with the so-called 'Troubles'. Other notable plays from Northern Ireland include Stewart Parker's *Spokesong* (1975), which filters the hard edges of contemporary reality through the unobtrusive

setting of a bicycle shop, and Bill Morrison's ambitious political farce *Flying Blind* (1977).

There was a major revival in Scottish playwriting during the 1970s in tandem with the discovery of North Sea oil, the rise in nationalism and the campaign for devolution. Hector MacMillan's *The Rising* (1973), Tom Gallacher's *The Sea Change* (1976) and Stewart Conn's *Play Donkey* (1977) probe the fall-out from these issues. *The Great Northern Welly Boot Show* (1972) celebrated the victory of the Clydeside shipbuilders' occupation; it was written by Tom Buchan, designed by John Byrne and starred Billy Connolly (a former welder in the shipyards). Donald Campbell and Roddy McMillan used Scots dialect in their plays as did John McGrath in *Out of Our Heads* (1976) and *Joe's Drum* (1979). Scottish women playwrights also achieved significant breakthroughs in the 1970s, including Marcella Evaristi with *Dorothy and the Bitch* (1976) and *Scotia's Darlings* (1978).

In 1969, Giles Havergal was appointed Artistic Director of the Citizens Theatre in Glasgow (a role he occupied until 2003). He launched a new artistic policy from 1970 with his co-directors, Philip Prowse and Robert David Macdonald. The 'Citz' produced glittering and often controversial reinterpretations of the European canon with exquisite design and decadent theatrical panache. Alongside this, the management implemented a policy of low-price tickets. In spite of the loss of its studio space, the Club, which burned down in 1973, the theatre secured its reputation as a producing house of international distinction by the end of the 1970s.

In Wales, there was significant development in theatrical infra-structure during the decade. The Brecknockshire Theatre Company, later Theatr Powys, was founded in 1972, the new Theatr Clwyd opened in 1976 and the Torch Theatre in Milford Haven in 1977. The Chapter Arts Centre, which opened in Cardiff in 1971 as a focus for alternative theatre in Wales, became one of the most vibrant arts venues in the UK. Two seminal companies also emerged in the mid-seventies: the experimental Cardiff Laboratory Theatre, established by Mike Pearson in 1973, and Paupers' Carnival, founded by Dek Leverton and Vanya Constant, in 1975. The Welsh-language plays of Urien William and the demotic comedies of the

Gwynedd-based William Samuel Jones won popular audiences, the latter performed at Theatr y Gegin in Criccieth before its closure in 1976.

International influences

Writing in 1974, J. W. Lambert paid tribute 'to the arrival in England during the 1960s of a number of young Americans, who proved a good deal more constructive in the theatre than did many of their fellows in our universities'.[116] He was referring, of course, to Haynes, Berman and Marowitz, but also to companies such as the Living Theatre, La MaMa, the Open Theatre and the Bread and Puppet Theatre, all of whom had visited London by 1970. William Gaskill states that these companies 'invaded our consciousness' with the same force as the visit to London of the Berliner Ensemble in the 1950s.[117] The work of Rosalyn Drexler, Leroi Jones, Michael McClure, Robert Patrick, Martin Sherman and Megan Terry carried the influence of American writing to Britain, and Sam Shepard was virtually a house dramatist at the Royal Court: six of his plays were performed there from 1969 to 1980.[118] The London performance of *Women in Violence* by the visiting Spiderwoman Theater from New York in 1978 inspired British feminist practitioners such as Michelene Wandor, while the American directors Nancy Diuguid and Nancy Meckler made outstanding contributions to the British alternative theatre movement.

From continental Europe, Lambert notes the influence of, among others, Günther Grass, Fernando Arrabal and Sławomir Mrożek.[119] The French director Simone Benmussa directed *The Singular Life of Albert Nobbs*, with a cast including Susannah York, in a much-lauded production at the New End Theatre in 1978. Arguably, however, the single most influential European on the development of British alternative theatre was the remarkable Dutchman Ritsaert ten Cate, who founded the Mickery Theatre in 1965. The Mickery exerted an inestimable pull on British practitioners including Howard Brenton, the People Show, 7:84 and the Pip Simmons Group. In its early incarnation, it occupied the site of a farmhouse in the village of Loenersloot, a short distance from Amsterdam: it began as an art gallery but performers from all over the world were invited to stage pieces. Brenton, whose 1972 play *Hitler Dances* evolved from his time at the Mickery, evokes the atmosphere of his first visit, in 1970, while stage-managing a Portable tour:

> It was a wonderful hide-out. There was a barn, converted to a theatre. There were lofts and outhouses surrounded, danger-ously for the ecstatic and the stoned who soon flocked there, by canals. [. . .] (you'd see some South American or San Francisco show on before yours and think, 'Jesus, and back in London they call *us* wild?')[120]

Ten Cate also organised a touring circuit for visiting groups – the 'Mickery tour' – which helped to raise much-needed funds for British theatre companies.

After its foundation in 1975, the Theatre Writers' Union (TWU) strengthened the links between British practitioners and their overseas colleagues. The union was active in campaigns connected to east Europe and South Africa. In 1977, the TWU worked with Equity in organising statements to be read out from the National Theatre and the RSC in support of Charter 77, the movement for human rights in Czechoslovakia co-founded by the playwright Václav Havel. It also worked with Amnesty International to support dissident writers in Latin America and led the boycott of apartheid South Africa from 1978, urging British writers not to allow their plays to be performed there.

One of Britain's eminent theatre directors left the country in 1970 in an act of self-imposed exile. In order to pursue his explorations of theatre within an internationalist frame, Peter Brook left the RSC and established the International Centre for Theatre Research (CIRT) in Paris with Micheline Rozan. His group travelled widely in the Middle East and Africa with a multi-national ensemble and its productions included *Orghast in Persepolis* (1971–2) and *The Conference of the Birds* (performed in six African countries, 1972). The company took over the Théâtre des Bouffes du Nord in Paris in 1974, transforming it into a centre for intercultural exchange and exploration.

Conclusion

Looking back on the 1970s from the vantage point of 1980, Itzin observes that 'the forces were reactionary and showed signs of becoming positively repressive'.[121] In the same year, the publisher John Calder writes 'of a shift from the eclectic and tolerant attitudes of the sixties to the new hardness of the eighties'.[122] David Edgar, too, notes the 'subtle privatisation of concern [. . .] as the "we" decade turned into the "me" decade, the Pot generation matured into the Perrier generation'.[123] The election of the Conservative government in 1979, with its commitment to monetarism and right-wing social policies, marked a traumatic defeat for the British left.

However, to dwell on the narrative of decline, to over-emphasise Francis Wheen's image of the 1970s as 'a long Sunday evening in winter', is to eclipse the transformations in a decade that also bestowed an egalitarian legacy. Alternative theatre paved the way for the explosion of women's playwriting in the 1980s and a surge of work by black and Asian practitioners. During the decade, the content and formal conventions of established theatre were challenged, creating an appetite for innovative and experimental work. In spite of their remorseless economic travails, the regional theatres and national subsidised companies gained in confidence and ambition, producing the work of playwrights who addressed contemporary concerns by placing individual lives within the echo chambers of history. The 1970s might best be understood, therefore, as the decade when British theatre artists sought to actualise, through the struggle of making and presenting new kinds of performance, a more equitable way of doing life.

CHAPTER 2
INTRODUCING THE PLAYWRIGHTS

The four key playwrights included in this book – Caryl Churchill, David Hare, Howard Brenton and David Edgar – were all born during the years 1938–48. They are thus part of a generation whose formative experiences were shaped by the terrible sacrifices of the Second World War and, following the Labour Party's unexpected landslide victory in the general election of 1945, by the social transformations that followed the establishment of the welfare state in the immediate post-war period. During their childhood, the British Empire entered its death throes, Cold War hostilities accelerated under the grotesque shadow of the nuclear bomb, and continuing wartime austerities were intermixed with hope for a better and more equitable society exemplified in new state institutions like the National Health Service (NHS).

With the exception of Edgar, who studied at Manchester, all of the playwrights attended either Oxford or Cambridge universities and gained early experience of making theatre within the privileged environment of student life. Their political maturation was sharply accentuated by the revolutionary upheavals of the late 1960s, especially the student protests of May 1968 in Paris, which were rooted in frustration at the perceived squandered opportunities and political retrenchments of the preceding generation.

In 1971, reflecting on the most promising theatre writers of the 1960s, the critic John Russell Taylor heralded the appearance of what he called a 'second wave' of dramatists.[1] If, as he argued, the 'first wave' comprised those architects of the 'New Drama' associated with the Royal Court in the 1950s – playwrights such as John Osborne and Arnold Wesker – this 'second wave' (he included the young Hare and Brenton among them) represented a new species of dramatist hotly attuned to the political realities emergent at the turn of the 1970s.[2] As noted in the previous chapter, these writers were unfettered by state censorship after the historic abolition of the Lord Chamberlain's responsibility for licensing plays in 1968. They were the beneficiaries of a surge in public funding for the arts and they came to prominence within the heady atmospherics of an alternative theatre movement which was committed, in many cases, to democratic, politically engaged and collaborative ways of working as well as to broadening the audience through touring, often to non-theatre venues. This ascendant 'second wave' also absorbed an eclectic and international range of theatre influences: from Osborne and Edward Bond to Harold Pinter and Samuel Beckett, from the continental avant-garde, especially Brecht's Berliner Ensemble, and innovative directors like Joan Littlewood and Peter Brook, to US performance troupes such as the Living Theatre and La MaMa.

In the first years of the decade, a period convulsed by economic and political instability, all four playwrights produced some of their first and finest professional writing for theatre. Then as now, they shared a commitment to the centrality of theatre's role in the public sphere, its capacity to shape discourses on national identity, the movements of history, and the febrile politics of class, gender, sexuality and race. In spite of their generational similarities, however, it is important to trace the distinctiveness of each playwright's early career. The following offers a brief introduction to the four playwrights, setting the context for the detailed analysis of their work in Chapter 3.[3]

Caryl Churchill

> At the beginning of the decade, she was a writer beginning to attract attention. By the end, there was no doubt about her international status. But throughout this time, one characteristic is apparent and that is a readiness to experiment and to take risks, both in the form of her work and with the theatres and companies she became involved with.[4]

Churchill (b. 1938) spent some of her childhood in Montreal, Canada, but she studied at Lady Margaret Hall, Oxford University, graduating in 1960. As a student, she wrote *Downstairs*, a one-act play performed by the Oriel College Dramatic Society in 1958 and subsequently at the *Sunday Times*/National Union of Students (NUS) Drama Festival. This was followed by her first full-length play, *Having a Wonderful Time*, which was given a student production by the Oxford Players at Questors Theatre, Ealing, in 1960. Her first performed radio play, *You've No Need to be Frightened*, was presented as a 'play for voices' in a student production by Exeter College Dramatic Society in 1961. The bold experimentalism of Churchill's early writing is exemplified in *Easy Death* (staged by the university's Experimental Theatre Club in a student production at the Oxford Playhouse in 1962), which uses song and verse, and is composed (ingeniously) of two plots running at different speeds.

Philip Roberts observes that 'Churchill [. . .] spent the sixties as a somewhat solitary writer, mainly in the world of radio'.[5] Indeed, eight of her radio plays were broadcast from 1962–73. The medium of radio appealed to Churchill for a number of reasons: it facilitated the performance of her plays at a time when there was no alternative theatre circuit; radio drama is challenging to write, requiring precision and discipline to meet the demands of deadlines and time slots; and the rhythm of work also allowed for an element of flexibility at a time when Churchill was raising a family (she married in 1961 and gave birth to three sons through the decade). The telescopic imagination and surreal dynamism at work in her radio drama is perhaps best represented in Churchill's first professionally produced play, *The Ants* (1962), which was broadcast on the BBC Third Programme (an arts-focused national radio network which was later incorporated into Radio 3), and *Identical Twins* (1968), both of which explore childhood, the opacity of language and the ambiguous premises of identity to unsettling effect.

Geraldine Cousin notes that Churchill's radio plays are 'amongst the most powerful and moving examples of [her] work'.[6] In the early 1970s, however, Churchill became impatient with the dominance of monologue in radio and its disposition towards existential and introspective subject matter. As she put it in a 1972 *Guardian* interview, 'I felt this [. . .] Becketty thing happening: [. . .] I was going to finish up with a play that was two words and a long silence'.[7] The focus of her writing thus moved from 'words' to 'events', opening up new territories of social and historical subject matter, and a more dialogic style.

The turning point came in 1972: in Churchill's words, 'my working life feels divided quite sharply into before and after 1972, and *Owners* was the first play of the second part'.[8] *Owners*, commissioned by theatre producer Michael Codron, was staged at the Royal Court Theatre Upstairs: this was her first professional stage production and the beginning of her lengthy association with the theatre. In 1974, she was appointed the first woman Resident Dramatist at the Court and, the following year, *Objections to Sex and Violence* became her first main stage production there.

Another turning point occurred in 1976 when Churchill began collaborating with theatre companies for the first time. This also marked an intensification of her feminist commitment: 'During the Seventies, there was a context for thinking of myself as a woman writer. Other people were thinking of me in that way and I was becoming more interested in women's issues. I became more aware of myself then as a woman writer.'[9] She wrote three major plays in 1976: *Traps*, *Vinegar Tom* and *Light Shining in Buckinghamshire*. *Vinegar Tom* was produced by the feminist company Monstrous Regiment at the Humberside Theatre, Hull, directed by Pam Brighton; *Light Shining*, staged by Joint Stock at the Traverse Theatre, Edinburgh, marks the beginning of her productive association with the director, Max Stafford-Clark. The experience of working with Joint Stock was transformative: 'My habit of solitary working and shyness at showing what I wrote at an early stage had been wiped out by the even greater self-exposure in Joint Stock's method of work.'[10]

Churchill sustained her association with both Joint Stock and Monstrous Regiment into 1978. That year, she contributed to the latter's uproarious revue *Floorshow*, intermixing songs and sketches in a witty deconstruction of the business of glamour. She also drafted *Cloud Nine* after a workshop with Joint Stock, which was directed, the following year, by Stafford-Clark at the Dartington College of Arts before going on tour. In 1981, *Cloud Nine* was produced at the

Theatre de Lys in New York where it ran for two years – thus confirming Churchill as a writer of international distinction.

Her engagement with feminism through the decade led to her participation in milestone events such as the Women's Theatre Festival in Leicester in 1975. She was also a co-founder of the Theatre Writers' Group, later the Theatre Writers' Union (TWU), in 1975. Churchill's outrage at the censoring of her television play for the BBC, *The Legion Hall Bombing*, in 1978, led directly to a TWU campaign against censorship in theatre and the organising of a one-day conference on 'Political Censorship in Alternative Theatre' that year. In the late 1970s, she also wrote *Softcops*, inspired by Michel Foucault's *Discipline and Punish* (although not staged until 1984); *Seagulls*, which was given a rehearsed reading at the Royal Court many years later (in 2002), and *Three More Sleepless Nights*, which opened in 1980 as a lunchtime production at the Soho Poly. In addition, by the end of the decade, Churchill was active on behalf of the Royal Court Young Writers' Group.

David Hare

Educated at Jesus College, Cambridge, Hare (b. 1947) was involved with various university drama groups including the Amateur Dramatic Club (ADC, with whom he played Montjoy in *Henry V*), the Marlowe Society and the Independent Theatre which he ran with his friend Tony Bicât. Hare also ran the film society and cinema was his early passion; indeed, for a short time in the late 1960s, he assembled library footage for the renowned documentary-filmmaker Richard Dunn for the British Pathé Pictorials series.

Hare and Bicât founded Portable Theatre in 1968. The company took its name from the then ubiquitous 'portable' radio and their main aspiration was to tour new writing to non-theatre venues. Portable was one of the first of the new fringe companies to tour beyond the capital and other cities; it was also, unusually, a writers' theatre. Portable productions were oppositional to the status quo but the target of hostility was culture rather than politics. As Bicât recalls:

'[Portable] was anti-bourgeois, anti-Conservative and anti the conventional theatre, but it was slightly vaguer about what it was *for*. [. . .] Left-wing, confrontational, aesthetically radical [. . .] foul-mouthed, certainly [. . .] Does that make political theatre?'[11] The confrontational style of Portable – Richard Boon's term is '"artistic terrorism"' – was prioritised over intellectual or thesis-driven content.[12] Unsurprisingly, the focus on shock provoked unease amongst conservative theatre critics of the time: J.W. Lambert's disdain is apparent from his thin-lipped description, in 1974, of Portable's 'strong leaning towards the zestful projection of schizophrenia and sadism'.[13] In addition, Portable shows were often derided as adolescent doom-mongering. Peter Ansorge felt, in 1975, that the company tapped rather too eagerly into the culture of paranoia that gripped literary fiction in the early 1970s:

> There is something to be learned from Saul Bellow's plea to his fellow writers in his novel *Herzog* [1964], that 'we must get it out of our heads that this is a doomed time, that we are waiting for the end. We love apocalypses too much, and crisis ethics and florid extremism with its thrilling language.' The Portable writers, half in love with easeful crisis, might do a lot worse than to pin this message from an American novelist over their writing desks.[14]

Portable's first show was *Inside Out*, an adaptation of the novelist Franz Kafka's diaries. It was compiled by Bicât and Hare and staged at Jim Haynes's Arts Lab in Drury Lane in October 1968 (and remounted the following January). The play was submitted to the Arts Council's new play scheme and Portable received a grant. Funding was increased in subsequent years, enabling the directors to commission playwrights including Brenton and Snoo Wilson; by 1971, the grant reached an astonishing £8,000 (nearly £80,000 today).[15]

In a continuation of the literary orientation of Portable's subject matter, Hare then wrote *Strindberg*, adapted from the playwright August Strindberg's diaries. This was produced in 1969 at the Oval House (with the actor Maurice Colbourne in the title role) alongside

John Grillo's *Gentleman I.* Hare's first original play was the one-act *How Brophy Made Good,* also in 1969, which he co-directed with Bicât. *Brophy* departed from the writerly focus of previous plays and honed the pared-down, uncompromising aesthetic associated with the company. Portable produced Brenton's *Christie in Love* at the Oval House in November 1969 and the Royal Court Theatre Upstairs the following March while Brenton's next play, *Fruit,* also directed by Hare, toured in 1970, often doubling with the production of Hare's new play *What Happened to Blake?* Influenced by La MaMa, *Blake* was also performed at the seminal 'Come Together' Festival at the Royal Court in October 1970.

In its first year, Portable toured over 30,000km, often securing bookings by sending press releases to schools, universities and army camps. By 1971, the group had three pieces showing at the Edinburgh Festival Fringe: Chris Wilkinson's *Plays for Rubber Go-Go Girls,* the group-written *Lay By* and Wilson's *Blow Job.* The Arts Council wanted Portable to remain small in scale, and it resisted the company's desire to create a reduced number of larger, collaborative and political shows in bigger venues. As Bicât and Hare became preoccupied with other projects, the company was increasingly ensnared by Arts Council bureaucracy and poor accounting, and was finally dissolved in 1973 (although Portable Theatre Workshop, under the leadership of Malcolm Griffiths, continued as the influential Paradise Foundry). Reflecting on his time with the company, Bicât comments: 'Our success was in showing that there was an audience around the country for new work and that it could be staged and toured comparatively cheaply. My feeling was that our failure was in never quite achieving a style that matched some of the innovation in the writing.'[16]

Hare worked as a script reader at the Royal Court from late 1968 and succeeded the playwright Christopher Hampton as Literary Manager from 1969–70 and then Resident Dramatist from 1970–1. The experience of working on his early plays and adaptations forced Hare to confront the challenge of writing complex characters: 'when I came to write *Blake* it was a good deal more complex, a mixture of my own approval and disapproval that I just couldn't handle'.[17] He proceeded to anatomise these tensions in his major plays of the 1970s.

Howard Brenton

The son of a former policeman turned Methodist minister, Brenton (b. 1942) showed a fondness for abstract painting at school but decided against applying to art college because he wanted to be a writer, and so chose to study English. He wrote a biographical play on the life of Hitler when he was seventeen years old and, early on, discovered a talent for writing comedy. He was also particularly enthused by the plays of Osborne and John Arden.

Brenton studied at St Catherine's College, Cambridge. While at university, he wrote a piece inspired by the writer Jean Genet called *Ladder of Fools* (1965) for the ADC Theatre which was presented in a double bill with Grillo's *Hello–Goodbye Sebastian*. The play included a rather disastrous twenty-minute final speech that caused the audience to leave in droves.

In 1966, he wrote a short farce called *Winter, Daddykins* and toured this piece to Dublin with the director Chris Parr and a group of ex-students from Central School and Cambridge. Around this time, he also worked as a stage manager and bit-part actor in repertory theatres: 'I played corpses discovered behind sofas, postmen delivering death threats, and I have a memory of standing in fisherman's thigh-length waders and sou'-wester, holding a three-foot-long *papier mâché* salmon in my hand and saying the line, "The old lady's dead".'[18] Outside of theatre, Brenton was employed as a labourer in factories and kitchens, and had previously worked as a teacher in Yorkshire.

In August 1966, the one-act play *It's My Criminal* was his first piece to be shown at the Royal Court as part of a double bill on Sunday evening. It was badly received but the then artistic director, Bill Gaskill, gave it support and found Brenton a job as a stagehand. Following this, Brenton joined the Brighton Combination, one of the great companies of the British counterculture, as an actor and writer – an experience that unleashed a tide of theatrical adventurism in his writing: in 1968, for example, the Combination's auditorium was turned into the inside of a giant's stomach for his adaptation of François Rabelais's *Gargantua*. At this time, he also began working on a play about Winston Churchill (which would later become *The Churchill Play*).

In 1969, Brenton wrote his trilogy of 'Plays for Public Places' – *Heads, Gum and Goo* and *The Education of Skinny Spew*. Chris Parr, director of *Winter, Daddykins*, had been appointed Teaching Fellow in Theatre at Bradford University and invited young writers to write plays for his students: Brenton, Edgar, Grillo and Richard Crane were among them. Brenton's 'Plays for Public Places' were performed before and after rock concerts and he was also commissioned to write for the Bradford Festivals: *Wesley* (1970) was staged in the 900-seat Eastbrook Hall, a Methodist chapel, while *Scott of the Antarctic* (1971) was performed on the Mecca ice rink.

Aware of his increasing range and experience, the Royal Court contacted Brenton to renew its acquaintance and *Revenge*, his first full-length play which he had been working on for three years, was the result. It was staged at the Theatre Upstairs in September 1969 and Brenton subsequently obtained an Arts Council grant. *Revenge* is a farce about crime, gangsters and the law; it is influenced by *King Lear* but totally rejects naturalistic psychology (the cast includes the maudlin Voice of Brixton Gaol: 'Oh England, what will become of you . . .?').[19]

Brenton visited Paris in 1969 after the revolutionary events of the previous year: he met with activists and this politicised his thinking. In an important interview published in 1975, he remarked that: 'May '68 was crucial. It was a great watershed and directly affected me. [. . .] it destroyed any remaining affection for the official culture. [. . .] It was defeated. A generation dreaming of a beautiful utopia was kicked – kicked awake and not dead. I've got to believe not kicked dead.'[20]

Portable Theatre contacted him when *Revenge* was in production at the Court and he was commissioned by the company to write *Christie in Love*. Many years later, Hare recalled that Brenton was planning to write 'a history of evil "from Judas Iscariot to the present day"'.[21] Brenton, in turn, stated in an interview published in 2000 that Hare and Bicât 'had a grand scheme of making a number of shows called *The History of Evil* – which seemed a really silly idea!

None of the plays got written, but *Christie* was meant to be one.'[22] At this time, Brenton was living in a basement flat near to the former home of serial killer John Christie and the idea for the play began to take shape. *Christie in Love*, arguably the most accomplished one-act play in post-war British theatre, is his first attempt to move beyond comedy: 'What I did was to write comic scenes, comic situations, but stretch them intolerably by using massive pauses or bad jokes, which an actor has to try and tell so badly that an audience doesn't laugh, even at its being bad.'[23] It won the John Whiting Award in 1969 and, for Bicât, '[i]t remains the best play we did'.[24]

Brenton's next play for Portable, *Fruit*, is a punchy political satire, written in response to the unexpected Conservative general election victory of 1970. In typical Portable parlance, Brenton calls the play 'a really great burst of nihilism'.[25] In one memorable scene, the protagonist, a thalidomide victim called Paul, smashes a television screen showing a party election broadcast. The play concludes with a petrol bomb thrown against the theatre wall and the script ends with an immortal authorial aside bedded into the final stage directions: '*God knows how we're going to get away with that.*'[26]

The screen-smashing and bomb-throwing in *Fruit* are symptomatic of the profound influence of the Situationists on Brenton, particularly as theorised in Guy Debord's *The Society of the Spectacle* (1967). Throughout his career, Brenton has lauded the critical perspicacity of the Situationists: Marxist-inspired, countercultural, anarchorevolutionaries, with roots in the Continental avant-garde, whose critique of public life, culture and mass consumerism was deeply influential on the left-wing activists of 1968.[27] In Brenton's theatre, the Situationist desire to rip apart the 'spectacle' of public life manifests in the collision of styles in *Magnificence* and in the fierce rhetorical tropes that circulate in many of his 1970s plays. At the end of Act One of *Epsom Downs* (1977), for example, which is set at the eponymous racecourse, the Ghost of the suffragette Emily Davison tries to persuade Margaret to kill the Queen, who is visiting as part of her Silver Jubilee celebrations:

Push the copper over. Crack the windscreen with your knife.

[. . .]

England at peace on Derby day. It is just a picture, thin as paint. Slash it.

[. . .]

See the dirty wall behind.[28]

By the early 1970s, Brenton had collated an impressive and wide-ranging amount of experience in theatre. He had worked with the Brighton Combination, Portable, Open Space, Oval House, University of Bradford, Traverse Theatre Workshop and the Royal Court. Gaskill commissioned Brenton to write another play, which was to become *Magnificence*. The piece was challenging to write because the subject was personal and specific to his own generation, but Brenton delivered the manuscript in June 1972. By this time, he was Resident Dramatist at the Court. There was significant resistance to the play at the theatre: large rewrites were required, the powerful Court director Lindsay Anderson protested against its wilful desecration of the 'unity of style' and there were wrangles about which space it was suitable for.

Magnificence, Brenton's breakthrough play, lays bare the legacy of 1968, his doubts about revolutionary action and the despair that fuels terrorism:

When the May '68 dream of mass revolt, of a popular, celebratory transformation of Society proved to be merely that, a dream, it decayed into the nightmare of handfuls of 'urban terrorists', the Angry Brigade and the Red Army Faction. A perverted reading of Debord's book inspired them and they destroyed themselves, turning many away from the sunlit, great, democratic idea behind the May '68 revolt.[29]

Magnificence is thus tailored precisely to the experience of the Royal Court audience: public-sector workers and former students from the same milieu as the characters in the play – 'bedsit-land,' as Brenton put it, 'which was very strong in the Seventies'.[30] The play sets in motion Brenton's preoccupations for the rest of the decade and beyond: individuals who pursue their ideals single-mindedly, 'admirable, but doomed' fanaticism, and the fall-out from disillusionment and failure.[31]

David Edgar

Edgar (b. 1948) graduated from Manchester University as a student radical at a time when youth rebellion was sending shockwaves around the world: 'one felt at the centre of things,' he reflected in interview in 1979, 'in the same way that a young, upper-middle-class Englishman with a pilot's licence in the 1940s might have felt at the centre of things'.[32] After his graduation, Edgar worked as a journalist at the *Telegraph & Argus*, a local newspaper in Bradford, from 1969 to 1972. He was the assistant reporter during the exposé of the corrupt businessman John Poulson, which quickly became one of the defining scandals of post-war British public life.[33]

Edgar's early playwriting was nurtured by Chris Parr at Bradford University. He wrote *The White and White Springbok Show*, inspired by the anti-apartheid protests at the time of the controversial South African rugby tour to Britain and Ireland in 1969–70, but Parr was not keen on the play. Edgar followed this with *Two Kinds of Angel* (1970), his first professionally performed piece. Its style was influenced by the structural gymnastics of Brenton and Grillo, and later plays like *Acid* (1971) absorbed what he described as the 'attitude of contempt and disgust, particularly expressed in sexual terms' of Portable Theatre.[34] His first full-length play, *Bloody Rosa* (written for Manchester University at the Edinburgh Festival, 1971), was focused on the revolutionary socialist Rosa Luxemburg. Working with Parr on the Bradford Festivals, Edgar was cast in the roles of Almighty God in Brenton's *Scott of the Antarctic* (1971) and Captain Bligh in Richard Crane's *Mutiny on the Bounty* (1972).

Edgar transitioned into full-time writing with the collaboratively written *England's Ireland* (1972). He was paired with Brenton during the creation of this project and travelled to Pembrokeshire to meet the group of writers the day after leaving his job in journalism. He spent time working on the play with them and then returned to

Bradford to continue writing for the socialist agitprop company General Will.

General Will toured five of Edgar's forensic and witty agitprop plays during the high tide of industrial militancy in the early 1970s: *The National Interest* (1971), *The Rupert Show* (1972), *Rent or Caught in the Act* (1972), *State of Emergency* (1972) and *The Dunkirk Spirit* (1974). During this period, Edgar also wrote two dazzling political parodies for the Bush Theatre: *Tedderella* (1971 and 1973, a pantomime-parody of Britain's entry into the Common Market) and *Dick Deterred* (1974, Shakespeare's *Richard III* interpreted through the lens of Richard Nixon and Watergate). Edgar's first television play, *The Eagle Has Landed*, was made for Granada TV in 1973, while his first original radio play, *Ecclesiastes*, was produced in 1977 for the BBC.

As the industrial crisis receded and the left began to suffer major defeats, Edgar questioned the viability of agitprop theatre. His later agitprop pieces, including *The Case of the Workers' Plane* (1973) and *Events Following the Closure of a Motorcycle Factory* (1976), were unhappy experiences. He also moved away from allegory (*Death Story*, 1972, and *O Fair Jerusalem*, 1975) and abstraction (*Baby Love*, 1973) as ways of discoursing about politics in theatre. In his fascinating essay 'Public Theatre in a Private Age', Edgar sets out the new theatrical priorities shaping his playwriting from this point:

> Social realism is obviously a synthesis – dare I say it, even a dialectical one – of the surface perception of naturalism and the social analysis that underlies agitprop plays. To explain, it is first necessary to be recognisable, and only then, having won the audience's trust, to place those recognisable phenomena within the context of a perceived political truth. It is indeed in this combination of recognition with perception that the political power of theatre lies.[35]

The intersection of the personal and the political was especially important in *Destiny* (1976), a play focused on the rise of fascism in Britain. *Destiny*, which was written over a number of years, carries an underlying agitprop structure but the overall aesthetic is social realist – the better to stimulate the audience's 'recognition with perception' of the contemporary resonance of its subject matter.

During the 1970s, Edgar was Fellow of Creative Writing at Leeds Polytechnic (1972–4). He wrote plays for Bingley College of Education and was Resident Playwright at Birmingham Rep (1974–5). The theatres he was most closely associated with during the decade – Birmingham Rep and the RSC – exemplify his desire to reach audiences beyond the politically committed. In the second half of the 1970s, Edgar began writing for *Searchlight*, the anti-Nazi journal, and the Institute for Race Relations; he also became a public speaker for the Anti-Nazi League from 1977, wrote an enormous range of articles on public issues, especially race politics, and co-founded the TWU in 1975. By January 1979, Edgar had three plays running concurrently in London: *The Jail Diary of Albie Sachs* at the Warehouse, *Mary Barnes* at the Royal Court and *Teendreams* at the ICA. He was also teaching Playwriting at Birmingham University and mentoring new writers including Louise Page and Terry Johnson. In 1978–9, towards the end of a very busy and productive decade, he spent time in the US on a Bicentennial Arts Fellowship – an experience that furnished raw material for his later two-play cycle *Continental Divide* (2003).

CHAPTER 3
PLAYWRIGHTS AND PLAYS

CARYL CHURCHILL
By Paola Botham

> We must find a balance that doesn't impose form and poetry unrelated to the details of life nor pile up details without finding form and poetry.[1]

> [S]ocialism and feminism aren't synonymous, but I feel strongly about both and wouldn't be interested in a form of one that didn't include the other.[2]

Introduction

In five decades of relentless theatrical experimentation, Caryl Churchill has always let her plays speak for themselves. Yet the two statements above seem to capture the spirit of a dramaturgy which otherwise has been in constant reinvention. The first comes from her seminal essay 'Not Ordinary, Not Safe' (1960) which, according to Philip Roberts, reads 'as a kind of manifesto'.[3] The second is taken from an interview in the 1980s, when the feminist cause was in danger of being hijacked by neoliberal ideology. Together they describe a body of work in which political commitment goes hand in hand with artistic audacity; in which 'the details of life' cannot be separated from 'form and poetry', nor gender equality from social justice. This complex balancing act was a mark of Churchill's early theatre career in the 1970s – starting with *Owners*, her first professionally produced stage play – and so it remains, despite the unpredictability of her creative directions.

Some analyses of Churchill's trajectory, however, tend to overemphasise discontinuities. Looking back at *Owners*, many commentators have stressed that this is 'not yet a feminist play', unlike the 'mature' work the dramatist started to produce later in the same decade.[4] Conversely, it has been implied that after *Softcops* (1978), a work inspired by the philosopher Michel Foucault, Churchill should no longer be considered a socialist-feminist playwright. Jane Thomas, for instance, claims that political readings of Churchill 'are often unable to account for certain gaps and contradictions in the texts'; instead, she examines Churchill's plays as dispassionate studies of power in the Foucauldian mould.[5] Similarly, Daniel Jernigan concentrates on the apparent 'ambivalence' of Churchill's political sympathies, suggesting that, after *Softcops*, she has become a postmodernist artist who recognises the impossibility of social change.[6]

Those who place Churchill firmly within feminist theatre have sometimes underestimated her unique style in order to highlight a more general feminist aesthetic. In this vein, Churchill's formal experimentation has been associated with French psychoanalytic feminist theory and the resistance against the masculine 'phallogocentric' order. Nevertheless, as Harry Derbyshire points out, Churchill's drama (even her more oblique twenty-first century plays) involves political analysis and operates 'in a mode in which ambiguity is not always valued'.[7] The adoption of Brechtian techniques in Churchill's 1970s work underlines the rational dimension of her theatre. Recently, however, Dan Rebellato has countered this interpretation, arguing that the drive behind Churchill's creative output has always been a search for the non-rational. In his view, 'Churchill's stylistic maturity is bound up with a particular fascination with how the purely private – dreams, madness – might also be a vision of society'.[8] This is a romantic idea but it perhaps does not do full justice to the dialectical structures present in most of Churchill's plays, including her later ones.

Instead of offering a one-sided celebration of form against content, or ambiguity against clarity, this essay will examine how these elements interact within Churchill's work, focusing on three plays: *Owners* (1972), *Vinegar Tom* (1976) and *Cloud Nine* (1979).[9] It will also explore the socialist-feminist character of these pieces, which is central to their meaning and impact. Within the context of second-wave feminism (an umbrella term used to designate the development of feminist theory and activism during the 1960s and 1970s, as distinct from the earlier suffrage movement), Churchill can be considered not just a supporter but a 'feminist thinker' in her own right.[10] Crucial to the contextualisation of her ideas is the traditional distinction between three types of feminism: radical, bourgeois and socialist. Radical feminism postulates 'that so-called female qualities (nurturing, emotionality) are superior to so-called male qualities (aggression, competitiveness, individualism)' and advocates an absolute solidarity among women. Bourgeois or liberal feminism, in turn, 'sees the main challenge as equalling up with men', thus stressing 'individual achievement and success'. Socialist feminism, by contrast, links 'the concerns and struggles of women with other kinds of oppression or inequality, such as those of class, race or culture'. Therefore, 'it recognises that fundamental social changes are necessary for a world in which difference and fairness can co-exist'.[11] Churchill's drama actively pursues this latter goal, questioning the essentialist undertones of radical feminism and the capitalist compromise of the liberal version.

With the retreat of Marxist thought in the 1990s, 'socialist feminism' was recast in the broader concept of 'materialist feminism'. Within it, a strong trend of neo-Marxist feminist philosophy developed in the US, which has been identified as Critical Feminist Theory. Combining 'the universal ideals and normative judgments of modernism, and the contextualism, particularity and skepticism of postmodernism', Critical Feminist Theory has put identity politics under scrutiny.[12] Nancy Fraser, for instance, argues that the feminist movement needs to move beyond a disproportionate concentration on cultural 'recognition' of identity/difference and remember 'the insights of equality feminism concerning the need for equal participation and fair distribution'. For Fraser, feminism's motto should be '[n]o recognition without redistribution' and its best formula, 'socialism in the economy plus deconstruction in the culture'.[13] This is exactly the kind of feminism envisaged in Churchill's plays. Recognition without redistribution underlies the destructive 'liberation' of Marion in *Owners*, while an anti-essentialist politics of identity deconstruction emerges as the only antidote to the material and sexual oppression portrayed in both *Vinegar Tom* and *Cloud Nine*.

Owners

The starting point of Churchill's professional career as a stage writer, *Owners* also launched her enduring association with the Royal Court Theatre. Less than two years after the play premiered in its studio space 'Upstairs', Churchill became the theatre's first female Resident Dramatist (1974–5) and later a tutor for its Young Writers' Group. The majority of Churchill's works have been presented at the Royal Court since then, yet the beginnings were fraught with problems. The lead actor in *Owners*, Jill Bennett, injured her foot during the preview period and had to be replaced. Director Nicholas Wright was not pleased with his own contribution, and neither was Churchill's agent, Peggy Ramsay, who wrote to her client: 'I was dreadfully unhappy about the production of your play Upstairs and have still not got over it. I find it difficult to even talk to Nick Wright.'[14] Churchill's personal circumstances were difficult too, as she had written the play in four days while recovering from a miscarriage.[15] Despite all these complications, *Owners* managed to impress the critics. Beyond habitual reservations about the dramatist's refusal to observe 'classical standards', she was praised for her 'amusing' dialogue and 'poetic imagination'.[16]

Many scholars place *Owners* within Churchill's formative period, as an interesting but not fully accomplished theatrical project. In terms of form, Churchill was already breaking the rules of naturalism by introducing bizarre plot twists and extreme character traits into perfectly recognisable situations (hence some reviewers' dismay at her unruly dramaturgy, a reaction which suggests early-1970s sexist prejudice). Nevertheless, the play is not considered original but 'Ortonesque' in style and Churchill herself conceded that her characters may have lacked nuance and that she would now 'take them more seriously'.[17] Judged in its own terms, however, as a savage farce on both capitalist and gender oppression, *Owners* can be readily included within Churchill's socialist-feminist corpus. Paradoxically, if it is unfortunate that the play has had few revivals, it is even more regrettable that its critique of the politics of 'ownership' is still as pertinent as ever.

Commenting on the Young Vic Theatre's staging of *Owners* in 1987, at the height of the Thatcherite economic boom, critic John Vidal noted that the play had become 'starkly relevant'.[18] More recently, in 2004 and 2008, two rehearsed readings of *Owners* were organised by the Royal Court as part of larger Churchill 'events'. The latter was scheduled to commemorate the dramatist's seventieth birthday, yet it also coincided with a new speculative property bubble bursting and the latest greed-induced global economic crisis. But *Owners* is, of course, not just about property. In his first review of the play, Michael Billington criticised Churchill for throwing 'everything in [it] bar the kitchen sink' and regarded the play's excesses as 'Churchill's weakness'.[19] With the benefit of hindsight, *Owners* can be seen instead as a rich catalogue of Churchill's longstanding preoccupations: capitalist exploitation, gender and sexual politics, identity, ecological damage and the fear of a terrifying future (usually signalled by the word 'frightening').These various topics are integrated within two core thematic strands which Churchill openly identified at the time: 'There was one idea going about landlords and tenants, and then another about western aggressiveness and eastern passivity.'[20]

Housing was an important issue in early 1970s Britain, which interested the emergent group of political dramatists writing alongside Churchill. David Edgar, for instance, addressed this subject directly in *Rent or Caught in the Act* (1972), as did Howard Brenton, indirectly, in *Magnificence* (1973). For Churchill, the 'details of life' in this case came from her experience of being 'in an old woman's flat when a young man offering her money to move came round' (p. 4). In *Owners*, this is what Worsely attempts with Lisa, a pregnant woman who shares a small rented flat with her husband Alec, two more children and her elderly mother-in-law. Worsely's initial offer of 'two hundred pounds' to displace the family in order to allow for property development is disguised as help: 'Turning you out? What an old-fashioned idea. I was hoping I could do you a favour' (p. 17). However, when Alec refuses to move and Lisa realises that the money would not get them very far, Worsely resorts to threats of 'adjusting' the rent and even removing the stairs and the roof for building work (p. 19). In tackling the ideology of private ownership, the play engages with socialism's central concern, that is, the unequal distribution of wealth. At the same time, it maps the divided territory of many of Churchill's subsequent works, a world split 'by the dreadful disparities capitalism creates between those who own and those who owe'.[21]

The play also questions capitalism at a philosophical level, contrasting the attitudes of former lovers Marion and Alec as representative of the Western and Eastern traditions respectively. Marion, the property speculator who employs Worsely, is the embodiment of the Christian hymn quoted at the beginning of the play: 'Onward Christian soldiers, marching as to war' (p. 3). She has an insatiable appetite not only for houses but also food – 'I'm always hungry' (p. 27) – and consumer goods – 'I hate old clothes. I love to throw them away. And get new ones' (p. 21). A logical extension of her voraciousness is the way she relates to people. She tells her husband at a strip club, 'If you want a girl, Clegg, I'll buy you one' (20). Marion is prepared to do anything to resume her affair with Alec, including tricking Lisa into signing adoption papers after her son is born. For Marion, Alec constitutes an object of desire and the baby is simply a functional item. Alec, in contrast, personifies the radical passivity of the Zen poem which Churchill juxtaposes to the Christian epigraph above: 'Sitting quietly, doing nothing. Spring comes and the grass grows by itself' (p. 3). Alec's response to Worsely – 'I'm not moving' (p. 18) – epitomises his stance in life. He has given up work and is completely devoid of desire. He tells Marion: 'I don't know what I could lose that would make any difference to me' (p. 28).

In 1982, Churchill said she had been 'strongly influenced by Buddhism' as an undergraduate and later found herself 'constantly coming back' to it: in 1989, Mark Thacker Brown built on this insight to suggest that many of Churchill's plays up to that date could be 'better understood when viewed in light of Eastern traditions and assumptions'. The most interesting aspect of Brown's interpretation was his tacit recognition that Churchill's engagement with these beliefs was not religious but political: Buddhism, as well as Taoism, Hinduism and Jainism, offered the playwright 'a formidable opposition to the acquisitiveness of Western capitalism'.[22] Even more intriguing is the fact that Churchill uses a fundamentally non-dialectical mode of thinking within a dialectical dramatic structure. This is explained in her own justification for Alec's existence in *Owners*: 'He's there really because of the interest I had in the Taoist Chinese idea of being: of not actually doing or achieving anything, but just being. I'm not proposing this as a marvellous answer, but *by putting it alongside the other system, I hope that each will question the other.*'[23]

Owners is full of references to Eastern ideas, which inform recurrent themes in Churchill's playwriting well beyond the 1970s and 1980s. For a start, there is a contrast between the chronological plot development – punctuated by the ever-increasing injuries in Worsely's body as he continually fails to commit suicide – and a more cyclical time, marked by the birth of Alec and Lisa's baby and the death of Alec's mother (whom he disconnects from the hospital drip as an act of kindness). In terms of setting, however, this cycle of life runs parallel to the inescapable cycle of capitalism, which moves from '*Clegg's butcher's shop*' (p. 7), about to close in the first scene, to '*Clegg's new butcher's shop*' (p. 64), already opened in the last. As opposed to Clegg's 'butchering' business, which also colours his view on gender, the alternative (Eastern) cyclical time derives from a respect to the rhythms of nature and all its inhabitants. In this sense, *Owners* announces the ecological anxieties key to later plays such as *The Skriker* (1994) and *Far Away* (2000). Churchill's unease about the effects of a utilitarian (Western) approach to the environment is encapsulated in Marion's main speech, directed to Alec, which combines elements of the Protestant ethic with those of scientific/ technological discourse:

I know the bible stories aren't true but that makes their meaning matter most. God gave him dominion over every beast of the field and fowl of the air. Gave the land to him and to his seed forever. Doesn't evolution say the same? Keep on, get better, be best. Onward. Fight. How did man get to the moon? Not by sitting staring at an orange. Columbus, Leonardo da Vinci, Scott of the Antarctic. You would be content on a flat earth. But the animals are ours. The vegetables and minerals. For us to consume. We don't shrink from blood. Or guilt. Guilt is essential to progress. (p. 30)

Churchill's distinctive notion of identity is also linked to Eastern thought. As Brown explains, 'Buddhism and Taoism agree that individuality is an illusion and that permanence in this world is unattainable'; moreover, 'the desire for such worldly stability is the root cause of suffering in both the Buddhist and the Taoist traditions'.[24] According to Brown, this desire, symbolised by those characters who try to 'own' things and people, is subtly undermined in Churchill's later productions by astute theatrical devices such as: more than one actor playing each character (*Light Shining in Buckinghamshire*, 1976), actors switching characters in the second act (*Cloud Nine*, 1979), doubling (*Top Girls*, 1982) and multiple roles (*Fen*, 1983). In *Owners*, possessing is an aspiration for everyone, apart from Alec, but the ultimate failure of self-ownership is signified by Worsely's unsuccessful suicide attempts. Here, again, Churchill's philosophical reflections are connected to political meaning, namely, the anti-individualism of her socialist position and the anti-essentialism of her feminist one. She would return to the problem of identity in *A Number* (2006), where the introduction of cloning delivers perhaps the most significant challenge to a conception of selfhood as stable and unproblematic.[25]

Despite the strong link between philosophy and socialist-feminist politics in Churchill's work, *Owners* is not often regarded as particularly concerned with feminism. This argument tends to be corroborated by a comparison between *Owners* and *Top Girls*, where the former's 'gender-inflected critique' is not considered as developed as the latter's 'mature, materialist-feminist inquiry'.[26] The close resemblance of these two plays, which are a decade apart, derives from the presence of 'active' women at the centre: Marion in *Owners*, Marlene in *Top Girls*. Both these protagonists have achieved career success by uncritically embracing capitalist values. Thus, far from enacting a naive celebration of 'bourgeois' female accomplishment, the plays highlight the dangers of disassociating feminism from socialism. *Top Girls* is a more structurally sophisticated piece, yet *Owners* is more complex than most commentators would credit. Its analysis of gender, as Helen Keyssar emphasises, is 'neither predictable nor reducible to a single argument'.[27]

According to Lisa Merrill, even though both Marion and Marlene 'use and abuse others to get ahead', only Marion 'always appears to be a monster'.[28] But Marion, like Marlene in the first scene of *Top Girls*, is initially introduced as an extraordinary woman within a male-dominated environment. As the play opens, Clegg, whose extreme chauvinism was influenced by Churchill's reading of Eva Figes's *Patriarchal Attitudes* (1970), fantasises about murdering his wife. He is not prepared to accept that '[s]he can stand on her own two feet' (p. 8) and deplores the fact that she did not even succumb to institutionalisation: 'When Marion was in hospital they tried to tell her she'd be happier and more sane as a good wife. [. . .] But she wouldn't listen. She came out of there with staring eyes and three weeks later she bought her first house' (p. 10). As Rebellato points out, the critique of psychiatry and its repressive methods was an important countercultural issue at the time.[29] Without justifying her ruthlessness in any way, Marion's past makes her less one-dimensional. Nevertheless, she ends proclaiming total identification with a capitalist and patriarchal version of progress.

Like Marlene, who abandons her daughter to pursue a career in London, Marion doesn't recognise a biological maternal instinct: 'Because I'm a woman, is it? I'm meant to be kind. I'm meant to understand a woman's feelings wanting her baby back. I don't. I won't' (p. 63). Unlike *Top Girls*, however, where Marlene's sister Joyce represents a caring and socialist alternative, the maternal Lisa in *Owners* is as compromised as Marion. Her powerlessness may turn her into a victim (ignored by Alec, threatened by Worsely, deceived by Marion, sexually exploited by Clegg), but she sides with the 'owners'. She tells Worseley in the second scene: 'Of course nobody with a decent place would want us in it. I wouldn't myself if I was letting rooms' (p. 17).

Then she says about the baby: 'I don't care if he's well or nearly dead. What good is it to me him being well in Marion's house?' (p. 49). *Owners* avoids an essentialist reading of motherhood by dissolving the link between biology and care. In fact, the only character who is actually seen on stage looking after the baby is Clegg, the 'loutish butcher with an unexpected nurturing streak'.[30]

The play escalates into the 'Churchillian' terror of the last scene, in which Worsely announces that Alec and the baby from the family downstairs have died in the fire he caused following Marion's and Clegg's separate instructions. Here, at last, the Cleggs appear to be united by their brutality and Marion, now a fully-fleshed 'monster', is not sorry but amazed by the force of her own power. Alec, in turn, loses his life after finally becoming 'active'. By going back into the burning property in an effort to save a child that is not his own, he proves to have meant what he said to Marion earlier, that he didn't 'necessarily' love his children more than anyone else's (p. 47). Although ultimately unsuccessful, Alec's attempt gestures towards what critical feminist theorist Seyla Benhabib calls an 'ethics of justice', the required counterpart of an 'ethics of care'.[31] Worsely had secretly returned the baby boy to his own mother Lisa, but the baby girl who dies in the fire signals an alarming future. As a socialist-feminist play, *Owners* implies that collective action is the only way of avoiding this horrifying prospect. If there is any hope on offer, it is not in the individual 'motherly' love tied to gender stereotypes, but, rather, in the daring act of caring about 'somebody else's' children.

Vinegar Tom

After Churchill's 1972 Royal Court debut, the next defining moment in her career occurred in 1976. She wrote three plays that year – *Traps*, *Vinegar Tom* and *Light Shining in Buckinghamshire* – and began a process of collaboration which would remain her working method for the following two decades. *Light Shining* was the first of a number of projects developed with Joint Stock Theatre Group and also the start of Churchill's successful theatrical partnership with director Max

Stafford-Clark. *Vinegar Tom* resulted from her association with feminist touring collective Monstrous Regiment, formed in 1975 by
women who, having experienced a 'relatively raw deal' as performers
in fringe theatre, were hoping to reverse 'the conventional balance of
power between the sexes'.[32] Like Churchill, they were interested in
combining artistic innovation with political ideas. By the time of their
chance meeting on a march in early 1976, both playwright and
company were thinking about the same subject: witches. For a group
whose name came from a 1558 pamphlet by Scottish Reformation
leader John Knox, 'The First Blast of the Trumpet Against the
Monstrous Regiment of Women', the historical witch-hunts were an
obvious topic of inquiry. The 'Monsters' gave Churchill 'a list of
books' which, together with those she was already reading for her
seventeenth-century Joint Stock play, led to an unsettling realisation:
'The women accused of witchcraft were often those on the edges of
society, old, poor, single, sexually unconventional' (pp. 129–30).

Vinegar Tom takes a strong secular stance. As Elin Diamond
explains, it presents witch-hunting as 'a function of seventeenth-
century religious fanaticism and an allegory of sexual and economic
oppression'.[33] In this sense, the play revisits Arthur Miller's political
critique in *The Crucible* (1953), where the Salem witch-hunt is seen as
a parable of the anti-communist hysteria of McCarthyism in the US.
However, *Vinegar Tom* is also a critique of *The Crucible* itself. In
Miller's play, the accusations sprout from Abigail Williams, a young
servant who lusts for her former employer John Proctor, the tragic
male hero. Abigail displays 'the qualities of beauty, lust, guile, fickle-
ness, and deviousness – typical constructions that comprise the object
of the male gaze', while Alice in *Vinegar Tom* 'endeavours to articulate
herself as a subject, as opposed to an object, of desire'.[34] Alice's casual
sexual encounter with an unknown man opens the play:

Man   Am I the devil?

Alice   What, sweet?

Man   I'm the devil. Man in black, they say, they always say, a
man in black met me in the night, took me into the thicket and
made me commit uncleanness unspeakable.

Alice   I've seen men in black that's no devils unless clergy and gentlemen are devils. (p. 135)

Being 'with the Devil' is the phrase used in *The Crucible* to allege witchcraft. In what is possibly the play's most famous scene, Abigail tries to save her own skin by confessing (and encouraging others to confess) to having seen female acquaintances 'with the Devil'.[35] On the contrary, Alice in *Vinegar Tom* refuses to take part in the man's fantasy and reverses the terms of the proposition. Not only is she *not* with the devil, but 'men in black' representing ecclesiastic and economic influence are where the real dangers lie. Alice would eventually become a victim of these powers when she is accused of witchcraft. As an underprivileged single mother, she refuses to conform: she is not a 'whore', but neither a 'wife', a 'widow' or a 'virgin' (p. 137). In another inversion of *The Crucible*, the charge against Alice comes from Jack, the sexually frustrated married farmer whose advances she had rejected. In Miller's play, Proctor has had an affair with Abigail but he repents and his marriage to Elizabeth is restored, even if his life is eventually taken by the witch-hunters. Proctor is the traditional flawed yet virtuous male protagonist who, unjustly condemned, prefers to die with honour rather than sign a false confession. In *Vinegar Tom*, Jack and his wife Margery – like Clegg and Marion in *Owners* – are only united by their dreams of economic prosperity. When their cattle start dying from a disease, they resort to blaming others in order to absolve themselves from what could be interpreted as God's punishment. 'If we're bewitched, Jack, that explains all,' says Margery (p. 152). Jack is relieved: 'Then it's not my sins. Good folk get bewitched' (p. 153).

Churchill's assault on marriage as a bourgeois institution is also reflected in the name given to the woman who actively participates in the hounding of others: Goody, the witchfinder's assistant. 'Goody', an archaic shortened version of 'good wife', is used in *The Crucible* to refer to all married women, most of whom (including Elizabeth) are unfairly charged during the course of the play. In *Vinegar Tom*, the name is reserved for the one who has been corrupted by economic gain as well as by the impossible conundrum of becoming either an accuser or the accused. Goody sides with the oppressors not only because there is money in witch-hunting, but also to avoid being turned into an alleged witch herself. 'Yes, it's interesting work being a searcher and nice to do good at the same time as earning a living,' she says impassively while holding one of the suspects so that her body can be pricked by the witchfinder. 'Better than staying home a widow. I'd end up like the old women you see, soft in the head and full of spite with their muttering and spells' (p. 168).

A similarly intolerable situation is faced by Betty, the landowner's teenage daughter, whose status allows her to evade the witch-hunt only by being forced into marriage. Following a rebellious spree, she is literally bled into submission by a male doctor: 'After bleeding you must be purged. Tonight you shall be blistered. You will soon be well enough to be married' (p. 149). Yet not even an unsavoury escape like this is available for those marginalised women who have been charged with witchcraft. Two of them are left awaiting sentence at the end of the play: Alice and her married friend Susan, who believes herself that she is a witch after having had an abortion. The other two – Alice's mother Joan, an ageing dispossessed widow, and Ellen, the healer who had given the abortive herbs to Susan – are hanged on stage.

Contrasting with Miller's naturalism, the structure of Churchill's play is episodic, comprising twenty-one scenes punctuated by seven songs. The musical numbers underline the contemporary parallels and should be delivered 'in modern dress' (p. 133). This makes *Vinegar Tom* a prime example of what Janelle Reinelt terms 'Britain's new feminist drama', built on a critical appropriation of Brechtian techniques.[36] Unsurprisingly, the first production was met with a mixed reaction. Michael Coveney from the *Financial Times* considered the songs a 'righteous overstatement', while *Plays and Players'* David Zane Mairowitz argued that 'the playtext is not strong enough to withstand the breaking of its rhythm and antagonism of the musical interludes'.[37] The fact that Mairowitz compared Churchill's play to *The Crucible* insinuates gender and political bias rather than stylistic preference. As Elaine Aston points out, the cause of Mairowitz's criticism of *Vinegar Tom* might be that 'Churchill does not choose to draw us into a harrowing, tragic study of a persecuted (male) individual, but [. . .] looks to a collective representation of woman-centred oppression'.[38] Even though Miller's play was created in defence of left-wing solidarity, its focus is a liberal reassertion of individual freedom, embodied in the heroic figure of Proctor. As the author himself admitted, 'the central impulse for writing at all was not the social but the interior psychological question', an impulse that also accounts for the representation of evil in the play as 'sadism'.[39] Churchill, instead, purposefully discards psychological, private explanations in favour of systemic, public ones: 'The pricking scene is one of humiliation rather than torture and Packer [the witchfinder] is an efficient professional, not a sadistic maniac' (p. 134).

Churchill's demythologising efforts in *Vinegar Tom* must be seen in the context of a playwriting phenomenon characteristic of the 1970s, namely, the rise of the history play. Although this genre has occupied a relevant place on the British stage since the Elizabethan era, the 'radical treatment of history', as D. Keith Peacock describes it, was an explicit aspiration for political theatre makers during this decade.[40] They drew their inspiration from new approaches within the discipline of history itself. Siân Adiseshiah identifies three common objectives for left-wing historians and playwrights at this time: an 'articulation of history as a political counter-action to a liberal historical consensus, a reconstitution of hidden historical narratives, and a deconstruction of the past as a static body of knowledge bracketed off from [. . .] the present'.[41] Historiography, that is, the reflection on history's own principles and methods, was also crucial for the feminist movement, and theatre companies such as Monstrous Regiment were particularly 'excited by the possibility of reclaiming the history play from women's point of view'.[42] According to Richard H. Palmer, two features of traditional history – and, by extension, of the traditional history play – were challenged in this period: the pretension of objectivity, which would give way to specific interpretations (including Marxist and feminist ones), and the emphasis on biography.[43] *Vinegar Tom* embraces both these challenges by expressing a socialist-feminist viewpoint and avoiding an excessive concentration on individual characters.

Mark Berninger's recent taxonomy of history plays is useful to understand the relationship between *The Crucible* and *Vinegar Tom*. As a 'realistic history play', the former 'contains a mixture of documented materials and fictional elements which do not contradict historiographical knowledge and the dominant interpretation of the events'. It also employs conventional formal devices such as a chronological presentation and stage realism. *Vinegar Tom*, a 'revisionist history play', defines itself against all of the above and presents an 'alternative' in terms of content and form.[44] Miller based his play on the historical record of the Salem witch-hunt but changed some details for dramatic effect. Churchill 'didn't base the play on any precise historical events, but set it rather loosely in the seventeenth century' (p. 130). Yet, as already noted, *Vinegar Tom* incorporated a significant level of research on revisionist historiography. In addition, at least one primary source, *The Malleus Maleficarum: The Hammer of Witches*, found its way directly into the text. This fifteenth-century treatise becomes a music hall double-act in the last scene. Its authors, theologians Heinrich Kramer and James Sprenger, were played in the original production by two female performers cross-dressed in top hats and tails. Most of their extremely misogynist lines were taken from the original document, concluding that 'All witchcraft / comes from carnal lust / which is in woman / insatiable' (p. 178).

The negation of female sexuality, both historical and contemporary, is a key theme in *Vinegar Tom*, generating an interesting counterpoint to *Owners*. In the character of Alec, Churchill had explored the potential (and limitations) of an East-inspired absence of desire as an alternative to the voraciousness of Western thought. In this later play, the main target is not the acquisitive but the repressive side of the Western Christian tradition, which has been constructed against women. An excess of desire in *Owners* turns people into possessions; in *Vinegar Tom*, it is the prohibition of desire that destroys lives. This focus on sexuality and the body – especially in the first two songs, 'Nobody Sings' and 'Oh Doctor' – justifies radical feminist readings of the text. However, even when *Vinegar Tom* appears as a case study for radical feminism, 'some elements of a feminist materialist analysis' are recognised.[45] In fact, if the play is considered as a theatrical whole, the materialist critique dominates its meaning. This seems to have been Monstrous Regiment's intention from the outset, as they encouraged Churchill to address the subject 'in a cool analytical frame of mind'.[46] The lack of logic of the witch-hunters' discourse is exposed by the highly rational Ellen, the 'cunning woman' (p. 132). Countering the stereotype of the herbal healer as a paradigm of feminine intuition, Ellen (like Alice in the first scene) represents the unheard voice of reason:

> I could ask to be swum. They think the water won't keep a witch in, for Christ's baptism sake, so if a woman floats she's a witch. And if she sinks they have to let her go. I could sink. Any fool can sink. It's how to sink without drowning. It's whether they get you out. No, why should I ask to be half drowned? I've done nothing. I'll explain to them what I do. It's healing, not harm. There's no devil in it. (pp. 169–70)

Drawing on one of Churchill's sources, Barbara Ehrenreich and Deidre English's *Witches, Midwives and Nurses* (1976), Adiseshiah claims that the assumed contrast between the 'scientific rationalism of the newly professional doctor' and the 'magic deployed by women healers' is itself a myth. Ehrenreich and English state that 'it was witches who developed an extensive understanding of bones and muscles, herbs and drugs, while physicians were still deriving their prognoses from astrology and alchemists'.[47] In the play, Ellen's threat to the system is nothing to do with magic, but rather with a skill that operates outside the budding capitalist economy and offers women a certain amount of control over reproduction. Thus, the effect of Churchill's revisionist approach to history is twofold: to uncover materialist dimensions of received historical narratives and to problematise gender binaries. At the same time, it allows for Brechtian 'historisation', that is, the possibility of judging the past from the point of view of the present (as well as seeing the present open to historical change).

The interaction between historical and current dilemmas is achieved mainly through the songs, which, as Brecht would advise, provide an ironical commentary on the action. 'If Everybody Worked as Hard as Me', for example, connects gender oppression to 'family' and 'country' (p. 160), with a playfulness that anticipates the tone of *Cloud Nine*. The same is true of the Kramer and Sprenger cross-dressed act, which – as Amelia Howe Kritzer suggests – reintroduces 'Brechtian distancing' immediately after the emotional climax of the story.[48] Other songs, however, deliver a more straightforward message. 'Something to Burn' links witches to 'blacks', 'women' and 'Jews' (p. 154); 'Lament for the Witches' poses the question: 'Would they have hanged you then? Ask how they're stopping you now' (p. 176) and 'Evil Women' confront men about their sexual fantasies. Monstrous Regiment's Gillian Hanna recognised that many members of the audience 'felt their intelligence was affronted' by the modern musical numbers, yet she deemed this strategy absolutely necessary: 'For every single intelligent man who can draw parallels, there are dozens who don't. It's not that they can't. It's that they won't.'[49] The explicitness of these particular songs incorporates a degree of didacticism to *Vinegar Tom* which is somewhat alien to Churchill's dramaturgy. Nevertheless, the play shares with the best of Brechtian drama that mixture of clarity and 'defamiliarisation' which invites the audience to re-examine their assumptions, and to look at both past and present in a new light.

Cloud Nine

Cloud Nine was Churchill's second collaboration with Joint Stock. The project started in September 1978, following the group's normal theatre-making pattern: initial collective workshops led to a (solitary) playwriting process and culminated in a final rehearsal/rewriting phase. During the first period, actors, director and dramatist 'read books and talked to other people', as usual (p. 245). However, having chosen sexual politics as their research subject, this time the company's starting point was far more personal. '[W]e each took turns to tell our own life stories and to answer questions on our own sexual experiences and lifestyles,' actor Antony Sher recalled years later. 'It was nerve-wracking to contemplate (and far more revealing than stripping naked would have been).'[50] Churchill and Stafford-Clark had purposely recruited performers who subscribed to different sexual identities, and the workshops put social attitudes and stereotypes under the microscope.

The final shape of the play, with the first act set in colonial Africa towards the end of the nineteenth century and the second in late-1970s London, was Churchill's own creation and emerged from two separate insights. One was theoretical: '[Jean] Genet's idea that colonial oppression and sexual oppression are similar.' The other came out indirectly from the workshops' explorations on childhood, where 'everyone felt they had been born almost in the Victorian age [. . .] with quite conventional and old-fashioned expectations about sex and marriage'.[51] These expectations are represented in *Cloud Nine* by colonial administrator Clive, the patriarch whose presence dominates Act One, together with his (highly hypocritical) declaration of principles: 'We are not in this country to enjoy ourselves' (p. 253). The fast-paced comedy of this section derives from the gap between prescribed rules and the characters' actual presence and behaviour, which is interrogated further by Churchill's celebrated device of cross-casting. As a 'man's creation' (p. 251), Clive's wife Betty is played by a male actor. Clive's black servant Joshua is played by a white actor because, likewise, he wants to be '[w]hat white men want' (p. 252). Conversely, Clive's nine-year-old son Edward is played by a woman to signal the failure of his attempt to comply with the norm: 'What father wants I'd dearly like to be. / I find it rather hard as you can see' (p. 252). Clive's two-year-old daughter Victoria, in turn, is portrayed simply as 'a dummy' (p. 248).

As the play progresses, a number of 'improper' desires are revealed: Ellen, the governess, is in love with Betty; Betty is in love with Clive's friend Harry; Harry is in love with Edward and has occasional sex with Joshua. In fact, not even Clive lives up to his own standards of respectability as he pursues a sexual liaison with Mrs Saunders, the widow who has moved in looking for 'protection' against a potential native uprising. Clive blames his adultery on Mrs Saunders – 'You are dark like this continent. Mysterious. Treacherous' (p. 263) – and women in general – 'There is something dark about women, that threatens what is best in us' (p. 282). His misogynistic discourse is redolent of Kramer and Sprenger's diatribe in *Vinegar Tom*, but with an added colonialist implication that equates female sexuality with 'darkness', highlighting the parallel between gender and race underpinning the play. Like Susan in *Vinegar Tom*, who becomes complicit in her own oppression – 'I'm so wicked' (p. 174) – Betty fully accepts her imposed negative identity: 'There is something so wicked in me', she tells Clive. 'I am bad, bad, bad' (p. 277).

When Joshua raises his gun at Clive, ending the first act, the play subverts the conventions of comedy by interrupting a marriage ceremony, the traditional plot resolution used to symbolise a happy restoration of order. But the wedding itself has already been exposed as a brusque attempt to force heterosexuality on to Harry and Ellen.[52] Here again, as in *Vinegar Tom*, marriage represents a form of coercion to suppress or 'cure' deviant behaviour. When an anxious Ellen asks Betty if sex with a man is 'enjoyable', Betty replies with Clive's words from the beginning of the play: 'Ellen, you're not getting married to enjoy yourself' (p. 286). Pleasure, especially for women, is out of the question within the parameters of Act One, rendering female desire not only forbidden but actually invisible. Ellen's passion for Betty is repeatedly ignored, reflecting the common belief that lesbianism was inconceivable for the Victorian establishment. Mrs Saunders is left asking 'What about me?' (p. 264) after Clive 'performs' under her skirt only long enough to satisfy himself. And Harry calls Betty '[s]illy' (p. 268) for wanting more than a platonic relationship with him. Frances Gray points out how this 'invisibility' is also underscored by a number of stage techniques, such as the doubling of Ellen and Mrs Saunders (who cannot meet), the representation of Victoria as a doll and the cross-casting of Betty, which implies that she 'does not exist in her own right'.[53]

Churchill's innovative use of cross-gender casting in 1979 has been linked to developments in feminist theory that would not materialise until the 1990s, in particular, Judith Butler's anti-essentialist understanding of gender as performative. According to American director and academic Rhonda Blair, the play deliberately employs this technique 'to illuminate gender-as-social construction'; in doing so, it anticipates Butler's assertion that 'the ground of gender identity is the stylized repetition of acts through time, and not a seemingly seamless identity'.[54] On the one hand, as Gray suggests, Betty is *absent* from Act One, emphasising the invisibility of women. On the other hand, the cross-gendered character *is* Betty, but he/she forces the audience to experience the instability and artificiality of gender identity, to appreciate its performative make-up (in real life) through theatre performance. Blair relates how her production of *Cloud Nine* failed to generate the desired effect in some spectators because they did not realise that the actor playing Betty was a man. She therefore insists that cross-dressing should function as a Brechtian alienation device, because 'the discrepancy between the gender of the actor and the gender of the character is where much of the meaning of the play lies'.[55]

In Act Two, the cross-casting involves only one character: five-year-old Cathy, who was doubled with Clive in the first production. The other child, Victoria's son Tommy, is permanently offstage (mirroring Victoria's non-existence in the first act). Betty, Edward and Victoria, now 'played by actors of their own sex' (p. 248), are twenty-five years older, but a whole century has elapsed and the action has moved to a London park. Taken together, the characters of the first and second act represent a wide range of ages and subject positions in a play that has been applauded for its inclusive approach to sexual politics. However, the metaphorical focus of the second part is a feminist critique of one particular gender role, that of 'wife'. Reiterating the commentary on marriage from Act One, the struggle of Lin (Cathy's mother), Victoria, Edward and Betty in Act Two can be summarised as a moving away from this given role in order to find autonomy, sexual fulfilment and more rewarding relationships. Lin has already left her husband, who abused her, and has come out as a lesbian. Victoria will eventually leave hers and embark on a relationship with Lin, who – unlike Martin – 'would [still] love [her]' (p. 302) when she moves to Manchester to start a new job. Edward has internalised the part of the 'injured wife' (p. 307) in his relationship with Gerry. When Gerry moves out, Edward transitionally becomes 'a lesbian' (p. 307) until he sheds his old identity and is ready, perhaps, to start again with Gerry on different terms. Betty leaves Clive, discovers masturbation and, as the play finishes, tries for the first time 'to pick up a man' (p. 320).

Even though, as Churchill explains, 'all the characters in this act change a little for the better', the play does not offer an unproblematic celebration of freedom (p. 246). A number of ghosts appear, demonstrating that the past still haunts the present: Lin's brother Bill (a soldier whose death in Northern Ireland brings back the spectre of British imperialism) and – from Act One – Harry, Maud (Betty's mother), Ellen, Clive and even Betty herself. As Kritzer remarks, 'Victorianism has not been entirely laid to rest, despite all the evidence of sexual liberation'.[56] Change is difficult and there are no easy answers to the old questions. One key issue which remains unresolved concerns child-rearing responsibilities and methods. The replacement of Lin and Victoria (scene one) with Martin and Edward (scene four) as main carers is 'a clear sign of progress'.[57] Yet when Cathy gets hurt under Martin's watch, Lin's complaints are met with this protestation: 'Why the hell should I look after your child anyway? I just want Tommy' (p. 318). One of the main themes from *Owners* resurfaces here, namely, whether it is possible to care for children who are not one's own. Confirming the utopian streak that many commentators have detected in *Cloud Nine*, the altruistic option prevails and Martin buys the bruised Cathy another ice cream. Still, the other side of the question, regarding *how* children should be raised, remains open. Lin 'can't work it out' (p. 303).

Unlike the silent Victoria in the first act, the cross-gendered Cathy 'is a tough little girl who won't be overly intimidated or otherwise imprisoned by feminine behaviour'.[58] However, like Edward in the first act, Cathy is slapped by her mother. It is hard for Lin not to repeat with Cathy what her own mother did during her upbringing, in the same way that Betty has struggled to release herself from the influence of Maud. The role of mother needs as much transformation as that of wife if the cycle of patriarchy is to be disrupted. In Act One, Maud constantly refers to her 'mama' while reinforcing the household rules. She tells her daughter, 'Betty you have to learn to be patient. I am patient. My mama was very patient' (p. 258). Then she shows her granddaughter Victoria how to smack her baby doll if she misbehaves, concluding: 'When I was a child we honoured our parents. My mama was an angel' (p. 275). In Act Two, Betty's monologue of late sexual awakening is directed against Maud as well as Clive. It was Maud who violently dragged her from under the kitchen table when she was touching herself as a child, which meant Betty 'never did it again till this year' (p. 316).

Betty's speech was famously moved to the end of the play in the first American production of *Cloud Nine* to maximise its emotional impact, but Churchill was not convinced: '[I]t threw so much emphasis onto Betty as an individual, while the other way seemed to be more about the development of a group of people, in the same way as the first act.'[59] It can be argued that the monologue itself, like Churchill's dramaturgy as a whole, contains an important collective dimension in terms of its critique of oppressive forms of motherhood that are inadvertently passed through generations. In its original position, Betty's speech is delivered immediately before her attempt to disrupt this harmful chain by offering Victoria (and Lin) an arrangement that even involves Maud in an alternative future: 'I have a little money from your grandmother. [. . .] I wonder if we could get a house and all live in it together?' (p. 317). Victoria rejects the idea, but the possibility of a different relationship between mothers and daughters has already been unlocked.

Despite *Cloud Nine*'s reputation as a bold feminist play, some scholars have claimed that it falls short of disrupting either racial ideology or heterosexism. Apollo Amoko criticises the responses to *Cloud Nine* for focusing 'disproportionately on what are perceived to be its "feminist accomplishments" to the near total exclusion of any in-depth or sustained examination of race and colonialism'.[60] After the lessons learned from the politics of difference within the feminist movement, it would be unwise to pretend that the play has anything to say about the experience of the colonised. Nevertheless, Churchill's attack on the discourse of colonialism and its overarching consequences is justified. James M. Harding also questions the subversiveness of the play in terms of sexual politics, claiming that it ultimately leaves 'dominant assumptions intact'. In his view, the use of cross-gender casting in Act One contributes to the erasure of gay and lesbian desire. For instance, when Ellen kisses Betty, the cross-dressing turns a 'transgressive lesbian moment' into 'a conventional reaffirmation of heterosexuality'. Much of the play's interpretation in this respect depends on how the final moment is read, when Betty from the first act embraces Betty from the second act: for Harding, this encounter 'subtly echoed the compulsory marriage at the end of act 1'.[61] Yet, as Marc Silverstein proposes, the embrace can also be understood as symbolising 'multiple forms of pleasure' presented non-hierarchically: auto-eroticism (Betty with herself), homo-eroticism (Betty with a woman) and hetero-eroticism (Betty with a man).[62]

Since its premiere at Dartington College of Arts in February 1979, *Cloud Nine* has prompted not only abundant academic discussion but also numerous revivals. The Royal Court brought it back within a year of its initial tour and then, in 1981, there was a first production in New York. Susan Bennett, who has written about changing perceptions of the play across the decades, affirms that in 1979 *Cloud Nine* acquired an 'almost immediate status as a contemporary classic'. It captured the imagination of feminists and, generally, of people on the left 'who were stunned and horrified by the rise to power of Margaret Thatcher'.[63] Thatcher became prime minister barely three months after the play's opening, promising a return to Victorian values. In 1997, as the long spell of Conservative rule was coming to an end, *Cloud Nine* was included in a season of 'classics' at the Old Vic Theatre in London, but some critics were not impressed. An outraged Charles Spencer wrote in the *Daily Telegraph*, 'this is a tiresomely tendentious, unpleasantly man-hating play which scarcely merits revival on the gay and feminist fringe'.[64]

More recently, the play has been produced at Sheffield's Crucible, directed by Anna Mackmin (2004), and at London's Almeida, directed by Thea Sharrock (2007). While a few reviewers were as dismissive as Spencer, these later revivals received a largely positive response. However, the debate about the status of the play as a modern classic continues. Many critics would agree with *The Times*'s Benedict Nightingale, who regards *Cloud Nine* 'as sharp about the contradictions of gender as anything that has been written since'; others, like Patrick Marmion in the *Daily Mail*, consider it a 'once-radical, now-fusty museum piece'.[65] To a contemporary audience, the second act probably feels as much a 'period drama' as the first (hence the use of a disco glitter ball in the Crucible production). Yet the play's non-judgemental attitude to two sexual taboos – paedophilia (Harry and Edward) and incest (Edward and Victoria) – may shock even now. More importantly, the still recognisable machismo-in-disguise of Martin in Act Two serves as a warning for those who believe the age of post-feminism has arrived. And above all, *Cloud Nine* remains one of the most inventive representations of anti-essentialist gender politics on stage.

Conclusion

In the 1970s, Churchill's drama was informed and nurtured by the development of left-wing activism and second-wave feminism, but the plays never wore their political or gender analysis as a straitjacket. Although Churchill's theoretical contribution was significant and often ahead of its time, her work maintained its artistic integrity and seductive theatricality. Moreover, her collectivist principles translated into collaborative methods of creation which enriched the material both on the page and in performance. Churchill's lack of complaisance – both politically and artistically – ensures the continuous relevance of these plays. I have suggested that they resonate with current materialist feminist thinking and in particular with the ethos of Critical Feminist Theory, which integrates modernist and postmodernist insights. Perhaps the most important affinity between the playwright and this contemporary feminist strand is the adjective 'critical'. In Churchill's work, an emancipatory impulse (striving for a better world) co-exists with a deconstructive one (dismantling easy political solutions). Churchill was, and still is, a socialist-feminist dramatist, but one who has never been afraid of questioning received assumptions of both socialism and feminism.

DAVID HARE
By Chris Megson

> I have become fascinated by the formal problems of film and
> theatre, which once had no interest for me [. . .]
>
> (David Hare, 1991)[1]

Introduction

The 1970s was an extraordinary decade for David Hare. He wrote
plays for small touring groups and the biggest stages in the country.
His work was performed by the two influential companies he
co-founded, Portable Theatre and Joint Stock, as well as by the Royal
Court and National Theatre, in the West End and regional theatres,
on tour, on Broadway and on film. During the 1970s, he also worked
prolifically as a director, wrote for television, and took up residencies
at the Royal Court (1970–1) and Nottingham Playhouse (1973). It
was a period characterised by extraordinary activity and also intense
critical reflection.

The focus of this essay is the formal development of Hare's playwriting in the context of the challenging and changing political
realities of the decade. The analysis will concentrate on three of his
major plays – *Slag* (1970), *Fanshen* (1975) and *Plenty* (1978) – because
they demonstrate Hare's evolving theatrical priorities during this
period and, as I will argue, exemplify how he tackled the 'formal problems' of writing for theatre at a time of political convulsion on the left.

Slag

> In all the plays I wrote in the seventies there is a powerful
> element of scorn. Scorn, I'd say, rather than anger, because I
> was impatient with an old England which had transparently
> collapsed, and yet the illusion of which still gripped our
> thinking and feeling.[2]

Slag, Hare's first full-length play, was commissioned for the Hampstead Theatre by the producer Michael Codron (although a shorter version of the play had been performed by Portable). It was staged at Hampstead in April 1970 and revived in May 1971 on the main stage of the Royal Court. The latter production, directed by Max Stafford-Clark, featured three excellent actresses – Lynn Redgrave as Joanne, Barbara Ferris as Elise and Anna Massey as Ann – and it scored 82 per cent at the box office.[3] In spite of its success, Hare has since endorsed Noël Coward's rather sardonic judgement on the play: 'five very good scenes and one bad one' (p. viii).

Slag represents one of the first incursions into the commercial theatre of a play from the generation of writers to emerge in the late 1960s; more specifically, it attempts to confront mainstream audiences with the pugnacious style of Portable Theatre. Peter Ansorge, writing in 1975, notes that the play was 'designed as a Portable show for the commercial theatre' and Richard Boon, likewise, observes that '*Slag* was written precisely as an attempt to lodge the Portable aesthetic behind the proscenium arch of the conventional theatre'.[4] The author's note to the play states that it 'is written deliberately with as few stage and acting instructions as possible' and '[b]lackouts should be instant, gaps between scenes brief, and scenery minimal' (p. 3). The pared-down design and frenetic pace of *Slag* carry the imprimatur of the Portable company, which Hare was still directing in 1970. The influence of Portable is also discernible in the literary pastiches bedded into the play: the first scene, for example, inverts the opening of Shakespeare's *Love's Labour's Lost* while the subsequent episodes of role-playing recall Jean Genet's *The Maids*.

These vestiges of Portable theatricality are part of a broader set of 'symptoms' that mark *Slag* as a transitional play in Hare's career. The music played in between the scenes – including Helen Shapiro's 'Walking Back to Happiness' (a saccharine chart-topper from 1961) and the work of the composer Henry Mancini (who created the score for iconic films such as *Breakfast at Tiffany's* in 1961 and *The Pink Panther* in 1963) – invests the play with a 1960s ambience; even the caustic one-word title, *Slag*, follows in the tradition of the monosyllabic *Saved*, Edward Bond's controversial play from 1965. Yet, although the play feeds off the anarchic and satirical impulses of the 1960s counterculture, it also anticipates the emergence of identity politics (especially feminism) and political fragmentation more readily associated with the early 1970s. With its attack on institutions, its blistering scorn for 'England' and its trio of erratic characters propelled by circumstance to the cusp of madness, *Slag* incubates some of the ascendant preoccupations in Hare's writing of the new decade.

The play is set in Brackenhurst, an English boarding school for upper-class girls. The action unfolds in six scenes covering a period from summer to January, during which time the number of pupils is reduced from eight to zero. In the opening sequence, which takes place in the school's Common Room, three women members of staff – Joanne, Elise and Ann (the head teacher) – take a ritual vow of sexual abstinence in order 'to register [. . .] protest against the way our society is run by men for men whose aim is the subjugation of the female and the enslavement of the working woman' (p. 7). They immediately start bickering over Joanne's attempt to link this vow to the creation 'of a truly socialist society' (p. 7) and focus is thus placed on the viability of the women's intent to create a new way of life. Socialism is positioned as the divisive issue within feminist politics and the women have different perceptions of the form their ideal society should take. Joanne dreams of a utopic socialism based on separatism, 'sexual purity' (p. 19) and a dismantling of patriarchy: 'Masturbation is the only form of sexual expression left to the authentic woman' (p. 21). In the pursuit of this conviction, she has renamed her study the Women's Liberation Workshop (parodying the feminist consciousness-raising groups that were mobilising at the time of the play's production) and replaced gym instruction with the teaching of Marxist dialectics (p. 14). Ann, aged thirty-two, is older than her two colleagues, and advocates a more humanistic, less ideo-logical, social model: she wants to 'build a new sort of school where what people feel for people will be the basis of their relationships. No politics' (p. 8). Ann reached adulthood in the 1950s while Joanne did so a decade later, and it is this generation gap that drives a wedge through feminist unity. It is notable that Joanne shows a visceral distrust of established culture common to the student activists of the 1960s: 'I wouldn't touch it eeurch. Culture eeurch' (p. 32).

In his introduction to the published play, Hare suggests that 'what dreamlike vitality the play does have is entirely from my imagining something about which, by definition, I can know nothing: what it's like to be in an all-female community' (p. viii). Hare's writing of *Slag* coincided precisely with the onset of the women's liberation movement in Britain and he was influenced by the publication of Germaine Greer's *The Female Eunuch* in 1970 (p. vii). In a major interview given in 1975 to *Theatre Quarterly*, Hare claims *Slag* was written 'in praise of women' but he also, with hindsight, concedes that its structure is too 'schematic' – a consequence of its small cast and claustrophobic setting – and 'that it's really a play about institutions, not about women at all'.[5] He has also contended that the play is an attack on the 'absurd idea' of 'feminist separatism'.[6] These perspectives interpret the play, variously, as a work of imaginative speculation on a radical feminist community, a response to the prospect of feminist liberation, a critique of radical or separatist feminism and an investigation of social institutions. In fact, the play recognises the diverse forms of feminism, from separatist to socialist, but sees each as reducible to a set of propositions ripe for satiric exploitation. At the same time, it offers a scabrous image of a decaying England. While Hare's negotiation of sexual politics attracted some critical opprobrium, as we shall see, *Slag* was also in the vanguard of a tranche of playwriting in the early 1970s that indicted the deleterious 'state of England'.[7]

Slag bears comparison with *If . . . .*, the controversial 1968 film directed by Lindsay Anderson (who was also a senior director at the Royal Court). *If. . . .* takes place in a boys' boarding school that incarnates, in miniaturised form, the operations of class society. The most important scene occurs when one of the pupils, Mick Travis (played by Malcolm McDowell), is flogged by his seniors – not because of his actions but merely for his desultory 'attitude'. Travis's flogging hardens his resolve to pursue justice through a new mantra: 'Violence and revolution are the only pure acts.'[8] In the final sequence of the film, Travis and his small group of student guerrillas set fire to the school on Founder's Day before raking the congregation with gunfire from the rooftops: Mick and his mates can be construed as cinematic prefigurations of terrorist groups such as Baader-Meinhof and the Angry Brigade (both founded in 1970). While *If . . . .* focuses on pupils and their turn to insurrection, *Slag* focuses on teachers and mediates its 'scorn' for 'old England' through satire. Crucially, however, just like the boarding school in *If . . . .*, Brackenhurst is conceived as a monument to English torpor and ossification. Here is Joanne's description of the school early in the first scene: 'Here, for example, at Brackenhurst, a distinctive sound. The heavy breathing that means nothing is happening. At Brackenhurst nothing ever happens. [. . .] The distinctive English sight of nothing happening and nothing going to happen' (p. 33). At this point, in a nearby class-room, the pupils begin to sing 'The Lord is My Shepherd' *'in agonized treble'* (p. 33). This moment has a wider resonance as one of the first examples in 1970s playwriting of English declinism: the evocation of England, rendered metonymically through its institutions, as turgid, life-denying, worn-out. In his 1975 interview, Hare comments that the play is 'about every institution I had known – school, Cambridge, Pathé, and so on. They are all the same. That is how institutions perpetuate themselves. With rituals that go on inside them – ever more baroque discussions about ever dwindling subjects.'[9]

In part, the satirical target of *Slag* is contemporary politics. At one point, Ann reads aloud a letter she has written to her mother: '"We have Mrs Reginald Maudling coming for speech day next year. Rather a catch"' (p. 87): Maudling was Home Secretary in the Conservative government at the time of the Royal Court production of the play. However, although the plot is premised in social reality, various surreal fantasies are played out, suggestive of sexual longing and repression. Ann refuses to let Joanne leave her job: 'This school', she intones, 'has some standards to keep up. And I will murder to maintain them' (p. 44) – it is uncertain whether this statement is disposed towards fact or hyperbole. In Scene Three, Ann and Elise duck Joanne's head in water to try to silence her radical feminist judgements on men and force her to accept what Ann insists on calling the 'inferiority' of women (p. 62). Repressed sexual urges erupt in Scene Four when Ann role-plays the part of a man seducing Elise: the latter claims to have fallen pregnant, with Ann as 'the father' (p. 80). Such sequences invest the play with an ironic and self-conscious theatricality that gestures towards gender as a socially regulated costume drama. Joanne attempts to rationalise Ann's 'fatherhood' with reference to evolutionary theory on the gradual elimination of the Y chromosome, which will lead eventually to the extinction of men (p. 78). Elise's 'pregnancy' is, as a result, hailed as the first of a new kind of exclusively female sexual reproduction (pp. 78–80).

The stormy interlocutions and fantastical game-playing come to an end with enrolment day of the new term, but no pupils turn up to register. Ann admits she was lying about her relationship with Haskins, the local butcher, in order to 'annoy' Joanne (p. 95) and she also admits to trying to poison her. Elise accepts that 'There was no virgin birth' (p. 96) and that her pregnancy was phantom. The final tableau is of '*Chronic unease, suspension, restlessness. Half a minute passes in silence*' (pp. 99–100). Joanne raises her arms, utters the words 'Well then –', and this is followed by an '*Instant blackout*' (p. 100). The play thus concludes with an equivocal image of frozen energy and feminist indeterminacy.

Some critics perceived the play as misogynistic and illegible in its gender politics. Michelene Wandor, for example, criticises *Slag* for recycling media hostility to the nascent women's movement: 'through the three women Hare constructs a montage of frigid, authoritarian, petty, man-hating nymphomania'.[10] What is less often remarked, however, is the way that Joanne, the youngest of the three women, becomes the linchpin and primary focus of the play. In the final scene, she interrogates her colleague: 'Why are the workers silent, Ann? Why does the revolution land with such a sigh? Twenty-five years the war is over, and everyone trying to get the workers to respond. And they won't. Where are the working women? Lulled by romantic love and getting home to cook the dinner' (p. 96). This is embryonic second-wave feminist discourse tied to an investment in socialism as an antidote to post-1968 political disillusionment. Ann responds that she was raised on 'R. A. Butler and the Beveridge Report, so I don't know what you're talking about' (p. 97). (Butler was a reformist Conservative politician in the post-war years while the Beveridge report, published in 1942, set in place the foundations of the modern welfare state.) Ann's comments in this final scene reflect the attitudes of many of her generation to the student activists of 1968: 'you don't even know what you want. Some unstated alternative that evaporates like your breath on the air' (p. 97).The play thus presents the generation of the 1960s (Joanne) squaring up to the generation that preceded it (Ann) in the very year that British feminists began, publicly and en masse, to contest the patriarchal stranglehold on culture. By April 1970, when *Slag* was first performed, Joanne's critique of the silence and compliance of British women and British workers was losing traction: the first National Women's Liberation conference was held at Ruskin College in late February that year and, within eight months of the Royal Court premiere, the miners launched their first momentous strike of the decade in January 1972. The play is of interest for its rapid-fire response to feminism, its calibration of Portable theatricality, and its evocation of English decline, but it quickly fell victim to the fast-changing sexual politics of the 1970s, and it is difficult to envision an audience for the play today.

Fanshen

Hare claims that *Fanshen* (1975), his major mid-decade play, provided a release for him because 'I was sick to death with writing about England'.[11] The sense of fatigue that rises from this comment is perhaps understandable. At the time Hare was working on the play, Britain experienced a three-day week to ration energy consumption and the miners began a national strike. Two general elections were called in 1974: the Conservative government lost power and Harold Wilson became Labour prime minister but only with a wafer-thin majority. There was fierce controversy surrounding the imposition of detention without trial in Northern Ireland and Direct Rule of the province from Westminster. On a range of fronts, the health, mandate and leadership of British democracy was being called into question. Looking beyond the skein of its esoteric content, *Fanshen* is attuned to the economic and political crises closer to home.

Joint Stock, the company which produced the play, originated in the desire of Max Stafford-Clark (who had spent six weeks in 1968 working with the experimental troupe La MaMa in New York), theatre producer David Aukin and Hare to form a travelling theatre company. They were joined by director Bill Gaskill, who had long aspired to create an ensemble of actors during his time at the helm of the Royal Court. The company – nicknamed 'the Royal Court in exile' by Edward Bond – was founded in 1974.[12] Stafford-Clark and Gaskill began running evening workshops at the Court which were initially focused on a book by Heathcote Williams, published in 1964, about Speakers' Corner in Hyde Park. *The Speakers* (1974) was Joint Stock's first production, notable for its unusual 'promenade' staging. The company's third project, *Yesterday's News* (1976), was a piece of pioneering verbatim theatre about mercenaries in Angola staged long before that form of theatre became ubiquitous across the UK more than two decades later.

The idea for the group's second production, *Fanshen*, came from the actress Pauline Melville who recommended a book by William Hinton on the Chinese Revolution. Hinton's book, as Hare describes it, 'tells how a backward peasantry was given the chance to use techniques of public appraisal and self-criticism to take control of their own affairs. At the heart of it is the eternal question of how a democracy should police itself to ensure that it is genuinely democratic.'[13] For Hare, this was an opportunity for 'chamber politics' – Hinton's filtering of the Chinese revolution through the experience of a small representative village, Long Bow, brought the subject within the purview of theatre.[14] The company also appreciated the optimism of this material at a particularly depressing time in domestic politics: here was a left-wing revolution that, by any estimation, had improved the lives of the population.

Joint Stock has wider significance in post-war theatre history for its ethos of collective working and political commitment reflective of the times.[15] As Boon observes, '[t]he group was to become a very significant force in the evolution of modern British theatre, not only through the plays it produced, but – and perhaps as importantly – through the working method it pioneered'.[16] The process commenced with an extended five-week improvisation workshop that included exercises on compressed storytelling. This was followed by four months of writing and a six-week rehearsal period. The actors explored the violence of the play, its roots in historical oppression and the attitudes of the characters to the unfolding situation.[17] Importantly, the process of social revolution dramatised in *Fanshen* extended beyond the play to the making of the production: as Cathy Turner notes, 'the company found in the play a way to explore the very concerns they had to address as a company: the process of negotiation, dialogue and group organisation'.[18] Indeed, the actors Will Knightley and David Rintoul, as well as Stafford-Clark, have explained how their work on *Fanshen* widened and deepened their own political awareness.[19]

The creation of the script, unlike in most theatre, was the purpose of the process, not the point of embarkation. There was a tension between the respect accorded to playwrights at new writing venues such as the Royal Court and Joint Stock's commitment to collective working that expanded the actor's involvement and held the writer to account. Hare was at the centre of a chaotic, at times exasperated, process of negotiation and disagreement, working out which direction to take with the copious primary material. Gaskill observes that '[t]he essential difference between this process and the work of nearly all other groups is that the writer maintains his [*sic*] control and authority over the material, even though the rest of the group has fed ideas, attitudes and characterization into it'.[20] Nevertheless, Hare remembers the first read-through of the play as 'a particular disaster' when his ideas were discussed by the company in a form of collective scrutiny that itself approximated the process of 'fanshen' enacted in the play (p. viii).

Fanshen is notable for its indebtedness to Brechtian techniques of theatrical distanciation. It is composed of twelve scenes or 'sections' that are divided into smaller units of action. There are no lighting changes; props and costumes, as the stage directions make clear, should be '*authentic*' (p. 5). The configuration of the performance space reflects the reach for analytic democracy in the play's content: the stage '*thrusts forward into the audience*' (p. 5), with spectators seated on three sides. The opening stage direction has the actors narrate the context of the play *until they form a whole picture of the village* (p. 5). Nine actors play around thirty parts, comprising the entire community and the adoption or removal of specific costume items marks a change in role; actors also move from 'inhabiting' the role they are playing to speaking about the character in the third person. Commenting on the minimalist approach to staging, Christopher Innes lauds 'the sense of spartan clarity that comes from reducing each situation to its essentials'.[21]

The image of a single man working in a field occurs at the start, middle and end of the play, suggesting a historical continuity in the condition of the labouring class in this society. In Brechtian mode, placards designate the central units of action, such as 'Asking Basic Questions' (p. 16) and 'The Forming of the Peasants' Associations' (p. 17). These scenes are interspersed with occasional longer monologues, accompanied by tableaux, in which other actors narrate the story. Throughout, the focus is less on individual psychology than the presentation of particular events within a process of organised social upheaval. The progression of scenes elaborates the process of revolution, or 'fanshen', which gradually extends from the privileged elite to the entire community of Long Bow. This process is not linear but cyclical and, indeed, the problems in the process become the focus of dramatic interest. For example, as the practices of 'self-report' and 'public appraisal' begin, the head of each family attends a meeting to identify his wealth and needs, which are adjudicated by a 'classification' panel comprising the poorest peasants (p. 53). There is a memorable sequence when the system struggles to cope with a self-employed blacksmith, and then a heroin dealer, who, it becomes clear, fall into each classification as a poor, middle and rich peasant all at once (pp. 54–9).

Hare illuminates the impact of 'fanshen' not just on the economy but also on the human personality. The play traces the shift from the redistribution of resources and assets in the name of equality to moral purification in the name of justice and retribution; in so doing, *Fanshen* exposes the challenge of holding leaders to account while recognising the necessity of leadership to drive reform. The preoccupation with social structures and eliminating poverty gives way to moral hysteria about individual probity. There is a dramatic flashpoint in Scene Eight that illuminates this issue. Hseuh-chen, Secretary of the Women's Association, is criticised by the villagers, not for her actions, but for the expression on her face: 'I submit to the people,' she replies after a pause, 'I will try to correct my face' (p. 71). The moment carries an echo of the punishment visited on Mick Travis for his 'attitude' in *If. . . .* In Anderson's film of 1968, puritanical authoritarianism has its source in a British public school; in Hare's play of 1975, it is a reflex of the revolutionary left. The point illustrates the play's sober and interrogative attitude to the contradictions of revolution. In an earlier scene, Yu-Lai, leader of the revolution, strikes Hsien-e, a landlord's daughter, and treats her like a slave (p. 40). The limits of justice and democracy are thus clearly marked: in respect of the treatment of women and women's right to divorce, there is a need for 'fanshen' to extend to the 'private' as well as the 'public' sphere. The revolution is thus constituted in an unending and relentless process of individual and communal appraisal. As Secretary Liu puts it: 'There are no breakthroughs in our work. There is no "just do this one thing and we will be there". There is only the patient, daily work of re-making people. Over each hill, another hill. Over that hill, a mountain' (p. 95).

The conclusion of the play presented particularly sensitive challenges. The difficulty for Hare was that, unlike Hinton, he was not invested ideologically in the material: '[Hinton] was a Marxist, and I wasn't' (p. ix). Hare's struggle was to loosen the grip of ideology on the mediation of the play's content – 'there's no way that this material is ever going to be resolved in the sense that conventional dramatic material can be resolved' – while remaining faithful to the historical process set out in Hinton's book.[22] In Scene Eleven, Secretary Ch'en addresses the Second Lucheng Conference and argues that the process of 'fanshen' has gone too far: 'the attack has been overdone' (p. 96). The original aim was 'the abolition of the feudal system. And that we have achieved' (p. 97). Goods and land are to be returned to the middle peasants '[a]nd we must ensure that landlords are given enough land to make a living' (p. 97). The final image of the play shows the villagers hoeing as the work team returns to Long Bow to inform the population of yet another change in policy, as the cycle of reform continues.

Fanshen was staged in April 1975 at the ICA in London (after opening in Sheffield), and televised by the BBC six months later. It was also revived in 1975 at the Hampstead Theatre and at the Oval House in 1977, and toured widely. The production attracted criticism from the Marxist left, some of whom walked out, and the Chinese Embassy complained that the violence of landlords was not emphasised enough.[23] Nevertheless, it remains one of the seminal theatre events of the 1970s, primarily because of its innovative mode of production, documentary provenance and collective commitment to the material. The fact that a play focused on communist revolution became Joint Stock's most celebrated and profitable money-spinner is one of the more arresting paradoxes of the 1970s theatre economy. The irony of this was not lost on Hare: *Fanshen*, he observed, 'became our *Mousetrap*'.[24]

'The Play is in the Air'

Hare's playwriting underwent a process of transformation in the 1970s triggered by a number of factors. These included his sense of disillusionment with the left, the new opportunities opened up by larger spaces such as the National Theatre and the political challenge of working on *Fanshen*. It is worth pausing at this point to consider the terms and implications of Hare's own reflections on his playwriting through the decade.

In his 1975 interview, reflecting on his early plays, it is notable that Hare asserts repeatedly the primacy of content in the experience of theatre. His description of Portable, for instance, draws attention to the 'deliberately and apparently shambolic style of presentation, where people simply lurched onto the stage and lurched off again, and it was impossible to make patterns. That is to say, we worked on a theatrical principle of forbidding any aesthetic at all.'[25] In a much later interview, given in 1990, Hare elaborates this point at length:

We had lost faith in [. . .] institutions, we thought that Britain's assumption of a non-existent world role was ludicrous, and we also thought that its economic vitality was so sapped that it wouldn't last long. So, we wanted to bundle into a van and go round the country performing short, nasty little plays which would alert an otherwise dormant population to this news. And by doing so we hoped to push aside the problem of aesthetics, which we took to be the curse of theatre. People were more interested in comparing the aesthetics of particular performances than they were in listening to the subject matter of plays. And we thought that if you pushed aesthetics out of the way by performing plays as crudely as possible [. . .] you could get a response to what you were actually saying.[26]

Howard Brenton makes an identical observation in an interview from 1973: '[Audiences] became theatrically literate and the discussions afterwards stopped being about the plays' content and began to be about their style.'[27] Portable Theatre thus made a fetish of 'crudity' – which is conceived here as pared-down 'rough' staging, allied to rhetorical directness, unimpeded by the conventions or etiquette associated with commercial theatregoing. It is this 'crudity' that, as we have seen, finds residual expression in *Slag*. 'I had no patience for the question of how well written a play was,' Hare recalled in 1981. 'I was only concerned with how urgent its subject matter was, how it related to the world outside.'[28] What emerges from these commentaries is a sense of the primacy of content vitalised by its link to the 'world outside'. It is little wonder, then, that Hare kept a certain distance from the Royal Court throughout this period: as he puts it, in a revealing formulation, 'the Court in the early seventies was primarily an aesthetic theatre, not a political one'.[29]

Some evidence backing up Hare's concerns about 'aesthetic theatre' is to be found in the reactions of critics to his early plays. Reviews were often characterised by bewilderment and an attempt to corral his work into the established parameters of theatrical realism. Randall Craig, for example, offers this summary in an article published in 1972:

> Mr Hare's style is now clearly identifiable, being a mixture of surrealist fantasy and murderous topical sarcasm. He is a sharp-shooter training a deadly eye on the trendy society and the hypocrisies as well as the fake sincerities of modern marriage. His flaws [. . .] are those of an impassioned visionary: his language will take flight now and again into a world of its own, away from the characters who speak it, and he sometimes scores points at the cost of probability.[30]

There's a clear nod here to Portable theatricality ('surrealist fantasy [. . .] murderous topical sarcasm') but Hare is marked down for falling short of realism ('scores points at the cost of probability'). More significant, perhaps, is Craig's relative inattentiveness to content: the emphasis is placed on 'Mr Hare's style' and on the fact that his writing seems to burst the seams of dramatic situation, putting pressure on the realist frame. This critical preoccupation with style at the expense of content was widespread in the early 1970s and led many writers of Hare's generation to seek an escape from what was becoming, in their view, an increasingly ghettoised fringe dominated by introspective discussions about 'aesthetics'.

It is also worth emphasising that, throughout this intense period of activity, and in addition to his own writing, Hare was working as a director of new plays. His roll-call of projects is impressive and the following is indicative, not exhaustive. In 1971, he directed Snoo Wilson's *Blow Job* for Portable Theatre, adapted Pirandello's *The Rules of the Game* at the New Theatre in London and instigated the collaboratively written *Lay By*. The following year, *The Great Exhibition*, his new play, was produced at Hampstead and he directed the controversial, group-written *England's Ireland*. In 1973, Hare co-wrote (with Brenton) and directed *Brassneck* to mark the appointment of Richard Eyre as the new Artistic Director of Nottingham Playhouse and Hare was appointed Resident Dramatist there. That year, he also directed Wilson's *The Pleasure Principle* in London and Sir John Vanbrugh's *The Provoked Wife* at the Palace Theatre, Watford. In 1974, his play *Knuckle* was staged in the West End – a major achievement – and he directed Trevor Griffiths's huge play about revolutionary politics,

Marxist theory and the failure of 1968, *The Party*, for a National Theatre tour. Six months after the opening of *Fanshen*, Hare's *Teeth 'n' Smiles*, which he also directed, opened at the Royal Court in September 1975. Hare directed Brenton's *Weapons of Happiness* at the newly opened National Theatre on the South Bank in 1976: a landmark victory in their joint endeavour to import the political consciousness of fringe theatre into the new citadel of established culture. He directed Tony Bicât's first play, *Devil's Island*, for the Sherman Theatre, Cardiff, in 1977. And in January 1978, *Licking Hitler*, his television film for the BBC which he also directed, was broadcast while *Deeds*, written with Brenton, Griffiths and Ken Campbell, opened at the Nottingham Playhouse in March – the month before the opening of *Plenty*. To repeat: this represents only a sample of his work.

Having amassed this huge range of experience – as a director, writer, script reader and mentor to other playwrights – Hare acquired a deeper appreciation of the possibilities and challenges of the writing process. This latter point is evident from his 1975 interview:

> To write a play at all you have to work extremely hard on what you believe about the subject – and the writing process is finding out the truth or otherwise of what you believe by testing it on the stage. [. . .] It's a rigorous discipline, playwriting, in the sense that you need to answer questions which are never answered by polemic or journalism or propaganda. [. . .] Now our decline is so voraciously discussed; but the means of discussion are failing us. That's to say, journalism, however intelligent, will always fail you.[31]

Crucially, Hare's contention that theatre is a site of judgement and scrutiny – and the opposite of journalism – remains consistent in his discourse from this point on. For Hare, 'theatre is scrutiny': it is the best, perhaps the only, forum for bringing public affairs under collective deliberation.[32]

On 5 March 1978, Hare elaborated these ideas in a lecture delivered to a theatre conference held at King's College, Cambridge. The event – his first foray into public speaking – was attended by many socialist theatre practitioners including David Edgar and John McGrath.[33] Hare has published the lecture in various forms which testifies to its centrality in his canon of non-theatre writing.[34] According to one first-hand report from the conference: 'He [delivered the lecture] with such an air of contempt that it left many members of the political theatre movement reeling as if from an unexpected, undeserved blow. Hare had not quietly sold out (he had arguably not sold out at all), but aggressively put himself on a platform to point an accusing finger.'[35]

This controversial lecture, usually titled 'The Play is in the Air', is important for a number of reasons. First, picking up the theme from his 1975 interview, he reasserts the differences between playwriting and journalism, and underlines theatre's role as a crucible of scrutiny:

> the theatre is the exact opposite art to journalism; the bad journalist may throw off a series of casual and half-baked propositions [. . .] which may or may not amuse, which may or may not be lasting, which may or may not be true; but were he [sic] once to hear those same words spoken out loud in a theatre he would begin to feel that terrible chill of being collectively judged and what had seemed light and trenchant and witty would suddenly seem flip and arch and silly. (pp. 113–14)

Second, Hare dismisses the viability of satire in the contemporary political context: 'consciousness has been raised in this country for a good many years now and we seem further from radical political change than at any time in my life' (p. 115). This jettisoning of satire amounts, of course, to a strategic disavowal of the kind of playwriting represented by *Slag*. Third, and more controversially, he assails the intractability of Marxist activists forever predicting a revolution that has manifestly failed to transpire ('It is hard to believe in the historical inevitability of something which has so frequently not happened', p. 117) and castigates what he sees as the delusional tendencies of Marxist drama ('Why do we so often have to endure the demeaning repetition of slogans which are seen not as transitional aids to understanding, but as ultimate solutions to men's problems?', p. 117).

Finally, Hare uses the lecture to explain the change in his own approach to writing plays:

> When I first wrote, I wrote in the present day, I believed in a purely contemporary drama; [. . .] It took me time to realise that [. . .] if you write about now, just today and nothing else, then you seem to be confronting only stasis, but if you begin to describe the undulations of history, if you write plays that cover passages of time, then you begin to find a sense of movement, of social change [. . .]. (p. 121)

His conclusion is categorical: Marxist drama, exemplified by but not limited to the explosion of agitprop theatre in the early 1970s, is no longer equipped to make sense of change in contemporary Britain. The playwright's obligation, therefore, is to situate historically 'the extraordinary intensity of people's personal despair' (p. 122) and to embed the exploration of individual psychology within broader landscapes of social experience.

In the aftermath of the Cambridge conference, Hare was accused of 'selling out' and, during the lecture itself, he was heckled by an audience member who shouted out 'Did Piscator die for this?' in an emotive reference to the great left-wing German theatre director (p. 111). Having cut himself adrift from Marxism, Hare's turn to the 'undulations of history' is exemplified in his next play, *Plenty*, which opened at the Lyttelton Theatre in April 1978 – one month following his intervention at Cambridge.

Plenty

The staging of *Plenty* – 'one of the most significant productions in the life of the National Theatre', according to Richard Eyre – coincided with a period of ideological fragmentation on the left, which was reflected at the Cambridge conference.[36] In the preceding couple of years, the Labour government's social contract with trade unions came to an end and the government's application for loans from the

International Monetary Fund (IMF) amounted to a national humiliation. The Grunwick strikers conceded defeat in July 1978, the
Conservative Party's advertising campaign ('Labour Isn't Working')
was launched in August, and rumblings of a so-called 'Winter of
Discontent' gathered momentum from November. Hare's play
bestows a historical frame on the pronounced sense of lost opportunity at this time.

Plenty consists of twelve scenes that stretch over nineteen years
from November 1943 to June 1962. During this period, Susan
Traherne, the central character, ages from nineteen to thirty-eight
years old. The episodic structure of the play throws into relief the
contrast between the idealism associated with the past and the
compromises of the present. Events in Susan's life are projected against
a broader canvas of post-war history, such as the Festival of Britain
(1951) and the Suez Crisis (1956), while the settings range from
France and Belgium to Whitehall and Pimlico in London. The ambition of the play is reflected in Hare's exploitation of the large-scale
spatial and technical resources of large-scale theatre: in Scene Two, for
example, a stage direction stipulates that '*Susan runs on from a great
distance*'.[37]

Hare's account of the conception of *Plenty* is revealing – 'I just
remember writing in my diary the words "A woman over Europe",
and then having the visual image of a woman sitting in an overcoat on
a packing case, rolling herself a cigarette, with her husband lying
naked at her feet' (p. xiv). This motif of transience and male subordi-
nation is actualised in the opening image of the play, set in Easter
1962, in which Brock, Susan's husband, lies naked and asleep on a
mattress as she prepares to walk out on their marriage. The first line,
spoken by Susan's young friend Alice, is an uncompromising expression of English declinism: 'I don't know why anybody lives in this
country' (p. 377). The sense of finality and failed expectation that
attends Susan's departure strengthens the contrast with the following
scene which moves back in time to 1943. Susan, now aged nineteen,
is working undercover for the Special Operations Executive (SOE) in
St Benoît, France, during the Second World War. Hare focuses on her
covert interaction with an agent codenamed Lazar and their dialogue

is fuelled by a potent cocktail of danger, quiet flirtation and, above all, a sense of mission and purpose.

The play integrates psychological veracity with social analysis by unfolding, through the mostly chronological ordering of scenes from this point on, Susan's experience of drift and alienation in the post-war years. As Lib Taylor argues, '[f]or Hare, Susan's depression is representative of Britain in decline, but its expression through her personal sense of dislocation from society chimes with a central tenet of the women's movement: that the Personal is Political'.[38] Scene Five, for example, takes place on London's Embankment during the Festival of Britain in May 1951 (the scene is set across the river from the site of the National Theatre complex, adding a local frisson to the London production). Susan has been working on the festival project and is now considering a job in advertising. In this scene, she invites Mick, a working-class trader, to father her child: she does so because she knows him, but only as an acquaintance, and would prefer not to be 'dishonest' by having anonymous sex with a stranger for the purpose of becoming pregnant (p. 417). Their conversation circles around the sexual mores of the early fifties and Susan's attempt to reject or downplay these: 'England can't be like this for ever' (p. 418). The following scene, in which Mick and Susan meet again, is set in the latter's residence in Pimlico on New Year's Eve, 1952. In the gap of time between these two episodes, it becomes clear that they have had awkward sex in clandestine places, including '[s]crabbling about on bombsites' (p. 426), but no pregnancy has resulted. Mick, insecure about the possibility of his own infertility, begins to rail against Susan and her housemate, Alice. In a fit of incandescence, when he calls her 'actually mad' (p. 428), Susan fires a gun four times over Mick's head.

The escalation of Susan's personal despair is linked explicitly to the denigration of national politics. By Scene Seven, it is October 1956 and Susan and her beleaguered partner Brock are hosting a diplomatic dinner at the time of the Suez Crisis. Suez is the symbolic moment in post-war history when Britain's attempt to launch an imperial offensive against Egypt, in connivance with France and Israel, was dealt a terminal blow through an onslaught of international censure. At the start of the evening, Susan's deliberately insincere reassurance of her guests that no mention will made of the Suez affair ruptures the patina of etiquette that normally holds such evenings together: 'Nobody will say "blunder" or "folly" or "fiasco". Nobody will say "international laughing stock". You are among friends [. . .]. I will rustle up some food' (p. 431). Susan's idealism, fermented in the self-sacrifice of war and the SOE, takes another blow as she discovers the personal cost of the double standards that are endemic in British public life. Scene Nine moves to the Foreign Office (FO) where, according to the stage directions, '*a mighty painting*' hangs imposingly on the rear wall (p. 452). This is 'Britannia Colonorum Mater' ('Britain, Mother of Colonies') which to this day hangs in the FO as a kind of visual reification of British imperial adventurism.[39] This portentous image provides an ironic counter to what takes place in the scene, as Susan pleads with Charleson, the Chief Clerk at the FO, to promote her husband Brock who has struggled to reconcile his professional and personal responsibilities. Susan then raises the temperature of the conversation by threatening to kill herself should her request fall on deaf ears. She makes this threat, however, only after Charleson justifies his inaction with the following: 'As our power declines, the fight among us for access to that power becomes a little more urgent, a little uglier perhaps. As our influence wanes, as our empire collapses, there is little to believe in. Behaviour is all' (p. 459). His comments naturalise the abdication of principle from the conduct of high politics and insist on the new hegemony of pragmatic opportunism. In fact, this exchange between Charleson and Susan is a lodestar in 1970s theatre because it carries the critique of institutional stagnation to the heart of the nation state. Charleson represents a new breed at the FO, casting aside the old-school chivalry and patrician codes of honour represented in the play by the antiquated diplomat Leonard Darwin, in favour of an urbane and expedient *realpolitik* that brooks no questioning.

The penultimate scene moves forward to June 1962, which follows chronologically from the first scene of the play. Susan is reunited with Lazar, the agent she encountered in the French countryside in Scene Two. They embark on a fumbled liaison in a seedy hotel bedroom – '*sparsely furnished and decaying*' (p. 470) – in Blackpool. By this point, Susan has left Brock and is on the cusp of psychological meltdown.

Her conviction that beliefs still matter is tempered by a dread of exposing herself to further disillusionment: 'I want to believe in you,' she says to Lazar, 'So tell me nothing. That's best' (p. 473). Their tryst takes place in the dark, Susan smokes grass and her mumblings fragment into incoherence.

The transition from this tableau of enervation to the final scene of the play is one of the most heart-wrenching in modern theatre. As Susan slides into drug-induced unconsciousness, Lazar swings open the door of their squalid hotel room to make his exit. Then: '*Where you would expect a corridor you see the fields of France shining brilliantly in a fierce green square. The room scatters*' (p. 475). Music begins to play as soon as he opens the door and Scene Twelve returns us to the countryside of St Benoît in France. It is August 1944, a golden rural landscape, and the time of Liberation. Susan is nineteen years old and dressed as '*a young French girl*' (p. 476); she meets a farmer who invites her to join his family for refreshments. The final line of the play is a paean to her exhilaration – 'There will be days and days and days like this' (p. 478) – which contrasts markedly with Alice's opening line of the play. Steve Nicholson regards this sequence as 'almost unbearable to watch'; for John J. Su, who criticises Hare's writing for surrendering to nostalgia at this point, it is best understood as a reverie of recollection, 'the final memory of a fragmenting psyche'.[40]

Hare's achievement is to open the spectators in the theatre to the full force of Susan's despair without requiring them to suspend critical evaluation of her actions. Christopher Innes describes Susan as 'a female idealist, the embodiment of utopian principle' but he also remarks that 'it is [. . .] possible to view her as a ruthless manipulator of others, made incapable of intimacy or self-fulfilment by attitudes which – however necessary for survival in occupied France – are destructive in a normal context'.[41] Janelle Reinelt argues that Susan is 'an almost-heroine' who divides opinion: for some spectators, she appears to '[demand] emancipation while proving unable to handle it', while others appreciate that 'she tries to find a different, honourable way to live in a depressing time'.[42] It is interesting to note that, when directing the play for its London premiere, Hare encouraged a strong identification with Susan and the production was less effective as a result: he and Kate Nelligan (who played Susan) 'were so pro-Susan we unbalanced the play'.[43] Nelligan and Hare returned to the material and, according to Innes, 'when the play reached New York [Nelligan] was showing Susan as an unreliable witness, pitiably half-aware of the unfairness in her outbursts against society'.[44]

The affective force of Susan's character, whose wartime service has left her ill-equipped to negotiate the drizzle of mediocrity (as she perceives it) in the post-war public sphere, is a testament to Hare's success in imbricating 'personal' and 'political', 'private' and 'public', aspects of experience. In its structure and historical sweep, *Plenty* is arguably the quintessential 'state of the nation' play of the 1970s.

Conclusion

The day after the opening of *Plenty*, Hare 'went to live abroad' and spent time in Australia; it was four years before he produced another stage play (p. xvi). By the end of the 1970s, he claims, 'I was lost'.[45] It took him from 1978 to the writing of *Pravda* (with Howard Brenton, 1985) to articulate a response to the Conservative ascendancy: there was, he recalls, 'snow-like silence in the early 1980s from socialist writers'.[46]

In subsequent decades, Hare's output has been prodigious. His plays include an examination of ethical retreat in the era of Thatcherism (*The Secret Rapture*, 1988), a monumental trilogy on British institutions (*Racing Demon*, 1990; *Murmuring Judges*, 1991; *Absence of War*, 1993), a monologue – which he also performed – on the subject of the Middle East (*Via Dolorosa*, 1998), a verbatim piece on grief, privatisation and the British railway system (*The Permanent Way*, 2003) and a large-scale quasi-documentary play about the build-up to the Iraq War (*Stuff Happens*, 2004). In addition, he has written and directed films (such as *Wetherby*, 1985) as well as producing film adaptations (such as his Oscar-nominated *The Hours*, 2002), published a number of volumes of essays, and, in 2011, he won the prestigious PEN/Pinter Prize. He was knighted in 1998, confirming his place at the epicentre of Britain's cultural establishment. The decision of the Crucible Theatre in Sheffield to commit part of its 2011 season to the staging of three of his plays, including a forceful revival of *Plenty* (directed by Thea Sharrock with Hattie Morahan in the role of Susan), testifies to the continuing appeal of his work in the contemporary repertoire.

In an essay published in 2010, marking forty years as a professional playwright, Hare looks back to the 1970s:

> When I set out in the theatre, I was part of a fringe movement that often sought to crash the problem of aesthetics by doing plays as crudely as possible. If you made no attempt to do things overly well, then people would not be distracted from what you were saying. But as the years went by, it became clear to me that I had not understood aesthetics. They were not your enemy. They were your opportunity. Style was the only means by which you could suggest that what you were writing about was something more than what you appeared to be writing about. Without style there was no suggestiveness, and with no suggestiveness, no metaphor.[47]

Hare's creative trajectory through the decade is compressed into this statement: his movement from 'crudity' to 'style', with the attendant shift in emphasis from the direct transmission of content in his early work with Portable to an embrace of 'suggestiveness' and 'aesthetics'. His use of the words 'style' and 'aesthetics' is intended to describe how his work resonates beyond the terms of its specific content to attain wider metaphorical resonance: Hare has long insisted that, while his plays are rooted in actuality, they are not slavishly obeisant to it. The assurance with which he articulates his practice as Britain's foremost theatrical scrutineer of public life has its source, to be sure, in the raging ideological debates and combative theatre ecology of the 1970s.

HOWARD BRENTON
By Richard Boon

'What's Stalin doing in a south London crisp factory?'[1]

Introduction

To look afresh from the perspective of 2011 at the work of Howard Brenton in the 1970s is to revisit myself as a young adult, a young theatregoer (and, in a limited way, a practitioner), and a young academic.

Fourteen years younger than Brenton, I came to his work when casting around for a subject for a PhD in 1979, having just graduated with a degree in English Literature and wandering rather blindly into an academic career. Late Shakespeare (too busy, cramped and competitive a field) and Brecht (all of him, and I had no German) were quickly abandoned. Then I was pointed towards a young(ish) dramatist, from a background not entirely dissimilar to my own, who had already established a substantial reputation for radical politics, controversy and theatrical daring. Brenton's professional career was already eleven years old, and had seen him move from the wildness and experiment of the Fringe in the late 1960s to mainstream stages at the Royal Court, the Royal Shakespeare Company and the National Theatre. In doing so, he had already been identified as part of a group which included David Hare, Trevor Griffiths and David Edgar – all, to different degrees, collaborators and friends, but together always a little too disparate in both politics and dramaturgy quite to be called a 'movement' – whose work seemed to be at the vanguard of political radicalism and theatrical innovation. Even if their 'state of the nation' plays never came to dominate the repertoires of the country's mainstream stages, they seemed, at least, to set a genuinely significant new political and artistic agenda. Brenton's work in particular, rooted in both traditional and revised Marxist thought, consistently mounted wide-ranging and violent attacks on what we were content to think of very straightforwardly as 'the establishment', whether it be Labour (still neither New nor Old) or Conservative, while exploring and testing to breaking point the nature of political activism (of which terrorism was seen as quite possibly a legitimate part), the limits of social responsibility, the threat to civil liberties and, increasingly, the nature and present influence of history itself. And he did so in increasingly ambitious forms, often taking theatrical risks that provoked audiences, divided the critics and gave sleepless nights to theatre managers. Humane, violent, idealistic, funny, bleak, angry, romantic, desperate, wicked, brave: Brenton, to me, was the most exciting of a new generation of politically motivated British playwrights that was self-consciously challenging and revitalising a moribund British theatre, and doing so by drawing not only on modern European influences (including Brecht) but on Shakespeare and in particular on the Jacobean theatre which had been for me one of the discoveries of my undergraduate degree.

Seven years later I had my PhD, somewhat misleadingly entitled 'The Plays of Howard Brenton' (it only got as far as 1973); by 1991 I had caught up to date and produced a book. *Brenton the Playwright* was the first and so far remains the only monograph on its subject and, as such, positive or not (reviewers fell into both camps), I suppose cannot have helped but influence (even, to some extent, frame) and provoke subsequent critical thinking about the dramatist – for good or ill.[2] Along the way I had directed a few of his plays, acted in a couple more, taught him to generations of undergraduate and postgraduate students, written articles, given conference papers, seen almost all his premieres and interviewed him on numerous occasions. I have come to count him a friend.

You have been warned.

Yet even as I began my PhD in 1979, history was shifting, and the world that both Brenton and I had grown up in was changing – at times, it has since seemed, beyond recognition. The election of the new Conservative government of Margaret Thatcher in that year marked the beginnings of a sea-change in the history of post-war Britain that is still happening and which has had profound effects not just on governance, economics, civic society and culture but also inevitably and consequently on the theatre – and indeed the academy.

The resurgent right shattered the broad political consensus that had ruled Britain since 1945, and found expression too in international politics, with the end of the Cold War and the collapse of communism in the late 1980s and early 1990s. As their friend and early-career mentor, Richard Eyre, commented, writers such as Trevor Griffiths and Brenton were 'robbed of their subject by the collapse of Socialism'.[3] Les Wade develops the point well:

> According to [playwright Mark] Ravenhill, 'Hare and the rest knew in the seventies what they were against. Now nobody knows and nobody cares.' Ravenhill's comment indicates not just a shift in British theatre; it recognises the profound changes that the 1980s and 1990s brought to British culture. Described as a post-ideological age, this time witnessed the ascendance of liberal democracy, the rise of global capitalism and the collapse of the socialist vision. Ravenhill's often-cited passage in *Shopping and Fucking* underscores the demise of 'big stories' that once governed modern life, including 'The Journey to Enlightenment. The March of Socialism'. The cultural situation Ravenhill identifies presented a dilemma for Britain's political playwrights. Demoralised by years of Conservative rule, many writers argued for political change but had come to question the viability of socialist critique.[4]

Hare – always possessed of an impresario's instincts – endured and even prospered, but Brenton in particular faced increasingly difficult times. In 1980–1 *The Romans in Britain*, after a barrage of negative headlines (the *Daily Express* was in particularly good form, with 'Fury over new sex play' and 'This disgrace to our National Theatre') and almost uniformly bad reviews (the play apparently came 'far closer to the sado-masochistic, pornographic literature of Soho than anything found in any English or Greek classic'), found itself the epicentre of a public – or at least a media – storm virtually unprecedented in British theatre history.[5] At issue was the staging of a scene in which a Roman soldier attempts to rape a young Celtic man, a priest. The scene attracted the attention of a number of well-established (and less well-established) right-wing groups, one of which, the National Viewers' and Listeners' Association (now Mediawatch UK), mounted an unsuccessful private prosecution of its director and two of its actors for procuring and committing an act of gross public indecency. Brenton himself was on trial only symbolically: as a dramatist of the 'permissive sixties' whose work had consistently and controversially challenged many of precisely those precepts of British history, politics and culture that the new politics was now seeking again to enshrine and reinforce, he was perhaps a convenient and obvious target for forces both outwith and within government. Although the prosecution collapsed in chaos and confusion, it left behind it sufficient uncertainty and anxiety to discourage any immediate thought of professional revival.[6]

Despite that, Brenton survived the 1980s reasonably well; he remained productive, and important plays found homes on the country's leading stages. By the later 1990s, however, he had fallen out of favour, to some extent at least as a result of his instinctive and unfashionably immediate opposition to the newly formed New Labour government of Tony Blair. He largely vanished from the larger stages, and what work he did produce was generally received poorly by reviewers; he was also consigned (although perhaps with less vehemence than was Hare) by some of the new 'in yer face' dramatists of the 1990s to a generation of 1970s dinosaurs whose 'lecturey' work had failed to deliver on its promises of helping bring about radical, leftist social change. And at the same time, the academy was already moving from the study of drama as a phenomenon that takes place largely in theatres (or at least dedicated spaces) to a more widely conceived notion of performance – drawing on sociology, psychology, anthropology, philosophy and other disciplines – as a means of analysing culture generally. To the postmodern eye, the play itself – particularly, perhaps, the political play – was coming to be seen as at best socially and politically complicit in a conservative and moribund theatrical establishment, and at worst philosophically and ideologically old-fashioned, even repressive, in its confinement, its boxing up, of the creative richness of experience. Fewer and fewer of us seemed to be teaching and researching theatre history generally and the modern political play in particular. In the age of Hans-Thies Lehmann's 'post-dramatic theatre', it became more than possible to sympathise with Brenton's predicament.[7]

In 2002, however, his voice began again to be heard more widely and his work received more positively, initially through his involvement with the BBC Television series *Spooks*. The last five years have seen a stream of new work: *Paul* (2005) and *Never So Good* (2008) at the National and *In Extremis* (2006) and *Anne Boleyn* (2010, revived 2011) at Shakespeare's Globe. In addition, 2010 saw his (second) adaptation of Büchner's *Danton's Death* at the National and his version of *The Ragged Trousered Philanthropists* transfer from the Liverpool Everyman to the Chichester Festival. He has also begun work on an adaptation of Philip K. Dick's *The Man in the High Castle* for the BBC, with Ridley Scott as executive producer. *Pravda*, his 1985 collaboration with Hare, was revived in 2006, again for the Chichester Festival (and subsequently Birmingham Rep), as was – at last – *The Romans in Britain* (at the Crucible Theatre in Sheffield; a production many thought stronger than the original).[8] Brenton is again putting big ideas on big stages; *Paul* and the Globe plays in particular deal with one of the great subjects of the moment, the nature of religious belief. And in doing so they address historically the very foundations of modern thought.

Brenton's bag

So the 2010s seem a particularly good place from which to re-examine Brenton's achievement in the 1970s. And as good a place to start as any is a bald list of the work he produced throughout the decade:

> 1970: *Wesley*, February, Eastbrook Hall, Bradford
> 'Fruit', September, Portable/Royal Court Theatre, London
> 1971: *Scott of the Antarctic*, February, Mecca Ice Rink, Bradford
> *Lay By*, August, Traverse Theatre Club, Edinburgh
> *A Sky Blue Life*, November, Open Space, London
> 1972: *Hitler Dances*, January, Traverse Theatre Club, Edinburgh

> *How Beautiful with Badges*, May, Open Space, London
> 'Lushly', August, BBC Television
> *Measure for Measure*, September, Northcott Theatre, Exeter
> 'England's Ireland', September, Portable/Mickery Theatre, Amsterdam

1973: 'A Fart for Europe', January, Royal Court Theatre, London
'Skinflicker', February, Almost Free Theatre, London
'The Screens', March, Bristol New Vic Studio
'Mug', June, Inter-Cities Conference, Manchester
Magnificence, June, Royal Court Theatre, London
Brassneck, September, Nottingham Playhouse

1974: *The Churchill Play*, May, Nottingham Playhouse
'Jedefrau', n.d., Salzburg, Austria

1975: *The Saliva Milkshake*, January, BBC Television
'Government Property', n.d., Aarhus Theatre, Denmark

1976: 'The Paradise Run', April, Thames Television
Weapons of Happiness, July, National Theatre, London

1977: *Epsom Downs*, August, Roundhouse, London

1978: *Deeds*, March, Nottingham Playhouse

1979: *Sore Throats*, August, Warehouse, London
'Warwickgate', n.d., Warwick Arts Centre

1980: *The Life of Galileo*, August, National Theatre, London
The Romans in Britain, October, National Theatre, London
A Short Sharp Shock!, June, Theatre Royal Stratford, London (professional), and, simultaneously, University Drama Studio, Sheffield (student/amateur)[9]

Several things are immediately apparent from this list: that whether the work be Fringe-based or mainstream, there are a number of key venues where Brenton found outlets for his work – and indeed, although not apparent here, a number of key collaborators, in writing (for example Hare, Edgar, Griffiths, Tony Howard) and directing (Hare again, Chris Parr, Max Stafford-Clark, Richard Eyre); that the first half of the decade seems busier than the second; and there is a movement from Fringe-based work to larger, more mainstream shows. There is an obvious relationship between the latter two points:

Brenton was writing fewer plays because he was writing bigger plays. *The Romans in Britain* is included here precisely because its writing heavily occupied Brenton, through several draftings, from 1977 onwards. But what, seen in overview, is also striking about the decade's output is the *variety* of work it encapsulates. *Wesley*, 'Fruit', *Scott*, *A Sky Blue Life*, *Hitler Dances*, *How Beautiful with Badges*, and 'Mug' can all be generally categorised as solo-authored Fringe work. The scabrous and provocative 'Fruit' was written for Portable Theatre, which Brenton had joined in 1969 with the seminal *Christie in Love* (and where he first met Hare), as were the richly controversial and oft-banned *Lay By* and 'England's Ireland'; but these were multi-authored collaborative pieces, in which Brenton's voice was one among many (on both occasions, six fellow writers contributed). It was on the Portable work that Brenton's already growing reputation largely rested. 'A Fart for Europe' and *Deeds* were also collaborative, although less ambitiously, with one and three partners respectively. 'Warwickgate' marked a return to the mass creative ensemble with no fewer than nine hands on the tiller, while *A Short Sharp Shock!* was more modestly produced in collaboration with only one partner. Both arose from Brenton's time as Writer-in-Residence at Warwick University and both, like the earlier 'A Fart for Europe', can be described as 'occasional' pieces: that is, work produced as an immediate response to contemporary events. 'Skinflicker' was a first film, made, to all intents and purposes, under the aegis of Portable. 'Lushly', *The Saliva Milkshake* and 'The Paradise Run' were television dramas. *Measure for Measure*, 'The Screens' and 'Jedefrau' were adaptations of Shakespeare, Genet and von Hofmannsthal, *The Life of Galileo* a translation of Brecht. *Epsom Downs* was made with the Joint Stock Theatre Group and as such is in many ways *sui generis* (most of the writers who worked with that company – because of its very particular process – produced work that differed, often significantly, from the style of their typical output). 'Government Property' was first produced in Denmark, while *Sore Throats*, which at the time seemed something of an aberration in both subject and form, turned out to be the first of a trilogy of utopian-themed work that was to take Brenton well into the 1980s.

What we are left with are those plays that effectively moved Brenton from the Fringe on to the mainstream stages and into the eye of a wider public: *Magnificence* (Royal Court, 1973); *Brassneck* (with David Hare; Nottingham Playhouse, 1973); *The Churchill Play* (Nottingham Playhouse, 1974, and subsequently revised twice for Royal Shakespeare Company productions in 1978 and 1988); *Weapons of Happiness* (National Theatre, 1976) and *The Romans in Britain* (National Theatre, 1980). These are Brenton's 'state of the nation' plays: ambitious in both scope and theatrical structure, tackling big and contentious themes and seeking platforms on some of the country's major stages.

The picture, however, is of course rather more complex than a simple chronology-by-date-of-first-production would allow (and, perhaps, than I allowed in 1991).

A few examples can make the point. *Hitler Dances* is both quintessentially a play of the Fringe in both its character and the nature of its making *and*, I argued in 1991, a vital progenitor of the epic, 'state of the nation' plays that were to follow. *A Sky Blue Life*, Brenton's treatment of the life of Gorky, is not only a very different Fringe play from *Hitler Dances* or the violent and brash Portable work, but had also been through several unperformed versions since a first stab was staged in 1966; on and off, a five-year project. *Magnificence*, produced in 1973, and the play which took Brenton on to a large public stage for the first time (although only if we discount the previous year's adaptation of *Measure for Measure* at Exeter's Northcott Theatre), was two years in the writing; but its themes, centred on the efficacy or otherwise of terrorist action as a political tool, were first rehearsed in a subsequently discarded television piece three years earlier, and later revisited in the Portable film 'Skinflicker' in the same year and in *The Saliva Milkshake*, first televised and then staged (the order is unique in Brenton's career) in 1975. Again, intermittently, this is a five-year engagement with the subject. And most complicated of all is the creative history around *The Churchill Play*.

This began in 1969. The image of Churchill, rising from the dead in his catafalque during his lying-in-state in Westminster Hall, first came to Brenton's imagination in that year, but it was an image he was at the time unable to develop into a workable play. Then, two years later, the BBC commissioned a radio play. Brenton produced 'Government Property', about a British concentration camp for political prisoners, prompted by contemporary civil rights abuses in Northern Ireland. The BBC declined, not entirely unexpectedly, to broadcast the piece, although it was heard in Denmark, Sweden and Norway. That play was then, at the suggestion of Jane Howell who had commissioned the Northcott *Measure*, turned into a stage play which was tried out in Denmark prior to a putative London production, where it was intended other writers would contribute new material as events in Northern Ireland unfolded. The London production never happened because of a lack of finance, but, by then, the original radio play had already inspired a screenplay for United Artists, 'Rampage', backed by David Putnam but never made (finance again). And, of course, with the creative and provocative insertion of the image of the resurrecting Churchill, it gave birth in 1974 to *The Churchill Play* itself. That play was then revised and revived twice, in 1978 and 1988, both directed for the RSC by Barry Kyle.

The Churchill Play is commonly and I still think rightly identified as a seminal play of the 1970s in particular and of modern British political drama generally. In a fashion more often associated with the work of Brenton's friend and collaborator Hare, it seemed, in its warning of a growing threat to civil liberties, to capture the *zeitgeist*. (In these days of CCTV, databases, mass surveillance and biometric passports, it still might.) But it also shows us something of the process of making playtexts, at least so far as Brenton was – and is – concerned:

> Your mental life is processional: there are things leaving the cavalcade and things joining on. Involved in all that, which come from the life you are leading, from what you think is important, from your allegiances, are several attempts to express what this movement is. The plays just take part in this stream. So ideas congeal and you begin to think of a play [. . .] I'm not a disciplined writer, I just write all the time [. . .] So it doesn't seem any miracle or anything particularly strange that

you should have ideas for plays. They're often condensations of several things that have worried or interested you, or got under your skin. The plays do often bear quite clearly the fact that they are impacted together and that's what's begun to make them work.[10]

Brenton is speaking in general terms here (and he omits the plain hard work – and the vital role played by 'that bald madam opportunity' – involved in simply getting the work out on to stage, screen or radio, something the importance of which should never be underestimated by the student of theatre), but his comments do seem particularly relevant to the nine-year-long cluster of interrelated projects of which *The Churchill Play* was the most prominent and important manifestation. And they also suggest the complexity of Brenton's creative process: ideas – often instinctive and vague, sometimes intensely personal and influencing the work in ways that will only ever be known to their author – emerge, grow, twist, spin, disappear, return, get married, divorce, metamorphose into something new, and all in an unpredictable and organically messy way.

Like many writers, Brenton habitually carries a shoulder bag containing the kind of notebooks, drafts, research materials and random scraps of paper that give physical form to this process. I was with him once when he realised he had left it in a restaurant. The degree of his panic was both shocking and immediately contagious. This was in the late 1970s – 1978, I think – and, dimly, it was only afterwards that it occurred to me he must have had bits of *The Romans in Britain* in there: maybe one or two of the several drafts Part Two went through, and perhaps the Stone Age axe-head and pieces of Roman pottery he used to move round on the floor in different patterns to help decide the play's structure. And *Sore Throats* might have been in there, too, although only in its final form: this was a 'straight write' that emerged complete in a couple of weeks.

We got the bag back.

'The View'

This kind of chaotic complexity should properly warn us against making too easy narratives of any playwright's career, but the overarching movement from Fringe to mainstream is clear enough. I think my 1991 treatment of Brenton's journey was over-defensive, too conditioned by a need to respond to those on the left who had accused him (and others) of having 'sold out'. So I was quick to point out that he continued writing for the Fringe, or as it was to become, the 'alternative' theatre, after 1973, and that he sought other outlets (television, the novel, poetry) in a conscious effort to reach as many audiences and kinds of audience as possible. And so he did. But he was himself unashamed about shifting the primary focus of his work into the established theatre, and I myself took insufficient account of the extent to which the cultural space occupied by the Fringe had already started to become and was further to become – of course with honourable exceptions – less radically politicised as the 1970s slipped into history. Speaking in 1973 – the year of *Magnificence* – Brenton argued, presciently as it turned out, that the 'hermetic' sealing off of the Fringe from society generally was reflected in its theatre, where audiences had become 'theatrically literate and the discussions afterward stopped being about the plays' content and began to be about their style'.[11] And a year later – the year of *The Churchill Play* – he said:

> I think the Fringe has failed. Its failure was that of the whole dream of an 'alternative culture' – the notion that within society as it exists you can grow another way of life, which, like a beneficent and desirable cancer, will in the end grow throughout the western world, and change it. What happens is that the 'alternative society' gets hermetically sealed, and surrounded. A ghetto-like mentality develops. It is surrounded, and, in the end, strangled to death. Utopian generosity becomes paranoia as the world closes in [. . .] you can't escape the world you live in. Reality is remorseless. No one can leave. If you are going to change the world, well, there's only one set

of tools, and they're bloody and stained but realistic. I mean communist tools. Not pleasant.[12]

It is worth noting (especially in 2010–11) that Brenton's argument here is essentially ideological, political: by implication it is, in the end, the social and political *usefulness* of his work in the 'real world' that motivates the move. And if the larger stages also represented not only larger and different audiences, then they also represented (seductively, I admit) greater creative and technological theatrical possibilities, the better to get the message across.

Yet it is also true that even in 1973 his views about the Fringe could seem more positive, suggesting it 'could be the one surviving democratic means of communication [. . .] the Fringe should never forget that'.[13] If this suggests political uncertainty and ambivalence on Brenton's part, then that is perhaps to be expected. It might account in part for his repeated revisions of *A Sky Blue Life*, with its examination of Gorky's agonised search for a meaningful role as a writer in a changing society. But perhaps the best place to explore Brenton's motivation in moving to the big stages is *Magnificence* itself.

I am going to approach the play by looking at a wide and varied range of contemporary reviews of its first production at the Royal Court in June 1973. For one thing, these help place the play in its immediate historical context. A number of reviewers rightly assume the play was inspired in part by contemporary terrorist actions by groups such as the 'Angry Brigade' (specifically, an attack on Robert Carr, Minister for Employment, two years earlier). Others place it in the theatrical context of the traditional commitment of the Court to developing new writing, noting in particular that Brenton was Writer-in-Residence and that his play was the first to be financed by the new Neville Blond Fund, which was designed specifically to support such work. We also learn in passing that it followed Bond's *The Sea* on the main stage, and the premiere of *The Rocky Horror Show* in the Theatre Upstairs. Away from the Court, reviewed at the same time were the UK stage premiere of *Grease* at the New London Theatre (with a then unknown Richard Gere), and two new farces, Jeremy Kingston's *Signs of the Times* (starring Kenneth More) at the

Vaudeville and *Who's Who*, by Keith Waterhouse and Willis Hall, at the Fortune. (If nothing else, this suggests the historical longevity of the musical as a popular form – *Grease* itself is revived in the West End as I write – although we should also note that, elsewhere in the West End, *The Mousetrap* was still a mere stripling, entering only its twenty-first year.) The National, still three years away from its new premises on the South Bank, was about to open Peter Shaffer's *Equus* and follow it with Wole Soyinka's version of *The Bacchae of Euripides* at the Old Vic.

Seen together, however, the reviews also give some indication of the critical narrative that began to develop around Brenton's work at this pivotal point in his career; a 'grand narrative' which, typically of its kind, once established takes some shifting. B. A. Young's review in the *Financial Times* in many ways offers a paradigm of Brenton criticism not only for this play but for years to come. It is worth quoting at some length (not least because, usefully, it offers a reasonably full and detailed account of the play's plot):

> As far as the interval, I believed that *Magnificence* might establish Howard Brenton as the Galsworthy of our time. Mr Brenton, being an anarchist, if not an Anarchist, would probably not relish the comparison; but as all too few of today's revolutionary writers realise, Galsworthy, wealthy and well-born, was one of the best agit-prop writers of the century. *Justice* effected a change in the law of the country, something none of the current underground writers has got near to. The theme of *Magnificence* is truly Galsworthian – as far as the interval.
>
> The play starts with a scene of stark realism in which a bunch of young people take over an empty house. We see at once that what they are engaged in is what Mr Brenton calls 'the politics of gesture'; they're not really homeless, they want to make an impression. The characters are nicely differentiated – Will, the light-hearted slogan-shouter, Veronica the bourgeois amateur Trotskyist, Jed the committed hater of the 'obscene spectacle' of organised living, Mary his faithful pregnant girl, Cliff the steady practical man. When he is not trying for

phonographic realism, Mr Brenton gives them some good dialogue; there is a splendid fugue for off-stage voices before they break in.[14]

Although Young feels that Brenton 'is not helped [. . .] by performances that suggest well-trained actors playing at being working-class', his account of the first scene still reads as largely accurate and sympathetic to the play's intentions, although what he perhaps misses is that the realism of the scene owes a more immediate debt to a specific Royal Court tradition of production style rather than to Galsworthy (all the reviews I have been able to find seem to miss this; the *Sunday Telegraph* sees similarities with Arnold Wesker, although the comparison intends no compliment) and that this was an entirely deliberate tactic on Brenton's part.[15] The social realism of the scene is adopted by the writer not just because it is the style which best articulates the particular content of the scene (always Brenton's guiding principle), but also because it enables a self-reflexive, ruefully semi-comedic dialogue about the arrival of an oppositional writer into the mainstream. This is a tactic Brenton goes on to use for all his big, solo public plays of the 1970s: motifs of occupation, invasion and imprisonment are present not just in *Magnificence* at the Court, but in *Churchill Play* at Nottingham and *Weapons* and *Romans* at the National.

Young, to his credit, recognises something of this when he says, 'Persuasively enough, at any rate, the conversation consists mostly of political dispute, in the course of which Will, depressed by the lack of impact their squatting has on the public, asks "Why didn't we come down here like a carnival?" Mr Brenton, to a degree unusual in his work, has done just that', and goes on to praise the power of the abrupt and disorienting stylistic shift to the cartoon-like black comedy of the second scene, where the squatters are violently evicted by bailiffs and Mary, Jed's girlfriend, loses the baby she is carrying as a result. Young recognises such 'quick changes of style' as entirely deliberate. To this extent at least he acknowledges Brenton as one of a group of 'underground', 'revolutionary' writers committed to social and political change and trying to bring something new to the theatre.

However:

> Jed ends, as he tells us in a narration at the end of the first act
> which summarises half of the next act, in prison, where his
> mind is debilitated by the use of drugs. Curtain. It might quite
> well be the end of the play.
>
> But no. The curtain rises again, on a totally new world. Two
> ageing homosexuals are talking in a Cambridge garden. One is
> a retired Cabinet Minister with a peerage and a fellowship at
> the college; the other, a younger man, is still in the Cabinet
> [. . .] The older man, splendidly played in decaying grandeur
> by Robert Eddison, dies in the back of a punt, having fulfilled
> no dramatic function; and we return to the young people
> assembled to meet Jed on his release . . .
>
> Jed now involves Will in a plan to catch the surviving politi-
> cian from the previous scene and blow his head off by fitting
> him with a cap trimmed with gelignite. The politician [. . .]
> behaves with uncommon bravery and kindness; yet when the
> fuse has failed to function and the scheme has come to ludi-
> crous failure, Jed gives vent to a furious tirade of hatred.

Young's sympathy and understanding seem now to have reached their
limits. That he can conceive of Jed's actions only in terms of an
uncomplicated, drug-addled personal hatred ('and a very unattractive
emotion that is; I hope Mr Brenton might grow out of it one day') is
comprehensible to a degree: Brenton himself admitted that he allowed
the ferocity of Jed's anger to unbalance the play. But it takes insufficient account of the particular political thought which motivated that
anger and its impact on the stylistic experimentation of the play: the
exact nature, as it were, of the 'carnival' that Brenton brought on to
the Court's stage. It is perhaps significant that Young's review omits
two of the play's key moments: Jed's hallucination of an encounter
with Lenin (scene five) and his story of a drunk throwing a bottle at
and puncturing a cinema screen, the resulting hole making the rest of
the film unwatchable (scene seven). The omission of the first is
surprising, as it is possibly the most striking piece of theatre in the

play. Lenin appears on a stage suddenly bathed in red, '*awash with banners and songs*' and '*moves through his heroic gestures*' as a '*wind machine blows a gale across the stage*'.[16] It is a *coup de théâtre*, designed deliberately to startle and provoke a Court audience used to cool, understated dramaturgies and performance styles, and its purpose is vividly to dramatise Jed's rejection of conventional Marxist-Leninist political strategy. This is the politics and the aesthetics of the Fringe being dropped with a loud thud on to the mainstream stage. What Jed offers instead of conventional Marxist thought is the subject of scene seven: political action rooted in a situationist analysis of society and culture:

> Broadly speaking, the situationists offered a reassessment of the traditional Marxist view of the relationship between the individual and society. The need to change society remained, of course, paramount; but conventional political struggle – not only parliamentary democracy, industrial relations and so on, but Marxist revolution itself – was rejected as no more than the deployment of tactics within an existing system that would remain fundamentally unchanged. That system was defined as 'the society of the spectacle'. The situationist analysis argued that the main agent of capitalist repression had ceased to be located at the point of production – on the factory floor – and had transferred to a point of consumption: the consumption of bourgeois ideology as transmitted through culture generally and the mass media in particular. The relationship between the individual and society was thus analogous to that between the spectator and the events on a screen: both were passive consumers of a two-dimensional charade. It was by shattering the hegemony of received images that individuals had of society that the ground-work of revolutionary change could be established; smashing the screen of *public* life would expose the realities of *private* and *daily* life beneath.[17]

Largely under Brenton's influence, it was situationist thought that had driven Portable work (*enabled* it, I am tempted to say), with his own *Christie in Love* and 'Fruit', and with the collaborative *Lay By* and 'England's Ireland'; these were pieces designed quite specifically and violently to 'disrupt the spectacle', to shock, appal and disgust audiences into seeing the world anew. This was the energy that Brenton now brought on to the Royal Court stage. *Magnificence*, in an important sense, creates its own spectacle in order to disrupt it. But it does so in an unexpected way, and one which Young fails to explain. Although Jed's bomb fails to explode as planned, it does so when he throws it to the ground in frustration, killing both of them. His magnificent gesture is itself bungled. The curtain line is left to his friend Cliff:

Jed The waste. I can't forgive you that.

A pause.

The waste of your anger. Not the murder, murder is common enough. Not the violence, violence is everyday. What I can't forgive you Jed, my dear, dead friend, is the waste.

Blackout. (p. 106)

Cliff rejects Jed's situationist-inspired terrorism in favour of long-term, committed 'corny work'; politically, the play should be his. But Brenton's use of situationist tactics as a dramaturgical device threatens to overwhelm the play's advocacy of the less dramatic, more hard-earned and long-term course of political action Cliff represents, and gives it theatrically to Jed. And that debate about 'real world' politics of course reflects Brenton's own self-questioning about the politics of his own theatre career.

Young claims to be at ease with Brenton's use of disruptive style changes ('as he has pointed out, Shakespeare did the same thing'), but he can still only read the second half of the play in terms of the 'terrible task' the director, Max Stafford-Clark, must have faced in attempting 'to sew together scenes in which so much wilful irrelevance is given its head'. Of course, this might be a logical enough view if Galsworthy is your model of a political playwright, but it has lost sight of the play's intentions. It is telling that Young misreads what

Brenton is attempting in his portrayal of Alice and Babs, the current and retired Cabinet ministers; the critic views them sympathetically, the writer as poisonously corrupt and self-serving. Equally, the critic teases his reader that he knows the real-life equivalents on which Brenton had based his characters; the writer is more concerned with showing a historical shift in political power in the contemporary Conservative Party from old-fashioned paternalism to something more dynamic, unforgiving and ruthless. (It is a prescience that also informs Brenton's collaboration with Hare, *Brassneck* – which opened at Nottingham a couple of months later – and Hare's own *Knuckle* of the following year.) Young seems to like the scene while at the same time believing it has 'no dramatic function'. What he does not see is an emergent dramaturgy that views theatrical style simply as a key to unlock the truth of a scene: 'I want to write about the old men who use a very elegant language, so I go straight into it. I don't worry about the style of the play or anything, just aim to get the truth of those men speaking to each other.'[18] And the 'truth' for Brenton is that the scene 'is an outright attack on Babs and Alice. If you attack something or a class get it right; you mustn't be stupid or shallow. I mean in this scene [. . .] people [. . .] are watching their *enemies*.'[19]

As with style, so with characterisation: the writing is not driven by preconceived notions of what human character, human psychology, are, but by the need to analyse a political mentality in action. The scene is the first of its kind in Brenton's original writing in dramatising the interplay between the private and public lives of the governing class, the better to understand the nature of 'the enemy'. (I say 'original writing' because if Brenton learned anything from adapting Shakespeare, it was surely to do with how to dramatise the interplay of private and public lives.) Accumulated psychological minutiae are less important than a detailed examination of how the need for power drives a series of status battles between two corrupt figures, battles which move seamlessly between the personal and the public spheres. As such Alice and Babs are a world way from the realities of life for Jed, Cliff and the others – and by implication the audience – and that is Brenton's point: stylistic disjuncture within the play dramatises, makes concrete, the nature of social reality outside it. Alice's and

Babs's scene is a play-within-a-play because the political class they represent is a world-within-a-world (or perhaps even a world-within-a-world-within-a-world, for both surely would have been members of the Bullingdon Club during Oxford days?).

Many of the play's reviewers (see, for example, local London papers such as the *Clapham and Lambeth News*, as well as the *Spectator*, the *Lady* and *Plays and Players*) view Alice and Babs with a greater or lesser degree of sympathy, and identify the scene as the best-written in the play; largely because, you suspect, its style falls – or seems to fall – within their established aesthetic world-view.[20] Almost all agree that Robert Eddison's performance as Babs was masterful, and no doubt it was. Young in fact contrasts the skill of his performance with what he has already identified (see above) as unevenness of the performances of the younger actors; but even here, as Philip Roberts has shown, there is more at work.[21] Fringe experience, philosophy and working process arrived on the Court stage not only in the shape of the hot expressionism of Brenton's writing but also in the shape of Stafford-Clark and a younger generation of actors whose whole approach to the business of playmaking – game-playing, improvisation, physical work, open-ended exploration and experimentation – differed radically from that of their more traditionally trained elders.[22]

The day after Young's review appeared it was precised in the *Financial Times*'s listings: 'ROYAL COURT – *Magnificence*. Intermittently impressive, intermittently infuriating, smoulderingly angry piece about the results of a badly-thought-out bit of "squatting". Opened Thursday.' It is a fair summary of his assessment, but also one which could have been condensed from the reviews generally, at least if the most hostile are set aside (Arthur Thirkell in the *Daily Mirror* 'can't remember when [he] last enjoyed a play at the Royal Court Theatre. I certainly disliked last night's offering called *Magnificent*. Hardly an apt title.' Well, no . . .).[23] Steve Grant's review in the communist *Morning Star* offers one of the better summaries of the play and its intentions, and homes in on the key question: 'To what extent is violence justifiable? Is it simply a futile, personal gesture or something more? As Jed, the central character, says to a surrealistic transfiguration of Lenin, rushing around the stage spouting tactics, "Yes, Vlad, but what can a poor boy do?"[24] More generally, his piece is – surprisingly or not – ambivalent in its judgements, noting in particular the problems encountered in getting it on at the Royal Court in the first place and the tension between its politics and those of the 'Sloane Square gin-and-tonic revolutionaries' making up the audience. The *Sunday Telegraph* was more confident that the 'tame, well-heeled Marxists in the audience clearly thought that Brenton was their man', and considerably less ambivalent in the fervent wish of its unnamed reviewer that s/he would be 'most unwilling' to see again 'such an abominably bad play'.[25] As we have already seen, Brenton himself was well aware of the tensions if not contradictions implicit in putting his particular brand of political theatre on to stages such as the Court's. Broadly, however, the thrust of the more critical notices is towards two main targets.

The first, predictably, homes in on Brenton's politics. The *Yorkshire Post* allows the writer his 'sincerity', but finds the play 'too strident and even old-fashioned in its one-sided radicalism', finally judging it to be 'little more than a worthy, youthful tirade'.[26] In the *Scotsman*, David Gow, who claims to be a 'long and consistent admirer' of Brenton's work, confesses to being disappointed with the play, and, pausing briefly to take a side-swipe at the Sloane Square audience (presumably by now beginning to feel somewhat punch-drunk and bewildered), ambitiously attempts to place it in the context of European political theatre:

> It says a lot for that peculiar kind of Court audience that they appeared to be enraptured by the 'politics' of the play, when, in fact, the astonishing naivety of the political ideas would be greeted with derision on the Continent. It is a sad fact that British writers as a whole have no feeling for ideology, or even ideas; and Brenton is the latest in a long run.[27]

Even if we accept that the history of mainstream British theatre of the twentieth century was characterised at least in part by its self-regard and insularity, this seems unduly harsh on, for example, Edward Bond and John Arden (both Court writers, and the former at least with an established reputation in Europe) and the earlier work of Joan Littlewood and Theatre Workshop, never mind Shaw (or even Galsworthy). And it seems harsher still on the susceptibility to leftist European and North American influence of pre-war underground theatres such as the Workers' Theatre Movement and Unity to their post-war analogues such as Portable in the 1960s. John Elsom in the *Listener*, again seeking a wider context within which to frame what proves to be an unremittingly hostile notice, bemoans the 'cliché-ridden' nature of political language generally and suggests that 'The design and assumptions of our political plays are wrong: they're intended to rally and hector, rather than to inform and stimulate, as if political involvement could only be measured by the number of flags.'[28] Both Gow and Elsom are implicitly reprimanded in a very positive and sympathetic piece in the *Amateur Stage*, which takes a similarly wide view but from a rather different angle:

> The importance of writers like Brenton is that he writes for his generation: more mature playgoers and critics will disregard that at their peril, even although many of the ideas and methods may be alien and unnerving to them. Here he is deeply and seriously concerned with the problems of active protest, violent demonstration and individual terrorism [. . .] this disturbing play throws up many issues which must worry revolutionaries and traditionalists alike – the corruption of idealism, the muddle-headedness of so many good intentions, the frustrations of agit prop leading to mindless annihilation.[29]

The second recurrent theme of the critical narrative relates to questions of style and structure.

Many reviewers recognise Brenton's promise as a playwright, but to a greater or lesser extent challenge his ability to control his subject matter – and even to construct 'proper' plays. The *Amateur Stage* again takes the positive view: 'encouraging, too has been the reception of critics generally, who in bygone years would have dismissed such a work as lacking a coherent plot or style'. It is a view, however, by no means entirely borne out by the evidence. J. C. Trewin in the *Birmingham Post* feels Brenton 'cannot really make a workable play of the material'. Trewin pops up again as the *Lady*'s reviewer to suggest that 'the construction is negligible and Mr Brenton has little idea of composing a narrative' (tantalisingly, he plays with the notion that this might be Brenton's intention as 'narratives are out of fashion', only quickly to move on). In the *Evening News*, Felix Barker finds Brenton's challenge of social injustice laudable and appreciates the experimental Court tradition to which the play belongs, but otherwise sees nothing new or inspired, only 'the same tired old mixture of angry political commonplaces' expressed through 'unrelated scenes that grope towards nowhere'. Not dissimilarly, the *Daily Telegraph*, in a rather strained metaphor, feels that Brenton 'keeps stamping out the dramatic fire as soon as it starts to burn for him. He has a sentimental message, and in his clod-hopping concern to kick it across to us, the flame goes out.' The *Jewish Chronicle* is a little more positive, acknowledging the importance of what the playwright has to say and deciding that the 'ramshackle construction ... only just holds the play together'. Like B. A. Young and others, John M. East, in his notice for the South London News Group (syndicated across the capital through local papers such as the *Streatham News*), sees the bulk of the play's structural problems as belonging to its second half: 'it is a pity that the tedium of much of Act Two destroyed one's appreciation of [the] play as a whole'. Perhaps the view most sympathetic to what Brenton was trying to achieve is R.B. Marriott's, who writes in the *Stage* that 'The technique of *Magnificence* is a kind of disorder ordered. So we have a scene moving well, towards a point, then a sudden switch off to something else. It is the same with character, dialogue, progress and atmosphere. The effect is gripping.'[30] The observation, interestingly, captures some sense – more than any other review – of the play's movement through *time*, of successive waves of discomfort and uncertainty playing on the audience's nerve ends or in its gut. This is surely what Brenton intended: a moment-by-moment connection with the audience that is unsettling and visceral. The larger point is that this was a new theatre struggling to push open a door into the old; struggling to *become*.

The point of all this is not to establish or comment upon the 'rightness' or 'wrongness' of critical views: any reviewer – any*body* – of course has his or her prejudices and the right to his or her own views, just as the newspapers, magazines and academic and professional journals for which they write have their own editorial standpoints. And these both inform and are informed by the wider political, social and cultural context, sometimes very obviously, sometimes with imperceptible subtlety. I have already made clear, I hope, that my own judgements have not been formed in some political or aesthetic vacuum. As is the case with any work of art, Brenton's plays are as they are seen, and they are seen through a variety of eyes. The point, rather, is to gain insight into the reception of a playwright's work at a crucial moment in his career and in the history of modern British political theatre, and it is particularly useful to the theatre historian that reviews tell us at least as much about the reviewer as about the reviewed. It is also, crucially, to attempt to demonstrate how an overarching critical narrative or discourse forms with which, like it or not, the playwright has then to live: there may be many pairs of eyes on the work which are individual, but those eyes come together to form 'The View'. The mechanisms by which this happens are not especially mysterious: critics read critics, reviewers chat to reviewers, practitioners share experiences, academics publish books (or write essays for books) and give conference papers. It is – we are – an industry.

In Brenton's case, then, we might crudely summarise the emerging narrative – The View in 1973 – thus:

1. that his radical politics simply alienated some reviewers;
2. that even those broadly in favour found those politics at times romantic in their utopianism, and while recognising they were sincerely held, saw them as simplistic and naive;
3. that his writing was uneven, but at its best poetic in its intensity;
4. that he loved taking theatrical risks that did not always pay off;
5. and specifically that the ambition of his ideas was not always matched, especially in terms of structural control, by his

technical skill as a playwright. This was true particularly of his second halves.

In fact, The View was half-formed even before *Magnificence*: reviewing Brenton's work to date in *Plays and Players* in 1971, John Russell Taylor concludes that Brenton was 'a hit-or-miss dramatist who hits often enough to be worth watching'.[31] And almost forty years later, Michael Billington's judgement in *State of the Nation* (and Billington has consistently been a 'critical friend' of the playwright) that there is something of the 'action painter' in Brenton perhaps demonstrates its longevity.[32]

The bear pit

What, in 1973, was Brenton's own response to the experience of having his first big play in the mainstream? I have already shown that the play itself knowingly and self-referentially plays to its own role as invader-from-the-Fringe. Its author might reasonably have expected a warmer welcome for it from the Court itself – according to Hare, 'one artistic director said [Brenton] should be taken out and buried in a hole in a field' – but his experience with Portable (especially the much-banned 'England's Ireland') had been a good schooling, and Portable's mission was, after all, quite specifically to make trouble.[33] *Measure*, the script of which had suffered when a nervous Northcott Theatre board enforced changes before allowing the production to go ahead, had also led Brenton to acknowledge that 'It taught me something, that your enemies know what they're doing [. . .] It was the first big theatre that I'd ever written for. I felt I put my head in the door and they had it off by the neck.'[34] By his own admission, Brenton believed the theatre to be 'a real bear pit. It's not the place for reasoned discussion. It's the place for really savage insights' so he can hardly have been surprised to have provoked negative reaction.[35] Indeed, his evolving theatre was rooted in deliberate antagonism, and it was in that antagonism that he saw political efficacy.

Nevertheless, I have sometimes wondered if he has come to regret that comment, for it is often and perhaps too easily repeated. It is undoubtedly a key component of The View, and as such, it is worth closer examination. The quotation above continues 'which can be proved at once by an audience saying "Yes that is actually true" at some level, not necessarily in a representative way. And theatre does teach something about the way people act in public.'[36] '[P]roved', 'by an audience', 'theatre does teach': these are not ideas or ambitions that automatically come to mind in a bear pit theatre, but they do speak to a view of what political theatre is and what it can be, a view of which some critics have taken less regard. An interview with Marriott in the *Stage*, published three weeks after *Magnificence* had opened and after the great majority of reviews had appeared, has Brenton endorsing the bear pit idea, but making it clear that he is not talking simply about what happens on stage, but also about what he wants that to provoke in his audience, which should itself be 'savage, with all kinds of prejudice and bad breath coming from [it]. It is not a bit delicate. You must pin down what you can yourself, and make your play reflect the bear pit.'[37] And perhaps he had read Young's review, for he goes on, according to Marriott, to suggest that a 'play such as Galsworthy's *Strife*, although what is termed well-intentioned, is totally wrong. "It may be good theatre, but it isn't about life." The most you can do in the theatre, Brenton thinks, is to "chuck a brick". Good brick throwers he named included Shaw, Osborne, Arden and Bond. "And you must keep your nose firmly on the street. The audience know if you don't. When your work gets rarified it loses everything worthwhile".'

The situationist brick-chucker, then, had an acquaintanceship with theatre history that included, perhaps to the surprise of some of his critics, Galsworthy and Shaw. And as I noted in 1991, *Magnificence* pays a knowing homage to Osborne's *Look Back in Anger*. The larger point is that Elsom's polarities of political theatre – 'rallying and hectoring' on the one hand, 'informing and stimulating' on the other – are posited as mutually exclusive. Why should political theatre not do both? Is this not precisely what Brenton is attempting in *Magnificence*?

Nevertheless, Brenton was under no illusion that he had found the exact form of his big, public play first time. I have already noted that he came to see that Cliff was, theatrically and therefore politically, an insufficient counterweight to Jed. He readily admitted too that audiences new to his writing might not have found the play clear, and hoped that it would become clearer as time passed. But he also wished to write a play that was clear from the beginning and to 'try a big play', with an 'epic structure, elegance and complexity'.[38]

His next big, solo piece was *The Churchill Play*, written for and performed at, not the Court or the National, but Nottingham Playhouse, run by Richard Eyre in part as a kind of greenhouse for growing Fringe playwrights on into the mainstream (it was here that Griffiths's *Comedians* and Edgar's *Destiny* were created). But if what Brenton was aspiring to was a 'big', 'epic' play that forced political concerns into the bear pit of his audiences (a kind of 'Brecht-with-attitude'), I am no longer sure that *Churchill* sits quite as comfortably within the kind of progressive, linear development I wanted to see in 1991. As I have suggested, its status as a seminal play of the 1970s seems to me incontestable, but in terms of Brenton's stated aspirations, the play's structural ambitions now seem smaller than they did at the time. It is a matter of form: Brenton's means here of smashing the Fringe into the mainstream tradition is the oldest of dramaturgical chestnuts, the play-within-a-play. That certainly allows him to debate the limits of agitprop, as his political prisoners mount their own production of the life of Churchill to 'entertain' a visiting parliamentary delegation, then use it as cover for a failed escape attempt; but the very familiarity of the form, its conservatism – which itself arguably blunts the play's political and theatrical edge – makes its value as an experiment in epic limited. That had come in fact, earlier, between *Magnificence* and *Churchill*, with *Brassneck*, the first 'Howard Hare' play, written with Hare and produced at Nottingham in September 1973, about which I have recently written elsewhere.[39]

Nevertheless, *Churchill* both crystallises and further develops certain themes and leitmotifs that had already begun to be articulated in Brenton's work, the continuing creative unpicking of which remains central to his project in the 1970s.

One focus is the sharper articulation, in the shape of the compromised camp doctor, Thomson, of the establishment-figure-with-a-conscience that had already stirred in earlier work, generated through Fringe experiments (*Revenge, Christie in Love*) with the kind of characterisation in which comfortably two-dimensional, satirical cartoon figures suddenly and bathetically reach out a real human hand and force a disconcerted audience to grasp it. The figure reappears with Ralph Makepeace [*sic*], the beleaguered factory owner in *Weapons of Happiness* and, most remarkably, in the figure of the increasingly unstable SAS assassin, Thomas Chichester, in *The Romans in Britain*. My earlier assessment of these figures was that they were 'agonised liberals', drawn by Brenton with a great deal of contempt but also some sympathy; they now seem to me harsher characterisations than that, my original judgement more a reflection of my own subject position than of what Brenton had actually written. (The real paradigm, perhaps, is the scarcely forgivable Jack, the brutal, emotionally stunted policeman of *Sore Throats*?)

The dominant image of *The Churchill Play*, however, is of course that of the great war leader rising from his coffin at the beginning of the prisoners' play to lay his dead hand on the present. The insult is immense and calculated, not just by the prisoners for their audience, but by Brenton for his. The great, untouchable Churchill, the play argues, in both his historical person and in the public icon he has become, enshrines and represents the possibility of a fascist future. He is not the first figure to be resurrected on Brenton's stage: the murderous Christie emerges blinking from burial under a mound of popular newspapers in the play which bears his name; a homeless old tramp similarly rises from his newspaper bed at the end of the first scene of *Magnificence*, his genuine predicament mocking the empty political gesturing of the young squatters. But perhaps the most significant resurrection before *Churchill* is that which occurs in *Hitler Dances*, where the war games of a group of young children breathe dangerous life into the rotting corpse of a German storm-trooper. I say 'most significant' because it seems to me that it is here that Brenton begins fully to understand the potential and power of his own image. It is by no means unreasonable to suggest not just that resurrection is a key leitmotif of Brenton's work for the decade, but that it is *the* key leitmotif: that it is, fundamentally, what much of the work is *about*. What comes out of the ground in *Hitler Dances* and *Churchill* to lay a mortifying hand on the present and hence the future is recent history. In *Churchill*, the idea is accounted for naturalistically: 'Churchill', after the initial shock, turns out to be one of the prisoners wearing a mask. But Hans, the storm-trooper in *Hitler Dances*, historically anonymous as he may be, is as real as any other character on stage, and his dramatised story is as 'true', 'real', 'believable' as that of the modern children to whom it is told and shown. And what enables that is a stage, a theatricality, conceived of as fluid, expressionistic and, to use Brenton's own term, 'phantasmagorical'.

When I began this essay I suspected I might find myself recanting on my earlier argument that *Hitler Dances* should be seen as a progenitor of the epic, state of the nation plays of the later 1970s. In fact I find the contrary. The way it imagines the stage, its use of twin narratives, its articulation of character and its development of the resurrection image might find their roots in earlier Fringe work, but most assuredly look forward to *Weapons of Happiness* and *The Romans in Britain* – for me, the pinnacle of Brenton's achievement in the decade and the fullest and most complex expression of his British epic theatre. And the key moment comes in the first scene of the second act of *Weapons*.

Here we see Josef Frank, an old Czech communist now working in a modern London crisp factory and the reluctant ally of its striking but politically illiterate young workforce, relive, in harrowing detail, his own torture and political recantation and that of his friend and colleague Victor Clementis. Frank's status in the play is already ambiguous: a note in the programme and in the printed text tells us that 'The real Josef Frank was hanged in Prague on the 3rd of December 1952'; this, then, is another of Brenton's resurrections, albeit one not seen on stage. For his fellow characters, Frank is simply a fellow worker, 'dirty old man' with odd habits, an odder accent and the more or less interesting aura of having a past. For the audience, he is that and more. He inhabits the play like a ghost, always half-lit on the edge of the action. The terrors of his past life erupt uncontrollably on to the stage, and with as much vivid reality as the scenes set in the present. Frank's memory of his friend's suffering begins to fade, with the bound and blindfolded Clementis sinking into the floor as the moment of his execution arrives. At that very moment, however, the present fights back, in what for the audience is a wildly disorienting moment:

Clementis   A few hours before his death even the worst man speaks the truth. I declare that I have never been a traitor or a spy. I confessed only to fulfil my obligation to working people and the Communist Party. It was my duty. In order that the Party survive our days of lies and fear to lead the working people to full happiness. Long live the Communist Party of Czechoslovakia.

Capital Radio   Hello all you nightriders out there.

A snatch of music. Mina Ripperton sings 'Loving you'.[40] **Clementis** *begins to sink through the stage.*

Janice (*off*)   Joseph?

Ken (*off*)   Oy Joey! Where you got to?

Clementis   I tried to keep my trousers up in court! I did not show my bum in disrespect!

Capital Radio   Insomniacs all, cold out there? Here comes Californian Sun.

The radio plays the Beach Boys singing 'Good Vibrations'. **Clementis** *has sunk to his chest.* **Josef Frank** *kneels beside him.*

Clementis   I've got a handful of raisins. In a matchbox. I'd give them to you if I were alive.

Clementis *disappears.* **Josef Frank** *looks upstage as* **Stalin** *comes out of the dark smoking his pipe.* **Ken** *comes out of the dark carrying a transistor radio.*

Ken (*to* **Josef Frank**)   What you doing? Sleep walking about the factory?

Stalin *walks away into the dark.* **Josef Frank** *watches him go.*

Oh go and tuck him up, Jan. Or whatever you get up to.

Frank   He wanted to give me raisins.

Ken   What?

Frank   Victor Clementis. In a matchbox. The last thing he said to me, before he died, in a corridor. You see . . . To keep raisins all those months, through the interrogation, the trial, the winter . . . That was an achievement.

A pause.

Ken   I don't know, old son. I just don't know what you're on about.

Ken *throws the transistor radio down the drain. A silence.*

Janice   What you do that for?

Ken   Can't stand the Beach Boys, can I?[41]

A Russian prison transforms into the factory floor, the scene of Clementis's death becomes a drain and the present washes the past away. It is an extraordinary sequence: as one resurrected figure sinks back into the past, another remains condemned to live – or half-live, at any rate – in the present while yet a third, one of the most recognisable and feared figures of the twentieth century, presides. Crucially, the phantasmagorical nature of the theatrical space – its establishment as the imagination given concrete form – enables the unproblematic co-existence of figures from different kinds of reality. I have already explained how the figure of Churchill in the play which bears his name is accounted for naturalistically; similarly, the appearance of Lenin in *Magnificence* is most conveniently interpreted as Jed's drug-fuelled hallucination.[42] But here Stalin is unashamedly introduced as the historical icon he is, and although icons are by their very nature two-dimensional this one is as 'real' as any other figure on stage. What Brenton has engineered, through the structure of his play and through the particular imaginative construction of the stage, is a world in which not only different places and time periods but also different types of 'character' can co-exist in dynamic, analytical interplay.

The weight of history seems intolerable, and to stand in ironic and damning contrast to the petty and inept politics of the present. History and politics here smash into the present both psychologically and literally, and challenge it to learn. But the present fights back. Brenton simultaneously condemns Ken's ignorance of history and endorses the need casually to shrug it off: the past is there to be learned from, not to crush hope. And it is Janice, the group's leader, who finally forces Frank to help their political action. Her relentless pressure on him – political, emotional and sexual – brings about a second resurrection, forces him to become fully human again. It kills him, but not before his old idealism fires one last time. The particular advice he gives to Janice is minimal but practical, and enables her to begin making the pragmatic, even ruthless quotidian decisions needed to begin her political education. The path on which she is embarking is Cliff's, not Jed's, and perhaps it is as hard won for her as it was for Brenton.

Brenton himself felt that 'the play was actually entering into an argument in a way in which a play of mine hadn't done before. I dreamed *Magnificence* would do it, but it didn't' and saw it as part of an ongoing mission to create political drama – a 'British epic' – devolving on an 'endless dialectic towards a real people's theatre. That is what we are all engaged in and building that is very, very difficult – building a theatre that is exclusively a popular socialist theatre.'[43] Those 'difficulties' were familiar. Brenton's 'occupation' of the new South Bank complex was a significant moment in his career and that of his fellow socialist dramatists: it was the first of their plays performed in the theatre, but that did not stop it attracting the hostility of the trades unions representing staff there. Nor did the production (directed by Hare) seem to do much to challenge the power of The View. It might have won a Best New Play award from the *Evening Standard*, but Charles Marowitz in *Plays and Players* argues that Brenton's own political prejudices limited its theatrical effectiveness. Marowitz engages with the play in a more serious, informed and detailed way than many others, but I cannot help feeling that his own political prejudices have a similar effect on his review. Somewhat immoderately, he accuses Brenton (and Hare) of an 'outrageous political naïveté' that 'makes one's flesh crawl', largely on the grounds that the play offers a utopian solution to the issues it raises. This he characterises as '"Let us technologically-unemployed-layabouts take over this derelict farm and live off the land".'[44] He refers to the Welsh farm to which Janice and her fellow workers have fled in the play's last scene, but takes no account (perhaps he did not notice) of the fact that Brenton could hardly be clearer in that scene that Janice follows Frank's advice not only in insisting the illiterate Ken learn to read and quashing the utopianist tendencies of others in the group, but also in realising that hiding in the country offers no solution and that they must return to the city. And it is a depressing if inevitable feature of The View that it is self-perpetuating: a later critic, more sympathetic to Brenton than Marowitz, none the less suggests that *Weapons* concludes with 'a counter-culture cop-out in the Welsh hills'.[45]

The kinds of tension between Brenton and the cultural establishment that grew throughout the 1970s came to a head in *The Romans in Britain*. I have no intention of rehearsing again the tedious furore that was generated around that play; I said all I wish to say in 1991. Suffice it to note that, whatever the political agenda that lay behind its persecution and prosecution (and I haven't the slightest doubt there was one), it seems clearer now than ever that what Brenton brought on to the mainstream stages in the 1970s constituted, in its rawness, its violence and its visceral, often disturbing theatricality as much as its politics, a nagging insult to the dominant aesthetic taste of the cultural and theatrical establishments. His politics might be utopianist, even romantic in their aspiration, but the world-view in which they originate is a harsher, more challenging and demanding one than the woolly minded humanism which many of his critics inhabit, a point made forcibly at the time by Edward Bond.[46] To this extent at least he can be seen as prefiguring the 'in-yer-face' playwrights of the 1990s. All I note now is that the play's eventual revival by Samuel West at Sheffield's Crucible Theatre in 2006 confirms both its quality as a great piece of theatre and how malevolent and silly was the fuss that surrounded its original production. And that West's production prefigured and to some degree prompted Brenton's successful return to our mainstream stages is an irony very much to be relished.

DAVID EDGAR
By Janelle Reinelt

Introduction

The 1970s was David Edgar's formative period as a playwright, a decade that he began as a young agitprop writer and activist, and finished as a major figure – an established and versatile dramatist and analytic critic of his age. The sophistication and scope of his writing grew exponentially over this period, while his commitment to direct engagement and political intervention also remained strong. Thus between 1976 and 1980, his playwriting included an epic state of the nation play for the RSC (*Destiny*, 1976), an agitprop play for 7:84 (*Wreckers*, 1977), a quasi-verbatim solo show (*The Jail Diary of Albie Sachs*, 1978), a social realist drama (*Mary Barnes*, 1978), and a nine-hour epic musical and international hit (*The Life and Adventures of Nicholas Nickleby*, 1980). Three of these five projects involved adaptation of original source materials, a special skill Edgar mastered and has continued throughout his career (most recently, the adaptation of Julian Barnes's novel *Arthur & George*, 2010). All of these 1970s dramatic writings were connected to Edgar's ongoing political commitments throughout the decade: to class-based labour struggles, to the British anti-racism and anti-apartheid movements, to a range of countercultural projects such as alternative therapies – and perhaps most clearly to a role as a public intellectual, illustrated by his writings in newspapers, journals and magazines, on such topics as the prospect of home-grown English fascism.

Dominic Sandbrook and Andy Beckett, historians of Britain's 1970s from conservative and progressive viewpoints respectively, both invoke the popular metaphor of the 1960s as a wild party and the 1970s as the hangover. Both also agree, however, that this view is too simplistic. In Sandbrook's words, 'Many things we associate with the 1960s only gained momentum in the first half of the following decade', while in Beckett's, 'For many politicised Britons, the decade was *not* the hangover after the sixties; it was when the great sixties party actually got started' (italics in the original).[1]

The 'hot topics' of the decade involved massive labour unrest, strikes and demonstrations; emerging new movements such as the Gay Liberation Front (1970), full-throttle second-wave feminism, and environmentalism; escalating violence in Northern Ireland, extending into England; and a variety of enterprises and experiences loosely grouped under the heading of the 'counterculture'. Collectives produced theatre or published magazines, operated book stores and cafés, set up drop-in clinics and rape crisis help lines. A large number of left-wing organisations and parties offered members the opportunity to organise around intense campaigns to press for sanctions against South Africa or, closer to home, to press for equal rights: in 1979, the Trades Union Congress (TUC) finally adopted and published the charter on 'Equality for Women within Trade Unions'.

All of these developments and many more made the decade a volatile and engaged time to be alive – and to be making theatrical art. In interview with Chris Megson, Edgar characterises the era in terms of the way its various agendas intertwined: 'There was this extraordinary counter-cultural mish-mash' – by which he means that very different values and viewpoints could be combined: 'I listened to The Searchers *and* I listened to progressive rock. I was a student revolutionary *and* I watched *Dad's Army.*'[2] Many people were active in multiple political projects, and had sympathy with others still. The mood of collective expansiveness and eclecticism during the early part of the decade (some would call it solidarity) was partially an effect of the rapid proliferation of projects for political and social transformation begun in the 1960s, but hitting stride in the 1970s.

Edgar has himself written a good deal about the 1970s, characterising not only the politics of the time but also its theatre, and exploring the contradictions operating in the arts arena for his generation of theatre people. In his 1982 essay 'Public Theatre in a Private Age', he identified what values he and his colleagues held in common in the 1970s (naming explicitly Brenton, Hare, Trevor Griffiths and Stephen Poliakoff): 'a belief in collaborative production processes, an aspiration to an audience wider than the usual metropolitan coterie, an open attitude to form, a concern with the public world and its relation to the private world, and a commitment to radical social change'.[3] Although by the end of the decade, the ability to maintain an extraordinary diversity of political commitments had been replaced by more sectarian and narrowly defined interests, and in theatre, by divisions into what Edgar calls 'art-college-based, visual, non-cerebral, performance art and the political, university-based, verbal, cerebral theatre', it seems important to stress, looking back, the overlapping agendas and passions that contributed to the excitement as well as the angst of the decade.[4] In the discussion of Edgar's work that follows, I will examine how these attributes manifested in Edgar's own theatre creations of the period.

In the previous chapter, Chris Megson has described Edgar's early theatrical development and his training as a journalist. His time in Bradford in the early 1970s, working at the *Telegraph & Argus* newspaper and writing agitprop and satirical plays for Chris Parr and then for the General Will, shows him participating in high-octane collaborations at both the newspaper and in his fledgling playwriting ventures. In 1972, he co-wrote *England's Ireland* with Howard Brenton, David Hare, Snoo Wilson, Tony Bicât, Brian Clark and Francis Fuchs – a fierce political play that found a way to blend the anarchic, surreal talents of someone like Wilson with Brenton's savage poetic vision – an example of the pre-split co-mingling of 'non-cerebral' and 'cerebral' talents. Edgar left the newspaper to pursue full-time playwriting, but he continued his political prose as a freelance commentator as well. The General Will eventually succumbed to the fragmentations of the later years of the decade – differences around the sexual politics and identifications of its members – but Edgar had participated in a wide range of projects by then, writing eighteen plays (five for the General Will).

This essay will focus on three major plays from the decade that demonstrate the range of Edgar's political concerns and the versatility of his dramatic means. *Destiny* (1976), *The Jail Diary of Albie Sachs* (1978) and *Mary Barnes* (1978) represent very well not only the panoply of important political concerns of the time but also Edgar's playwriting project as constituted throughout his career – an account in dramatic form of the way human beings engage with and behave in terms of the most basic questions of how to organise and govern themselves in modern societies. (Michael Oakeshott defines 'politics' in similar terms, as 'attending to the arrangements of a collection of people who, in respect of their common recognition of their manner of attending to its arrangements, compose a single community'.[5]) Before considering each of these plays in detail, however, I will briefly focus on virtually the last of his agitprop plays, *Wreckers* (1977). Coming just after *Destiny*, it sums up both the previous kinds of plays he wrote and shows the relationship between them and the features of dramaturgy that carried over into the newer material.

> Where were you
> In '72
> Where were we in '73
> And '74
> Easy
> Easy
> Easy to smash the law
> (*Wreckers*, Act One)[6]

The premise behind agitprop theatre is that activism can be stimulated by theatre that explains the underlying political structures that shape and control our lives in common and that it (agitprop) advocates ways to collectively take action to resist or oppose this hegemony. The emphasis on 'message' that is now more or less discredited – how dare the theatremakers think they have something to teach? – follows from the faith in ideology critique which had yet to be attacked in the name of poststructural undecidability. Yet *Wreckers* itself was hell-bent on showing how situations change rapidly, making any 'eternal truth' or 'party lines' highly questionable. Edgar describes *Wreckers* as an attempt to dramatise how, between the early and late 1970s, 'everything changed' and the euphoria of working-class gains in terms of successful strike actions and cross-sector solidarity began to collapse in light of divide-and-conquer policies of a government that did not so much attack workers (that was left to the Thatcher years) as compromise it from within. So while *Wreckers'* first act ends with the victories of 1974 when 'the miners they came out again / And showed Ted

Heath the door' (p. 23), the second act charts the gradual swing of Labour to the right, selling out the dockers and the militant workers by an appeal to prosperity and surplus. As the Labour MP says about his vote against the dockers: 'We are now having to choose [. . .] between social goals and the health of the wealth-making machine. Put simply, we have to choose between the interests of the needy and the interests of profitable industry. As the former depends on the latter, we really have no choice' (p. 43). The play is schematic, and agitprop in its clarity of analysis, but it is pragmatic and non-dogmatic about the rapid shifts that really-existing circumstances on the ground can make to political strategy worked out from the top.

This play, and the uncertain note on which it ends (there is no clear programme of how to fight back), figures a transition point in Edgar's work that was also clear in his stylistically different and marginally earlier 'breakthrough' play *Destiny*. From 1977 on, Edgar still wrote theatre with a clear analysis of the situation, and with clear political values that might be called 'left', but the programmatic of his earlier agitprop work was gone, and a new inquiring scepticism and insistent critique of the failure of the left to actualise its programmes becomes the main thrust of Edgar's writing for the theatre.

Destiny[7]

At the time of writing (2011), when David Cameron has announced the failure of multiculturalism and immigration has once again become a lightning rod for fears about employment and financial security, it is useful to see the back-story to *Destiny* as coming from a similar socioeconomic context that links hostility to foreigners with fears about the economy. Edgar wrote *Destiny* in response to the connections among racism, xenophobia and fascism that he perceived to be coalescing as Britain came to terms with the end of its Empire.

In 1948, the British Nationality Act had granted British citizenship to citizens of the British Commonwealth, and the first West Indian workers arrived in Britain to begin Commonwealth immigration. By 1951, 15,000 people had arrived from the West Indies.

Jumping ahead to 1976, and taking into account the recent arrival of East African Asians expelled by Idi Amin, there were still only 1.85 million 'non-whites' in the UK population, 3 per cent of the total – and 40 per cent of those had been UK born. Nevertheless, the influx could seem momentous and troubling since, as historian Tony Judt observes, 'What made the difference, of course, was that these people were brown or black, and being Commonwealth citizens, had a presumptive right of permanent residence and eventually citizenship in the imperial metropole.'[8]

In spite of the availability of jobs and the relatively low numbers of immigrants, the Commonwealth Immigration Act of 1962 limited non-white immigration to the UK through a system of employment vouchers. From 1968, UK citizenship was restricted to persons with at least one British parent, and in 1971 a further act severely restricted the admission of the dependants of immigrants already in Britain (with clear racial consequences). Judt concludes: 'The net effect of these laws was to end non-European immigration into Britain less than twenty years after it had begun.'[9]

Threaded through the same time frame, however, was the first Race Relations Act (1965), which prohibited discrimination in public places and in employment, and provided penalties for incitement to race hatred. A second act in 1968 strengthened the weak first act, extending protections to housing and employment. Moreover, by the time of the main narrative of *Destiny*, immigrant workers were sufficiently embedded in some levels of the workforce to organise in protest against discrimination – for example, the 1974 strike by Asian workers at Imperial Typewriters in Leicester, struggling against bias that favoured white workers.

Destiny predicted the emergence of a populist fascist tendency, represented by the character David Maxwell in the play but remarkably like Nick Griffin, the current leader of the British National Party (BNP). In the 1970s, the National Front (NF) – a racialised political party originating in the 1960s, and predecessor of the BNP – called for the repatriation of Commonwealth immigrants and advocated other anti-immigrant positions as well as opposing 'liberalism' and international organisations such as the United Nations (UN) and

North Atlantic Treaty Organization (NATO). The NF grew in strength from 4,000 to 17,500 between 1968 and 1972.[10] Although it never won any seats in general elections, it won some local elections and did well in some by-elections. Its growing strength can be measured by the 1974 general election when the NF had ninety challengers in the October contest, and could therefore have a party political broadcast on the BBC along with the major parties. Martin Walker, *Guardian* journalist, claimed in 1977, the year of the play's London run, that the NF was 'the country's fourth largest political party'.[11]

The recognition of the virulence and the threat of the NF came to the public quite slowly. In 'Thirty Years On', the introduction to the most recent edition of *Destiny*, Edgar narrates the gradual development of Britain's recognition that the NF was a Nazi organisation. He points out the tendency of even liberal commentators to think claims that the NF was a Nazi front were exaggerated, 'a grandiose Leftist fantasy'.[12] Edgar argues that it was not until 1979 that evidence had mounted up enough to convince the public, signified by BBC Radio 4's description of the NF electoral outcome as 'the fascist vote' (p. xi).

The NF engaged in thuggish demonstrations and assaults in immigrant neighbourhoods, especially in north-east London, throughout this period. A report from the TUC, 'Blood on the Streets: Racial Attacks in East London', documented over one hundred such incidents including two murders between 1976 and 1978.[13] Mobilisation to come out against this behaviour gained momentum, with popular music becoming a vortex for anti-fascist campaigners. 'Rock Against Racism' mobilised activists from the Socialist Workers Party and other left groups, left Labour Party members and lots of non-aligned young people, culminating in a demonstration and concert, co-sponsored with the Anti-Nazi League, in April 1978 that was attended by 100,000 marchers.

Thus *Destiny* was performed in the thick of this situation. Edgar was absolutely committed to the project of making the true nature of the NF unmistakably clear to the British public. In addition to *Destiny*, Edgar was active in anti-fascist and anti-racist organising, and after the success of *Destiny*, became a major public spokesperson on this matter, speaking at more than fifty events of the Committee

Against Racism and Fascism and the Anti-Nazi League during the decade. He also wrote articles for a number of publications with titles such as 'The National Front *is* a Nazi Front' (italics in the original).[14] He opposed the coverage of the NF campaign by the BBC (very uncharacteristic of Edgar, who is a lifelong free speech advocate) and he also reviewed a number of books on the NF between 1977 and 1982 that were, in his opinion, insufficiently critical or accurate in their portrayal of the party.

In *Destiny*, Edgar portrays a meeting of his fictional Nation Forward party leaders on the occasion of Hitler's birthday party in 1968 – the same day Enoch Powell made his infamous 'Rivers of Blood' speech. Shadow Defence Minister in Edward Heath's Tory government, Powell was a powerful orator who had spoken out against immigration as early as 1953. In Birmingham on this occasion he delivered a powerful protest to the Labour government's Race Relations Bill, which would prohibit racial discrimination in housing, employment and public accommodations. Quoting and echoing Virgil about the Tiber 'foaming with blood', Powell pointed to the 1960s race riots in US cities as a warning of what immigration was bringing to Britain as well. Although he was sacked the next day by Heath, and denounced in the press, a Gallup poll taken two weeks later gave Powell's position a 74 per cent approval rating from the general public.

In setting his fictional cabal on the same day as the Powell speech, Edgar is able to link them and to insist on the extremity of both Powell's and the NF's positions. Susan Painter, who has written an extensive and illuminating analysis of *Destiny*, calls this 'the most shocking scene in the play'.[15] Focusing on the two especially despicable politicians, Cleaver and Maxwell, Edgar demonstrates how brutally racist they are on the eve of their attempt to hide their true radical fascism by building a new party (Nation Forward). They quote Powell, engage in anti-Semitic jokes, attack communism and praise Hitler as they celebrate his birthday. Edgar portrays the Nation Forward leadership to highlight the grievous and extreme NF party by analogy; however, he focuses most of the play's attention on the other ordinary British white people who come to join the fictional party, dramatising why the NF is able to appeal to them. The strength of this analysis lies in the embodied positionalities of those who were being attracted to extreme positions because of their own lived experiences of economic blight and post-imperial bitterness.

Act Two: Scene Two stages a meeting of the Taddley Patriotic League (TPL), a community-based pressure group trying to increase its political clout by considering joining forces with Nation Forward. The scene is brilliant in its orchestration of the way public meetings and grassroots political processes work, by fits and starts. TPL's sound equipment does not work, they have to pass the hat to collect enough to pay the hall rent and they apparently have trouble publishing enough copies of their newsletter – they operate on a shoestring. Maxwell, whom we last saw at Hitler's birthday party, represents Nation Forward, but he remains silent while members say what they think about becoming part of NF.

The main speakers are as divided in viewpoints and affiliations as they are united in 'patriotism', and with it resentment and open hatred of immigrants. Mrs Howard, a high Tory, misses the sense of values and purpose she associates with the middle classes, and the decline of Empire. She notes the 'silent majority' who 'watch their green and pleasant land become more and more like an Asian colony' (p. 41). She mentions people on fixed incomes and complains about the unions. Attwood, who is a union man from the foundry, says he is just as patriotic as she is, although he has voted Labour all his life. Now, however, with 'the many turbans in the canteen', he is worried about jobs for whites. He is explicitly racist: 'And I'll be quite frank about the blacks, I hate 'em. And no-one's doing bugger all about it' (pp. 41–2). Liz, a lower-middle-class woman married to a lecturer at the local poly, lives in West Thawston, a heavily immigrant community, and she complains about property values and mortgages. Tony, who is unemployed, points out that Turner's antique business (where Tony used to work) was taken over by a big firm. He suggests that even though they all have differences, they also have a lot in common. Only at this point does Maxwell step in to make his pitch for them to join the party:

Of course we disagree on many issues. But more, much more, unites us than divides us. It's an old saying, but you can change your class and your creed. But you can't change the blood in your veins [. . .]. More seriously we all of us observe a gradual decay, disintegration, in our fortunes and the fortunes of our nation. And perhaps there is a reason – that we have a common enemy. (p. 42)

The dynamics of the meeting bring together people who might on other occasions refuse to associate. The anger, resentments and sense of loss of belonging on the part of the group lead them to affiliate with a smooth-talking man with a vision of a larger political cause. This scene remains pertinent in 2012 – because, while wholly credible for its time, it contains clear presentiments of the anti-immigrant climate at the current conjuncture of economic recession, large-scale cuts to social welfare, unemployment and anti-multiculturalism policy.

The style of the play is Brechtian epic in terms of its short complete scenes and social *gestus* (described further below). Its characterisation, however, draws on Georg Lukács's social realism, which Edgar explicitly acknowledges in describing his dramaturgical technique not only in *Destiny*, but in *Albie Sachs* and *Mary Barnes* as well:

That is, unlike symbolist or absurdist or agitprop plays, they present what aspires to be a recognisable picture of human behaviour as it is commonly observed – but, unlike naturalistic drama, they set such a picture within an overall social-historical framework. The characters and situations are thus not selected solely because that's how things are – but because they represent a significant element in an analysis of a concrete social situation. The most popular definition of this endeavour is by Lukács, who said that social-realism presents 'typical' characters in a 'total' context. (p. 45)

For the Taddley Patriotic League, it is clear how Edgar chose and sculpted characters in keeping with this statement, but the most compelling demonstration of his technique comes from the opening scene of *Destiny*, where he deploys characters in what might be called emblematic realism.

Destiny's first scene summarises and compresses the 'back-story', functioning as a prologue to the rest of the play. Set in 1947 on the eve of Indian independence, in a British army barracks in the Punjab, it begins with the voice of Jawaharlal Pandit Nehru, the first prime minister of India, proclaiming 'At the stroke of the midnight hour, when the world sleeps, India will awake to life and freedom' (p. 5). On the back wall of the stage, Edgar calls for a painting of the violent suppression of the Indian Mutiny of 1919. This short scene introduces four characters who are historical types: Colonel Chandler, ruling elite, sentimental and 'a little liberal' (p. 12), whose character is shown by his proposal of a drink with his subordinate Sergeant Turner, as well as the Indian Sikh servant Khera, only to order Khera to give his drink to newly arrived Major Rolfe before he can take his first sip. This bit of comic business is only one of the humorous ironies of the scene. Khera is quite purposefully slow in his responses (in a perfect Brechtian *gestus* of his resistance), seeming not to grasp what he is asked to do – infuriating Turner but amusing the Colonel who observes, 'quite a bright little chap, that one' (p. 9). If Turner is a beleaguered sergeant trying to get things in order for the British withdrawal and the one who most directly deals with the 'natives' (which is why Khera resists him so well), Rolfe is a born-in-the-bone military man who wants to visit his old garrison once more before he goes home. Turner asks the Colonel if 'they' (the Indians) will be able to come to England to live, and the Colonel replies that Attlee, Britain's Labour prime minister, is preparing the legislation since India is in the Commonwealth. Further, he defends this policy as 'an obligation. We are the mother country, after all.' Rolfe counters, 'I have some reservations' (p. 10). The army men leave Khera to finish packing the trunk and Khera, alone on the stage, gets the last word and gesture. Pouring himself a whisky, he looks at the painting of the Indian Mutiny and then turns out to the audience for a toast: 'Civis – Brittanicus – Sum' (in Latin, 'I am a British citizen'). A final jibe at the ignorant British who assumed Khera ignorant, it also ironises the end of the British

Empire through reference to the Roman Empire (and St Paul's 'Civis Romanus sum'). Through iconic imagery, but also detailed realist portraiture, these four men become the primary subject-positions through which we experience the rise of fascism in the play.

The Colonel, the most benign of the English bunch, becomes a Tory MP, 'dignified, worthy. Out of time': the second scene begins with his funeral almost thirty years after Indian independence (p. 12). His nephew, Peter Crosby, is now standing for his seat in parliament. While Crosby is similarly mild and patrician, he is part of a new conservative mentality. He is a business type, following the stock-market and missing the reference to Enoch Powell when Jim Platt, the works manager at the local foundry and chairman of the constituency, cautions, 'bear in mind that we're in Enoch country and you'll be all right' (p. 13). In the same way that his uncle's inclusionary gesture of offering Khera a drink gave way to exclusion in his next breath, Crosby will change from a moderate who appeals to the Nation Forward Party not to harass immigrants at polling stations to a frightened politician, half sick of himself and his party, who will nevertheless make a statement to the press the night before the election clarifying his position 'against any further coloured immigration' (p. 83).

Sergeant Dennis Turner has returned to become a petit bourgeois shopkeeper who gets squeezed by large business interests. Coming back from India, he has opened an antique shop. Disaffected by what he perceives as a loss of values and increasing threats to his livelihood from both business and labour, he is dispossessed from his shop by a large real estate developer. The man who comes to break the news is Monty Goodman, very obviously Jewish but not a good man. In a double irony, he is both working for a corporation that later may support the neo-Fascists, and reinforcing (by embodying) anti-Semitic stereotypes. In the course of the intimidation of Turner, Goodman threatens him with violence from the Caribbean workers employed on the building project next door. When Turner plaintively asks why the powers Goodman represents would destroy his livelihood, the response is brutal (anticipating Gordon Gekko, in the 1987 film *Wall Street*, by ten years): 'Cos we, we make our money out of money. We covet on a global scale. We got cupidity beyond your wildest dreams of avarice. And you, the little man, the honest trader, know your basic handicap? You're suffering a gross deficiency of greed' (p. 28). Turner eventually becomes the candidate of the fictional far right in Edgar's text, the Nation Forward Party.

Major Lewis Rolfe comes back to England and goes into business, but he also stands in the first round for Colonel Chandler's Tory seat against Peter Crosby. He loses and, feeling bitter, talks to his friend Kershaw, an industrialist who owns the local foundry, about the need for a strong, possibly military-based, class war against workers, unions and immigrants. When Kershaw demurs, Rolfe appeals to Kershaw not to betray the lower middle class and the NCOs:

> Who, on all counts, have been betrayed. Their property no longer secure. Their social status, now, irrelevant. And in the place of what's important to them, national destiny and hope, we've given them . . . You see, Frank, it's not true that we've lost an Empire, haven't found a role. We have a role. As Europe's whipping boy. The one who's far worse off than you are. Kind of – awful warning system of the West. And to play that role, we must become more shoddy, threadbare, second-rate. Not even charming, quite unlovable. And for those – the people that I come from, that despair is a betrayal. (p. 23)

Thus Rolfe, whose subclass was identified when we were told in the very first scene that he did not go to prep school, represents a particular class interest that invested heavily in patriotism and the idea of a strong military, and in the aftermath of empire and the Second World War, experiences the erosion of their values and sense of national identity as well as the humiliation of national decline. Rolfe has become rich and powerful by the end of the play, one of the businessmen who considers lending financial backing to Nation Forward after they have taken 23 per cent of the vote.

Khera takes up the offer of British citizenship and comes to England, where he works in Kershaw's foundry and eventually acts as shop steward for the union, which he helped establish. The Asian workers protest against discrimination in wages and promotion, and

Khera leads the effort to get the union to support a ban on overtime, and wins. The play shows him in a leadership position as the labour dispute progresses to a lock-out and to violent confrontations with the National Forward people, brought in by management to break the stoppage. He is a fully integrated British citizen – a poster child for a later policy of multiculturalism – but of course he is also subject to discrimination and abuse. His colleague, Prakash Patel, is deported for participating in the strike, since he is technically an illegal immigrant, having fallen through the cracks when the Immigration Act of 1971 closed the borders.

Thus by establishing these four characters as pivotal to the action (Peter Crosby acting as surrogate for his uncle), and also as contrasting social types who react and participate in the political situation in Taddley according to their specific context, Edgar emphasises the through-line from the fall of empire starting in 1947 to the moment of reactionary racism and incipient fascism in 1976. In combining a muscular episodic structure with sharp observation-based characterisation, Edgar forged the writing style he has employed in a large number of his most effective plays, from the 1970s through to the present, exemplified by *Albert Speer* (2000) or *Daughters of the Revolution* (2003).

The Jail Diary of Albie Sachs

In 1963 a young South African advocate was imprisoned for his activities in opposition to apartheid. Under the newly established Ninety-Day Law, he could be held without formal charges and interrogated for up to ninety days; then he could be rearrested and held for another three months (ad infinitum). Black South African activists had been detained and imprisoned repeatedly in this manner, and some, like African National Congress (ANC) leader Nelson Mandela, had been convicted and imprisoned for life on Robben Island. Sachs had defended a number of these political activists, and succeeded in keeping some of them out of jail. Now he, a Jewish white man, was undergoing interrogation and detention in a moment when the state was increasing its surveillance and persecution of those who defied the national system of apartheid.

Telling the story of Albie Sachs's time in prison through a theatrical production was a form of activism in 1978, of solidarity with the ANC's opposition to the apartheid regime. Edgar adapted Sachs's memoir, *The Jail Diary of Albie Sachs*, for the theatre, creating an intense psychological portrait of the young white lawyer challenged to uphold his political beliefs by not 'ratting out' his comrades. Although Albie Sachs holds out through serious privation and the incredible loneliness and self-doubts of solitary confinement, he finally gives in. In typical fashion, Edgar finds a way to affirm the aspiration and the amount of human strength Sachs marshals to face his situation, even though he finally falters. At the end of the play, as Sachs prepares to leave for England, a former prisoner whom Sachs defended three times comes to see him with this message: 'I brought you greetings. There are many people, hope that when South Africa is free, we'll see you once again in Cape Town. Many people, won't forget, the things you did for them.'[16] Living in exile in England and Mozambique, Sachs continued to work against apartheid, losing his arm and sight in one eye in a car bomb in Maputo planted by South African security forces. Albie Sachs did return at the end of apartheid to help build the 'New South Africa', becoming a Constitutional Court judge (1994–2009). He has written a number of books about his experiences, most recently *The Strange Alchemy of Life and Law* (2009).

By the late 1970s, when Edgar adapted the *Jail Diaries*, international protests against apartheid had been gathering strength since the 1960s. Consumer boycotts, academic boycotts, attempts to persuade the British government to stop all trade and investment (unsuccessful) all marked the Anti-Apartheid Movement (AAM). Rock Against Racism, noted above for its anti-racist activities in connection with protesting against the NF, also played a role. Jerry Dammers, one of RAR's leaders, wrote 'Free Nelson Mandela' for his band, the Special A.K.A. In 1986, Dammers and Dali Tambo, the son of ANC president Oliver Tambo, formed 'Artists Against Apartheid'. They invited a diverse range of artists and performers to take part in a Freedom Festival on Clapham Common in London. Over 250,000 people from all sections of British society attended. The theatre community was also involved in anti-apartheid work, beginning in 1963 when forty-five prominent British playwrights signed a Declaration announcing that they had instructed their agents to insert a clause in all future contracts automatically refusing performing rights in any theatre where discrimination on grounds of colour occurred. British artists organised boycotts of touring to South Africa and participating in South African productions, and in 1976 British Equity voted not to sell its programmes to South African television and not to cover performers going to South Africa with Equity contracts.

In the late 1970s, however, many people still did not know enough about the details of apartheid to join the efforts to pressure for change. The actor who played Albie Sachs in the original production, Peter McEnery, for example, had never heard of Sachs: 'I'm not really a political animal at all and I didn't know about Albie Sachs – not a lot of people did, though everyone knew about racism and apartheid at the time.'[17] He was attracted to the role because of its theatricality and its challenges – especially for the main character: 'the leading actor has to be onstage the whole time, so there's no going off for any reason whatsoever, and he has to maintain that through-line and learn it all as a demonstration of the art of theatre'.[18] It is interesting to contrast his point of view with that of Ann Mitchell who played Brenda in *Mary Barnes*, who had read R. D. Laing and Joe Berke before taking the role, and who was fully committed to the ideas of the community she helped portray. Thus it is possible to see a range of relationships between artists and materials in Edgar's plays of this period – political plays do not always entail politically engaged performances, but sometimes they do, and other times they affect those who perform in them.

The craft of Edgar's adaptation can been seen in the subtle additions and resequencing in his modifications to the memoir. Building suspense in some scenes, achieving irony by juxtaposition in others, he sharpens the dramatic qualities of Sachs's introspective memoir. The play is mostly about an individual's struggle with his own convictions and human limitations, but Edgar makes sure the sociopolitical aspects keep centre-stage. For example, the play opens with a fictional address by the twenty-nine-year-old Sachs to a meeting (probably of an anti-apartheid group), in which he explains the new Ninety-Day Detention Act which is being used against whites as well as blacks for the first time in an escalation of attempts to repress the opposition against apartheid. Sachs tells his audience that this law makes it clear how scared the government is in the face of their opposition: 'And that's not bad. It's good, that they're so scared, they're scared enough to use it on the whites, on us, because it makes *us* choose what side we're on, it tells us, and we didn't know, it tells us what it's like' (pp. 3–4; italics in original). Thus the audience addressed is a white audience, and the message is a challenge to choose sides and be aware of the import of the law. In an analogous move, the play is addressing British whites in the late 1970s (like Peter McEnery) who could be politicised by understanding the nature of the repression in South Africa through the paradigmatic treatment and experiences of Albie Sachs. In the following scene, Sachs repeats the phrase 'so this is what it's like' (p. 4) to himself shortly after seeing his cell. His private journey of discovery of what it is like begins with his own detention.

When compared with the horrors revealed to have been perpetrated at Abu Ghraib or in other military prisons in recent years, Sachs's treatment of solitary confinement, sleep deprivation and psychological abuse may seem almost quaint. But Sachs hears the beatings of the black prisoners held in adjoining cells, and what the memoir and Edgar's play makes clear is how institutionalised and state-sponsored violence – including psychological tactics – eats away even the most privileged and self-confident egos. Edgar also underscores a link between the individual and the community of activists by portraying how isolation as a tactic breaks down the connections to the larger movement: 'And I abhor its [apartheid's] cunning. What it's done to me, by splitting me from my comrades, isolating me. Removing me from that collective strength, that stops me from being just a white man with an upset conscience, places me in history, and gives my conscience scale' (p. 51). Questioning his own sanity at one point, Sachs shows how subjectivity defines itself only in relation to others, and how even a strong ego can deteriorate in the face of constant hostility and isolation.

McEnery stressed the theatricality of the play as one of the key aspects that attracted him to it. Sachs's diary contains the theatrical material that allowed Edgar's play to create further levels of meta-theatricality: Sachs had himself imagined writing a play to dramatise his situation, with himself as the actor speaking the line, 'So this is what it is like'. Edgar, having already imagined the first scene in which Sachs gives a speech to an audience (replete with the theatrical set-up), places Sachs's speculations about performing at the end of the first act and has Sachs/McEnery act it out as he imagines it. For the opening of the play, Sachs wants Africans on stage singing and he describes a stage set which would show prisoners seen through gauze cubes. He imagines speaking in direct address to the audience, and telling them of his ideas about writing the play, 'maybe even somewhere having the playwright writing it' (p. 48). However, he comes to think that the most crucial part would be to give his audiences a concrete idea of the experience of isolation. In his diary, Sachs imagines making his audience sit and stare at a blank screen for three minutes in silence. Edgar adapts this for an actual stage by shortening the time lapse to two minutes, and by using Sachs's body as the focus rather than a screen. McEnery describes the effect of this sequence in performance: 'I lay on the bed and then I'd start internally counting for say about half a minute, and then I'd turn over and say another half a minute. But the point is stillness, not movement or anything to break that. And the audience would, without fail, just focus; it was quite, quite extraordinary.'[19]

The real Albie Sachs was able to see the play in October 1988, and view his audiences experiencing this moment. He attended a special benefit performance at the Young Vic in which five actors who had previously been in the play in various productions were on stage as he himself sat in the audience. Edgar brought him up on stage after the performance to sustained applause, and later Sachs recounted his thoughts as he mounted the stage: 'Everybody is waiting, this is the moment where the evening ceases to be about a certain part of my life and actually becomes another part of my life.'[20]

The connection between the real Albie Sachs, David Edgar and the theatre has remanifested in recent times. In October 2011, Sachs spoke at a theatre conference at York University on 'Things

Unspeakable: Theatre and Human Rights' organised by Mary Luckhurst and Emilie Morin. Among the other keynote speakers was David Edgar.

Mary Barnes

Starting in 1965, and for several years thereafter, Mary Barnes, a woman who had been diagnosed as schizophrenic, came to live at a place called Kingsley Hall. There, under the care of psychiatrist Joe Berke, a follower of R. D. Laing, Barnes went through a process of regression therapy from which she emerged at least partially healed. She also developed a new creative vocation as a painter, and had begun to establish her identity as an artist. Today, one can still see her artwork online and, in 2010, a retrospective exhibition of her work took place in Hackney, east London, not too far away from where she lived at Kingsley Hall.[21] In 1978, Edgar adapted the memoir, written by Barnes and Berke, *Mary Barnes: Two Accounts of a Journey Through Madness*, for the theatre, writing one of his most compelling and successful dramas.

Who were Berke and Laing? What was Kingsley Hall? Who, for that matter, was Mary Barnes? In order to answer any of these specific questions, it is necessary to journey back to the late 1960s' anti-psychiatry movement, and to the social experiments of utopian communities attempted by many different constituencies in the 1960s and 1970s, as well as to the particular people involved.

The 'anti-psychiatry movement' is only one of the names for the large-scale revolution in how ordinary people came to deal with mental 'problems' from the 1960s on. Sometimes called the 'Human Potential Movement', other times 'Self-Actualisation', or identified by practices such as 'Awareness Training', 'Encounter Groups' or 'Transactional Analysis', many programmes and therapies associated with this movement became popularised through magazines like *Psychology Today*, which started publishing in 1967 for a non-specialist general public interested in alternative therapies, and mental health and wellbeing. Popular regimes such as Erhard Seminars Training (known as 'est') or transactional analysis (TA) were less radical and more populist than the concentrated and serious work being done by anti-psychiatrists such as Erving Goffman, Michel Foucault, Thomas Szasz and R. D. Laing. These social scientists, philosophers and practising psychiatrists (in the case of Laing and Szasz) criticised the medical community for its inhumane treatment of mentally ill patients in hospitals and asylums and for resorting to treatments that were more destructive than healing (heavy doses of drugs, electroshock therapy, lobotomy).

Many ordinary people followed some programme of therapy or training in order to improve their mental state and to reduce stress and anxiety – these were often group therapies, and varied widely in their effectiveness and authority. As self-help activities became widely available and popular among the Western middle-class world starting in the 1960s and lasting through to the 'New Age' therapies of today, radical attempts to criticise the medical establishment for inhumane treatment of those diagnosed as mentally ill, and alternative experiments with other means of dealing with mental illness, came to the fore along with the more popular practices. Mary Barnes, diagnosed as schizophrenic and hospitalised without any positive results, heard about Laing's radical egalitarian ideas about mental illness, and determined to be a part of his residential community where she might pursue a different path to healing.

Kingsley Hall, where Mary lived and was treated, was a therapeutic community established by Laing in London's East End. Between 1964 and 1970, a group of Laingian psychiatrists set up an exemplary community and treatment space where non-traditional forms of therapy could be developed and deployed. As with many 1960s collectives, this one aspired to egalitarian principles and to allow as much freedom as possible to patients to find and take their own paths towards recovery. Laing was the leading proponent of this alternative approach to madness. Through important publications as well as his clinical practice, he popularised the critique of psychiatry as commonly practised as an inhuman response to others' pain that did not help them and, in fact, often harmed them more than their original state of mind.

In a series of bestselling books (*The Divided Self*, 1960; *The Self and Others*, 1961; *The Politics of Experience*, 1967; *The Politics of the Family*, 1971), Laing set out the thesis that schizophrenia is the result of a 'divided self' formed of contradictory messages in early life, usually from one's parents, which leave the person in a contradictory double bind. Behaviour and especially language that might seem babble actually could be understood as a metaphorical code that signals this internal psychic impasse. Combining existentialism and Marxism, Laing understood psychosis as induced by a combination of social and familial interaction that shaped subjectivity: 'By the time the new human being is fifteen or so, we are left with a being like ourselves, a half-crazed creature more or less well adjusted to a mad world. This is normality in our present age.'[22] Laing was extremely prominent in the 1960s, achieving a kind of guru status in the anti-psychiatry movement and in popular culture. He lost most of his influence, however, in the 1980s because significant scientific research had since shown that schizophrenia can be treated, at least in part, through pharmacology and psycho-surgical techniques.

When Laing opened Kingsley Hall in 1965, the site contained a history which included in its earlier days serving as a community centre, a rallying point for pacifists, suffragettes, social/educational service campaigners – a very 'political' place – and even Mahatma Gandhi's residence in the 1930s, while he was negotiating with the British government. Laing's experimental community there began in 1965, was most intense during its first two years, then slowly faded until it lost its lease in 1970 and closed up shop, though some of its members continued its practices elsewhere.[23] Joe Berke, the American psychiatrist who was Mary's primary care-giver, had come over from the US to work with Laing.

The plan was to set up a living situation that offered so much freedom that it could accommodate the 'eccentric' and 'chaotic' behaviours often associated with schizophrenia. Efforts were made to eliminate all elements of hierarchy, authority, rules, organisation or any other distinguishing principles that might give some members power or influence over others (thereby making some more free than others). Not only does this type of community seek to expand freedom to the very fullest within its boundaries, it implicitly calls for the same change in the larger society, because it locates the source of 'schizophrenia' in the many ways in which the larger society (and its microcosmia, such as the family) is overtly or covertly repressive.

In the play *Mary Barnes*, the community also represents many other 'alternative' communities developed during the 1960s: most of them founded by people who felt themselves oppressed by conventional society and sought to make small-scale utopias where freedom was maximised for all. Sometimes this meant a collective farm growing organic food, or a spiritual group on an ashram, or an artists' collective living above a gallery space or in a warehouse.

Following Edgar's attention to the tendency of human beings to fall short of their ideals, and his commitment to what I have elsewhere called the principle of 'retrieval' – the necessity of keeping on keeping on even in the face of disillusionment and concrete setbacks – *Mary Barnes* is both about Mary's partial recovery and about the failure of the communal experiment to pull off a long-term realisation of its goals. The play juxtaposes scenes in Mary's room where her intense relationship with Eddie, her therapist, takes primary focus, with scenes in the common spaces of the house where communal meals, informal meetings and conversations take place, and where Mary displays her artwork as the play moves on in time.

The play combines intensely personal two-character interactions with scenes of volatile group dynamics to produce the most emotionally intense and at times almost chaotic play Edgar has ever written. The actors who played the key roles (Simon Callow as Eddie, the Joe Berke figure, and Patti Love as Mary) delved into creating their characters with what Callow has described as method acting intensity.[24] Mary demands total attention and unconditional love from Eddie, and pushes him to the limit again and again, acting as a small child in a middle-aged body. She smears her own shit all over herself and he cleans her up; she cuddles him as if he were her mother; she monopolises his time and attention as if she were the only person in his life. At one point, Mary throws a chair at another person in the house because Eddie has left her to take a phone call. When he comes back and sees what happens, he talks to her about it:

Eddie   It's cos I went away. And you were jealous. Threw the chair cos she was coming in on you. You felt possessed. That made you angry.

Mary (*whispers*)   No. Not angry with you, Eddie.

[. . .]

Eddie   Yuh, Mary, you were angry with me.

Mary (*whispers*)   No, no.

Getting angry.

No, you know I'd not be angry with you, Eddie!

Eddie   Mary, you look angry now.

Mary (*hits* **Eddie** *on the chest*)   No! No! No! Confuse me. No, not angry, Eddie.

Eddie   Hey, is that all you can hit, Mary?

Mary (*hits* **Eddie**)   No! No! No!

Eddie   Hey, I bet you can hit me more than that.

Mary (*grunting as she hits* **Eddie**)   Uh. Uh. Uh. Uh. Uh.

[. . .]

Eddie   Mary. You bit my ear. You hit me. Yuh? And I'm still here. And I bit you. And you're fine. Anger doesn't hurt me, and it doesn't kill you either. Both OK.[25]

Eddie and Mary interact in terms of an intense focused commitment to each other; as a result of this extraordinary 'therapy' and Mary's discovery of her art talent, she begins to get better. In this regard, the play pays homage to Laing's vision, Berke's healing skills, and Mary's determination and agency.

However, the group dynamics exhibited within the larger community counterbalance this affirmative vision. Hugo (the Laing figure) had suggested at the very outset that they should eat together every day in the public space. Consequently, Edgar stages two scenes that have deliberate resemblances to Last Supper meals and also to political meetings, like those other Edgar plays about how groups of people negotiate their living together: *Destiny*, *Maydays* (1983), *The Shape of the Table* (1990) and *The Prisoner's Dilemma* (2001). These dinner table scenes reveal ways in which a number of individual factors – age, ambition, personality, skills, empathy – combine with external events, ideological principles, prejudices, ritual and social dynamics to produce the patterns of cooperation and conflict characteristic of family gatherings, public meetings, and community events. Hugo has said: 'We must avoid hierarchies, chains of authority, unspoken rules. Or we should at least speak our unspoken rules' (pp. 97–8). This was certainly a major ambition of many countercultural groups during the 1960s, but outsiders were always sceptical about such equality being sustainable.

At the first of the two such dinners dramatised, the psychiatrists begin by bonding through focusing on the common enemy: conventional psychiatry. Brenda tries to alter the direction slightly by providing a traditionally Marxist position, suggesting that mental illness is a product of the reduction of humans to commodities. The male psychiatrists do not take this up, but one is prompted to tell of 'drapetomania', a piece of pseudo-science from the antebellum southern US which claimed that drapetomania was a mental illness which only applied to 'Negro' slaves, encouraging their fantasies about running away. Edgar may be being a little sly with this allusion: the historical creator of the notion of drapetomania claimed that it was caused by an excessive sense of equality between masters and slaves (though that point is not made in the play). Beth, one of the 'patients', partly gets this reference and responds to it. Her answer, though, leads to open conflict, first between Brenda and the 'shrinks', and then among the 'shrinks' themselves: Brenda continues to maintain her left-wing views about authority and state violence, but Douglas and Eddie begin to fall out about the role of perception in authority and violence, while Hugo attributes these evils to hypocrisy and self-deception. Mary responds to the increasingly conflictual atmosphere by picking a fight with Beth, and this is headed for serious struggle when the action is interrupted by the breaking of windows by people from the outside neighbourhood – expressing their unhappiness, so it is thought, with the community for bringing into their midst 'nutters, perverts, layabouts' (p. 119). In response to this vandalism, Douglas calls the police, and by calling in heretofore invalid outside authority, begins the erosion of their 'liberated zone'.

The second dinner scene, although it presumably takes place some time later than the first one, begins with Hugo trying to regain the earlier 'us against them' unity that the psychiatrists had at the beginning of the first meal, but Douglas is not having any of it. Douglas is hostile from the first, and subsequently Hugo matches him. Things deteriorate from there, Douglas charging the others with dishonesty for not acknowledging that there are informal rules structuring life in the community. Some of these have to do – from Douglas's point of view – with the excessive licence granted to Mary Barnes, who, he notes, has expanded from her room to fill the house with her paintings (which now cover many of the walls). He claims that she is, bit by bit, taking over the life of the community. This leads to open physical fighting between Mary and one of the other patients, and to Douglas's departure from the house. It also leads to Mary using biblical language and symbols (bread and wine) to take on a redemptive role in keeping with the Last Supper theme. This, too, because of her religiosity, seems to be part of her recovery process. These two scenes show the social dynamics internal to the group that make the goals of the community difficult to achieve while also drawing attention to the difficulty of fulfilling the ideals on which it was founded.

Ann Mitchell describes the experiences of the actors in the original production of *Mary Barnes*. She notes the actors' awareness of the dynamics I've been describing:

> It's clear this is a cast utterly committed to the work. Peter Farrago [the director] has the foresight and courage to let us talk and argue for a very long time. We're getting to know each other and what each will bring to the table. This company want and need to honour the very soul of this piece – we all have a personal connection of some kind with the material and soon we start to 'become' our characters. I'm playing the only female

therapist in the play, which means I end up doing a lot of mothering on and off the stage [. . .]. The actors playing the therapists begin to become powerful and competitive and the actors playing the 'patients' eye us warily![26]

The play and its production 'honoured' Mary Barnes and the remarkable community that nurtured her without ducking the difficult parts of the journey or sentimentalising the human failings that made their project difficult to sustain. Edgar finds a way to celebrate as well as critique the particular story and the wider generational impulse it represented.

Conclusion

By the end of the decade, Edgar had established himself as a major British playwright. His plays had been performed in Europe and the US, and a number were broadcast on television (including *Destiny* and *The Jail Diary of Albie Sachs*). Counting his agitprop plays, he wrote twenty-four full-length plays during the 1970s.

In 1980, he adapted Charles Dickens's massive novel, *Nicholas Nickleby*, for the RSC. Originally played over two nights, it featured more than one hundred characters. It was extremely successful in the UK and also on Broadway, winning the 1980 Best Play Award from the Society of West End Theatres and the Laurence Olivier Award, and in 1982 the Tony Award for Best Play. In the three decades since, Edgar has created a range of ambitious works for the theatre, including his response in the 1990s to the collapse of socialism in three plays set in eastern Europe: *The Shape of the Table* (1990), *Pentecost* (1994) and *The Prisoner's Dilemma* (2001). In addition, he has continued to write about British racism and multiculturalism in such plays as *Playing with Fire* (2005) and *Testing the Echo* (2008). He also continues to experiment with form, whether in the pair of plays designed to be produced together as *Continental Divide* (2003) about California politics, or in the short play *Black Tulips*, written for Nicolas Kent's collection of Afghanistan plays, *The Great Game* (2009).

Edgar's prose writings appear frequently in the *Guardian* and the *London Review of Books*, where he can be found writing about political issues, theatre past and present, or his own work. In 2011, he completed a four-year project – *Written on the Heart* – for the 400th anniversary of the King James Bible, which was produced in October by the RSC, directed by Gregory Doran. In February, some months before the actual production premiered, Edgar published a long article about the history and politics of the Bible's English translations and their relationship to the English Reformation, which constitutes the main focus of the play: Edgar dramatises the political implications of the translators' word choices, and the way the translations negotiate the religious and state battles of the time (late sixteenth and early seventeenth centuries).[27] His long career as a political thinker and writer continues apace.

CHAPTER 4
DOCUMENTS

This chapter focuses on the theatre of the 1970s in the words of those who created it. When preparing this book, I contacted a number of theatre artists involved in the original stage productions of the key plays featured in Chapter 3.[1] I invited them to share, in their own words, their memories of working on these shows and their reflections more generally on British theatre of the 1970s. The following is made up of the responses I received, along with original archival and interview material. Entries are listed alphabetically by surname.

James Aubrey

The actor James Aubrey played the role of the Constable in the original production of Brenton's Magnificence *(1973) at the Royal Court Theatre. The following letter, dated 5 June 1984, was written in reply to an enquiry about the production from theatre scholar Philip Roberts. Aubrey died in 2010.*

The overriding memory I have of *Magnificence* is of the wonderful Russian actor Nikolaj Ryjtkov who played Lenin and the old tramp. At the beginning of the evening, at least half an hour before the play began, Nikolaj would conceal himself under a pile of newspapers on the set. As there was no curtain the audience could see the set from the moment they came in – Nikolaj had to remain undetected and still for that half hour and again for about forty minutes into the show, when suddenly he would rise from the centre of the stage to the amazement of the characters and the audience. This is quite a common Brenton technique – I think he uses it in *Hitler Dances* (1972) – and is a startling effect. The reason one is impressed by

Nikolaj's discipline is this: he worked with Stanislavsky at the Moscow Art Theatre until 1936 when he was arrested for his knowledge and study of Esperanto. (Prior to this, out of interest, because of his resemblance to Lenin he would tour football stadiums all over the USSR reciting Lenin's speeches and imitating his mannerisms and speech – this after studying all the old newsreels. One of his 'tricks', which he used in Russia, he also incorporated into his performance at the Royal Court. He would cut out a maroon-coloured piece of tinsel in the shape of a tiny triangle and glue it to the eyelid of his right eye. As he walked on to the stage he would pace in a classic Lenin style and slowly turn his head towards the audience – he would then blink – the lights would catch the tinsel and his eye would flash red – to an astonishing effect.) Back to the newspapers: Nikolaj was in Siberia for eighteen years – starved and brutally beaten – his jaw was wired together, having been broken so many times. But the remarkable discipline of lying for over an hour under the newspapers came from being forced whilst in Siberia to grab whatever sleep he could and at whatever time during the day. He could lie down absolutely motionless for two, three, four hours and wake himself automatically whenever he chose. He was released in 1954 and escaped to the British Embassy in Austria whilst on an international Esperanto speakers' conference in 1957. He died in the late 1970s. I gave him Mao Tse-Tung's *Thoughts* in Esperanto on the opening night – he was visibly moved.

One's memories of productions inevitably I suppose are always subjective. I played the part of a police constable in a front cloth scene with Len Fenton – Brenton's father, as you may know, was a policeman. In the scene there was quite a lot of chat about 'fathers' – it so happened that my own father died during the run – that made the comedy quite difficult to play – but we got the laughs back after a few days – what troupers!

It was the second time I had worked with Max [Stafford-Clark, the director] – the first time was a disastrous production of [Peter Shaffer's] *Royal Hunt of the Sun* at the Palace Theatre, Watford. Max's technique, which is rare and admirable, is to encourage the actors to contribute and create, thereby creating a genuine ensemble. This I think we achieved. And of course carried on that tradition – i.e. of ensemble that the Royal Court has developed since George Devine via Bill [Gaskill]. Perhaps because it was my first production at the Court – I went on to do another four plays over the years – I wasn't aware of it being the end of the Gaskill era – but of course years later I appreciated that it was the passing on of the baton as it were to Max and beyond. It is still the best theatre in London.

Howard Barker

Howard Barker's playwriting of the 1970s is characterised by bitter satire, despair at the 'state of England' and mesmerising poetic intensity. His major plays of the decade include Claw *(Open Space, 1975),* Stripwell *(Royal Court, 1975),* Fair Slaughter *(Royal Court, 1977),* That Good Between Us *(RSC Warehouse, 1977),* Downchild *(written in 1977, staged by the RSC at the Barbican Pit, 1985),* The Love of a Good Man *(Crucible, Sheffield, 1978) and* The Hang of the Gaol *(RSC Warehouse, 1978). The following is an interview Barker gave to the author, hitherto unpublished, dated 13 October 1996.*

CM: Over a prolific ten-year period (from the staging of *Claw* in 1975, to that of *Downchild* in 1985), many of your plays foregrounded politicians as central characters. Why has the politician-character proved such an enduring fascination for you in theatre?

HB: The exercise of power – presumed or real – had a natural appeal to me before I had uncovered an urge to write tragedy, for which no social democratic political figure could be an appropriate protagonist. When I moved towards plays like *Victory* [1983] or *Power of the Dog* [1984] I had discerned that what I required was a narrative about the *evasion* of authority and not the exercise of authority. Until then, English political types figured extensively in my work because the failure to be heroic – surely what characterised all English politics in the 1970s – brought these individuals into the scope of satire. I was a satirist because I was trying to evade social realism. I had not found an aesthetic that would edge me beyond satire, and when I found it, the objects of the satire disappeared with it.

CM: In an interview with *Theatre Quarterly* in 1981, you identify *Claw* and *Downchild* – along with other plays including *The Hang of the Gaol* – as 'State of England' plays.[2] You also affirm that *Downchild* will be the last play of this kind. The departure from 'State of England' dramaturgy seems to have been a major turning point in your approach to playwriting in general, and dramatic form in particular. What prompted you to move away from writing about contemporary political malaise and institutional decline, and to move more forcefully into myth and history?

HB: One obvious reason was that too many people were doing it. It didn't require me. I had said it . . . I mean, I had said all *I* had to say . . . about the corruptibility of ideals, for example, about the erosion of meaning, the haemorrhage of meaning from grand and eloquent strategies. I had also been reacting against the specifically English milieu, which was small, contaminated with journalistic technique. I had come to hate news. The nearer drama gets to news the more poverty-struck it becomes. I ceased listening to news. I was also inventing a specific dramatic language for emotions and subjects behind the 'issue'. Perhaps also, the critical abuse which was poured over plays like *The Loud Boy's Life* [1980] made me shrink from the contemporary in the obvious sense (all my texts are obviously contemporary, but they are metaphorical . . .). This particular play was unrealistic . . . I saw I had to get even less 'realistic' . . . Furthermore, I do not think, in the end, it is worth an artist's while to engage with characters he essentially holds in contempt. I had not held Fricker [in *A Loud Boy's Life*] in contempt at all . . . but others I had . . . and this is what satire is, and I did not feel my emotions were properly engaged . . . I had to escape that. Also, I did not want to position myself as anyone's 'defender', a spokesman for anything. I do not think theatre is about social correction. Its civilising aspects did not seem to lie in this area at all. I had originally titled *A Passion in Six Days* [1983] 'The Curse of Debate . . .'. They wouldn't accept that as a title. But it was what I felt.

CM: In *The Loud Boy's Life*, *A Passion in Six Days* and *Downchild*, in particular, critics attempted to trace the relationship between plays and actual political events, between the characters and existing politicians. How far is this search for authenticity a distracting critical fetish? How far *were* these plays directly influenced by their contemporary political milieu?

HB: Critics are journalists. The entire contemporary political theatre was generated by journalistic instincts, far from my own. [Michael] Billington [theatre critic for the *Guardian*] loved to see the 'dramatisation' of an issue, a political event. This is a miserable function for a great art form. To 'dramatise' something is to confess the inability of theatre to be its own first cause. So if I had been inspired by a piece of news, I improvised wildly on the news, the news was never enough for me. I detest research. Research is for academics, not artists. This research destroys the autonomy of the drama, which cannot and should not be controlled by a political intention.

CM: Plays such as *Claw* and *Downchild* insist on the relationship between politicians and criminality. Other dramatists have explored this relationship but your plays – presumably since they do not adopt a party political stance – refrain from castigating it in a conventional moral way. Can you explain your interests in this relationship?

HB: I have never admired or hypervalued criminals. Nor have they exercised a fascination over me. On the contrary I find criminal life dull, itself exceedingly conventional. The prurience of bourgeois intellectuals in this field is repellent to me . . . it can be found at all levels of the intelligentsia, not least in the liberal institutions like the Royal Court. Of course there's a huge sexual investment in this, as in all close inspection of 'working-class' society. The proposition that criminals are in opposition to society is of course absurd. They are no more oppositional than rock stars. I suspect, looking back, to throw criminals and social democratic politicians of the 1970s into close relations only suggested to me a sort of mundane, sordid set of transactions typical of a moment of decadence . . . I can't refine it further than that. There is despair in all this, the plays seem to me a testament of despair. I haven't ceased to feel that, all I have done is to shift the place where I think drama operates to an area of tragedy as opposed to despair and tragedy is health, pain is health. 'Throwing light' on scandals is a poor occupation for a serious dramatist. It merely puts you into the endless conversation about public life, it isn't very brave, it doesn't test your tolerances because the entire audience is alongside you. They come equipped with moral conventions and you merely nourish them. For me, drama is about the rupturing of tolerances.

CM: Your focus upon *individual* characters within institutional structures, and your avoidance of stereotype despite the satirical impulse which underscores your 'State of England' plays, suggest that you are less interested in examining political dogma and more concerned with exposing those moments when personal ideological commitment is destabilised and public perceptions subverted. How far does this account for your statement that you are not a very good 'political' dramatist?

HB: It's quite true I had no fixed scale against which to measure the characters of these plays. I did not wish to make a play into a demonstration, a QED, even if I was certain of my own Marxist qualifications. I already dimly sensed that drama is about oscillation, it is tender, it is not solid, a hard weapon of struggle. I could never bring myself to gratify my own ideological prejudices, something always usurped it – the autonomy of the characters always asserted itself, pushing down the satire, as you suggest. What does Axt stand for in *A Passion in Six Days*, after all? It's hard to say. Certainly what he is looking for isn't available from a political programme.

CM: Would you like to see your 'State of England' plays revived with greater frequency?

HB: Perhaps in time they will be, but only when the 'issue' elements are rinsed out of them, when they seem to be about the melancholy of defused ambitions rather than any rage that might attach to them. I think *Fair Slaughter* could stand this now . . . the pity of Old Gocher's blind defence of dead and indeed – cruel – ideology, Downchild's sexual servitude, Scadding's faith in sexual love when all else has been betrayed . . . things like that . . .

Ian Blower

The actor Ian Blower played the role of Jack in the original production of Churchill's Vinegar Tom *(1976).*

What do I remember about *Vinegar Tom*? I remember the rehearsal room in Marylebone and Caryl's wonderful generosity when we were subjecting her work to a process not unlike worms turning over the compost. She would go away and come back with more and off we'd go again. I remember the creative energy in the room and the sense that something lay just within our grasp if only we could crack the code and bring it into being. I also remember the best fish and chip shop in the world (just down the road), numerous trips to the pub, and a discussion about Kramer and Sprenger.[3]

The best political work, of course, never mentions the word 'politics'. The final scene of the play, in which Kramer and Sprenger appear as music hall characters, cuts right across the songs and music that precede it with an 'in your face, there you are, that's what it's all about' sense of purpose. The doubters were won over and the scene stayed in the play. I suspect we didn't want the audience to get too comfortable.

My memory gets a little hazy after that but I do remember that, when we were on tour, the moment the lights went down and [the actor] Roger Allam said 'Am I the devil?' you could feel the hair rise on the back of your neck in anticipation of the journey to come.[4]

I recently read an interview with the producer of *Coronation Street* which said that the days were over when television drama could sit back and leave it to the imagination, and that it now had to compete with the juggernauts of 'event' and 'reality' television. In the days when content has taken a back seat to form in all aspects of our lives, I think back with great fondness to that little rehearsal room in

Marylebone and what appeared to us to be the seamless synthesis of both.

[Email to the author, 28 July 2011]

Howard Brenton

Howard Brenton gave the following interview to the author on 1 July 2011 in London.

CM: Your recent plays *Paul* [2005], *In Extremis* [2006] and *Anne Boleyn* [2010] are extraordinary meditations on the power of faith. Some of your earlier plays – *Wesley* [1970], *Magnificence* [1973], *Pravda* [with David Hare, 1985] – also focus on characters who pursue their passions or ideas to extremes in the uncompromising manner of Ibsen's Brand: 'all or nothing'. I wonder if extremity interests you because it opens a way of exploring the social structure and its limitations?

HB: Yes it is but you want 'all or nothing' characters because you're a storyteller. Dramatists go for extreme moments of stress on the stage to illustrate normal everyday life; it's nothing unusual. In the early 1970s, we were much taken with calling ourselves neo-Jacobeans, for reasons of publicity more than anything, and of course the model was good because you were able to loot the Shakespearean tradition for your own purposes and break the hold of Brecht on your mind. So extreme figures like Jed in *Magnificence* or Lambert in *Pravda* naturally came to mind.

CM: In the late 1960s, you worked with Chris Parr in Bradford and the Brighton Combination before that. *Revenge* [1969] was staged at the Royal Court and, of course, you wrote for Portable Theatre. What sort of possibilities did you see in theatre in those early days?

HB: The world felt very unstable in the late 1960s and early 1970s and your response as a writer was to try and destabilise the art which you tried to practise, you felt the need for new forms to express a difficult time. That made you think of a new Jacobean style or plays like *Magnificence* where you deliberately used clashing styles – one scene would be naturalistic, the next would be cartoon-like, and the two would clash, and you'd follow within each scene what the scene needed. It drove some people mad. I remember Lindsay Anderson exploding when he saw *Magnificence*, saying 'It has no stylistic consistency!' I said, 'No, it doesn't, Lindsay, of course it doesn't!'

The other night I went to this brilliant concert with Maurizio Pollini playing Boulez's incredible Second Sonata, which was written in 1948. Boulez pursued a scorched-earth policy: he said, after the Second World War, after the Nazis, no more Brahms! There was the same feeling when we were starting in the late 1960s, that's what we were after. Because of the feeling of instability: no more John Osborne, no more plays in rooms, no more boulevard or gag writing (although, of course, our shows are full of gags . . .). This may happen with every young generation, I don't know, but that sense of instability was very strong, and hopeful too. I remember in 1968 – it's awful to bang on about 1968 nearly fifty years later – but you really did think, 'Oh my God, there's going to be a revolution in France, the world is going to change *utterly*', but it didn't, and then there was a terrible fall-out as it all went bad and decayed into terrorist groups and confusion on the left. What happened then was the beginning of what we now can see as the first capitalist crisis when, unfortunately, Labour governments were in power.

CM: You were in Paris in 1969 and you've talked about the impact of the Situationists on your own thinking and the style of your work.

HB: Yes. There were two books which influenced me very strongly. One I found in the school library when I was fifteen: Sartre's little book called *Existentialism and Humanism* – a pamphlet which I think was actually a lecture that he gave in which he outlined the basic tenets of existentialism.[5] At the time I was a staunch Methodist kid, a young Sunday school teacher, and it just blew my mind, that little book, which I've still got and still read. Then later, in my twenties when I was beginning to write after '68, I read Guy Debord, also Raoul Vaneigem's *The Totality for Kids* which chimes in with Sartre's view of the world and is a brilliant aesthetic.[6] It wasn't meant to be an aesthetic but, to understand how you can write about the world, the Situationists said 'Look, public life is not lived in, actually, by any of us. It's a two-dimensional billboard but things can only be discussed in the terms displayed by the billboard.' It's like a printed circuit – which is old imagery now, a pre-chip notion – where you can't discuss things out of that particular framework, so you all have to pretend that you are operating in this world in order to get on and live your daily life, earn bread and work, but actually no one really believes in it or lives it. It's like learning that Tony Blair swears constantly, politicians are shouting at each other all the time. In public it's bland, assuring and false, but that bland assurance was the tone of the government in public. Once you realise that, what plays can do is put a boot through and try and explode this. Now these are dangerous ideas but great ideas always have a dark side: it gave the intellectual impetus to terrorist groups like the Baader-Meinhof gang and Red Brigades and others. They said if the spectacle is running us, let's actually bomb it.

CM: The focus on violence as a function of idealism is characteristic of your writing in the 1970s, most obviously in a play like *Magnificence*.

HB: It's difficult to explain to people today how feverish the atmosphere was in the emerging fringe theatre, how *hot* the evenings were, how you could get shouted at so easily. On the left this was happening increasingly, post-'68, when the dream of love and cooperation and all-together-ness, began to decay into factions, or even into despair or anger. You got caught in a kind of psycho-drama where you would be saying, 'You talk about being revolutionary, but what do you *do*?' I remember there was a famous occasion when Edward Bond of all people got up at a university meeting and said, 'Well, I hope that there are Marxists here', at which point someone stood up and shouted, 'You're not one!', and then a fight broke out and Edward had to leave. Now it seems absurd these days but that was the atmosphere that *Magnificence* was written in and I got caught in that psycho-drama. What do I do? Go and join the Workers' Revolutionary Party? Go and take up a gun and shoot a British soldier? I hated this debate because basically I'm a softie, I want peace, and so I dramatised the psycho-drama in *Magnificence* in order to make up my own mind. It came to what seems a banal conclusion but I think it's a true one which is that this is a tragedy of waste, and that a whole generation of leftists are destroying themselves by dreaming and bombing and taking up the gun.

CM: In the mid-1970s, didn't you have an encounter with members of Baader-Meinhof at a conference?

HB: Yes. Trevor Griffiths, the writer, and I and an American lawyer were asked to go and meet them. It was around 1977, I think. There was a problem in Germany which was a vicious one. In reaction to the problems caused to the West German state by urban terrorists like the Baader-Meinhof gang, they'd introduced a political vetting of public servants, particularly teachers. It was almost McCarthyite. You had to swear that you'd never had Communist links, or Communist persuasions, or knew any Communists – it was that bad. This was a conference set up by the Bertrand Russell Foundation to analyse this, denounce it, and publicise the problem. It was an excellent conference but, of course, there was an attempt to hijack it by the Baader-Meinhof people who asked to meet us. It was a very scary meeting because, just like with Jed in *Magnificence*, you were talking to people who had gone over a line and so it was impossible to have any discourse with them. They would say anything to achieve what they wished to achieve. It's what happened in the Soviet Union, where all that matters is the end, the means are up for grabs. So they will say they're democrats, say anything, to get you to do what they wanted, which was to go and see their prisoners in Stanheim, the jail where they were held. After some agonising, Trevor and I decided not to go. Trevor's mind is stronger politically than mine and he said, 'This is a trap'. It shows the psychological world you were living in at that time.

CM: Like other members of your theatrical generation – Griffiths, David Edgar, David Hare – by the mid-1970s you were becoming sceptical, to say the least, of fringe theatre.

HB: It may be a self-justification but it became possible to get plays on at the Royal Court and Peter Hall came and saw *Magnificence* and commissioned me to write a play which turned into *Weapons of Happiness* [1976] at the National. We were ambitious playwrights but, at the same time, this attractive idea of a counterculture – that you could grow a different way of thinking, a different kind of entertaining, which would have the utopian and the left libertarian ideas within it, and this would become so strong and overpowering that it would replace the official culture – that dream was becoming fragmented and dying out. You began to realise there's only one world and you'd best make your way in it. That was what we thought and we got some flak for that. Today, of course, the subsidised theatre is regarded in many circles as dangerously left-wing with countercultural organisations called the RSC and the National Theatre, and indeed the BBC is seen as a hot-bed of radicalism!

CM: You were the first of your generation to really push through and get big new plays on repertory stages. Nottingham Playhouse was clearly crucial for you at that time.

HB: In the arts, and particularly in the theatre, there are waves of generations, and because theatre is very much an entertainment which needs to be in touch with the zeitgeist, usually it's people in their twenties who ask the questions, who see the new forms, who actually do see what's going on around them and are able to express something about it or write stories or satires that can intervene. The theatre goes very much generation by generation. My generation was Richard Eyre at Nottingham, Max Stafford-Clark at the Royal Court, and Peter Hall, who is older but nevertheless strongly identified with new writing. We made hay for ten or fifteen years or so, and the same thing was happening at the BBC which produced some of my work. Then a new generation appears which is perhaps more in contact or strikes a note with its own audience. That's what happens in theatre.

CM: When you were at the Brighton Combination you attempted to set up a writers' space; in 1975, you tried to find a space that would stage your play *Government Property*, and you also tried to set up a writers' theatre at the Roundhouse in 1978. What kind of theatre were you dreaming of?

HB: I was trying to find new forms, new ways of expressing. There was a kind of faith – find a new form and you'll say the new thing that's true, you'll find the new truth. The two go hand in hand, and we were forever trying to do that through the 1970s. We couldn't make it happen, it was hard with a number of the projects. When I began writing in the 1960s, I wrote these short plays – *Gum and Goo*, *Heads*, *The Education of Skinny Spew* – also, later, *Christie in Love* [all 1969]. These plays were influenced by the thinking that, if you can get three actors, you can do a play anywhere, about anything, and that a handkerchief can be the sea, you can perform it to one thousand people sitting in a circle or ten people in the circle. They were little plays, a couple of them were done in intervals during rock concerts at Bradford University. Can you imagine a harder gig? That's why something like *Skinny Spew* is so outrageously farcical, just to get attention. That spirit sort of lingered on in the big, more formal, plays. I began to think about returning to it, to try to do that kind of writing again. There was always in the back of your mind that wonderful poem by Brecht about him seeing a soldier going off to war at the station and he says, 'Quickly I set up my theatre' – that's the chorus – and I always admired that spirit, which was the fringe spirit, the touring spirit of Portable Theatre and all the rest.[7]

I've always been interested in site-specific projects and companies like Punchdrunk have taken that up in a very strong way these days: that was what we were thinking of, that kind of experience. Back in 2000, I was asked to write a play for RADA. There was a wonderful derelict house owned by the voice coach called 'The Shipbuilder's House', now much refurbished and on the market. It was virtually derelict then and we had the idea of doing a play about Christopher Marlowe, encouraging the students to invent a new language for it. That failed, Health & Safety moved in. I wrote the play *Kit's Play*, which was done conventionally by the students in RADA's Jerwood Vanbrugh Theatre – it's about a modern Marlowe who eventually meets the old Marlowe, and I tried to write the last scene actually as he would have spoken; of course, they could barely understand each other. I had great fun with it but it was a play which dated very quickly because there was a lot about a dot.com company in it and the latest dot.com research which I got from a mathematician who was working for British Telecom, and all that passed of course.

CM: The Globe Theatre, I would imagine, also demands a rumbustious approach to theatricality?

HB: Yes, I feel very much at home in the Globe. I've done two shows there now. It's the default setting of the Globe that strait-laced critics can't stand. The default setting is vaudeville: in other words, you can easily go 'below the line', as Ken Campbell called it, and disgracefully mug an audience. The theatre wants you to do that, that's its default setting, so in other words you're working against that, you've got to get above that, you've got to mug but be better. Then if you're going to do something more tragic or more intellectually difficult, you've really got to be on your mettle or you lose them because of the theatre's default setting. The default setting of the Olivier or the Lyttelton is church, not vaudeville. That's the problem there. You can perform Ibsen's hardly-ever-performed three-hour *Emperor and Galilean*, you can get away with it because, although it's largely humourless and there are vast tracts of it which are not that interesting, the audience is in church and, of course, they're immensely grateful when someone farts in church – you're really away then.[8] That's the difference between the two theatres. I'm happier in vaudeville, with the vaudeville default setting, than I am with the church default setting, because in the church some of the work looks shocking, more shocking than it would look in the open air.

CM: What were your priorities in writing plays for bigger spaces in the 1970s – I'm thinking of *Weapons of Happiness* and *Epsom Downs* [1977]?

HB: With *Weapons of Happiness*, I'm still developing the idea of the British epic, the neo-Jacobean approach where you would have a realistic scene and then a scene which is more comic, or more vaudeville, and there's a mix going on in that play. It was also brilliantly designed by Hayden Griffin who understood that. So he would have a factory yard which was scrupulously realistic, inspired by photographs of an actual yard, then he had a scene in an office which was a painted flat with a real door but the light switch was painted – it was like a front-cloth because the tone of the scene needed that. There was an element that was site-specific because, in those days in the mid-1970s, a few hundred yards away behind the National Theatre, there were small family owned factories paying poor wages to small groups of workers all over that area of south London. They've all gone now. The world you were seeing at the Lyttelton Theatre was just beyond the back wall and we tried to make the audience aware that the London on the stage was very near.

Epsom Downs was interesting in the way that show came out of the 1970s. Max [Stafford-Clark] and I had an argument. Max is basically a miniaturist, he's happier in smaller spaces. He always accused me of 'gigantism', that was his phrase I think, maybe because I'm a big man, I don't know! I wanted to go to the Roundhouse, he didn't really, he wanted to do it at the Young Vic which is, for Max, the biggest theatre you need. You don't need anything larger than that – the Royal Court, Cottesloe, Young Vic, or a small studio theatre, that's Max's happy hunting ground. I had this vision of Joint Stock taking over the Roundhouse so we could launch shows there. Actually, when you build the audience, you can only get a few hundred into the Roundhouse so it wasn't how it turned out. There was that tension in the show. Joint Stock were going through their Maoist phase, where the company decided what to do, the policy, the programme. I had an idea for a play which was originally to be the successor of *Weapons of Happiness*. I went for an audition and I sold the company the idea of a play about the Derby set in the following year. They bought that. It was an extraordinary experience: the actor isn't auditioned, the writer is. It was a company of nine. But it then became apparent that, Maoist company though they were, they were also actors so everyone had to have an equal part, even down to line-counting. So I said, 'Right, you are each going to play five characters and we're going to have forty-five characters in this play', which put the damper on the whole thing a bit. That's how it happened, there are forty-five parts and the nine actors have five each, just about. This means that the play is frequently done by schools who can have forty-five kids in it. *Epsom Downs* came out of so many things that were going on in the 1970s.

I was also still pursuing my own aesthetic concerns which had gone from Bradford's simple circle, *Christie in Love* to *Magnificence* to *Weapons of Happiness*: I was still running those concerns of clashing styles. Your concerns roll on.

CM: I'm interested in your conception of British epic theatre as neo-Jacobeanism aligned to a popular political vaudeville.

HB: The sense always came from the idea that, just as you could make a circle with a group of half-drunk students in the middle of a rock concert and set up a theatre for fifteen minutes, so in a theatre of any size you can do anything, unlike in movies where you can't afford the budget. In a way, the theatre's budget-less. *Weapons of Happiness* was revived at the Finborough Theatre, a matchbox production: it was done on crates, no tank, no huge banners flying in when Stalin appeared, none of that, no motorcycle, they just sat across a crate![9] Fine, you can do it, you can *drum it up*. That sense never left me really, of what you could do. Of course, at the Globe, this is essential: the presence of the theatre is overwhelming. Even though you may dress up the odd pillar a bit, the theatre's an absolute given. For some reason, word painting is very strong there. You can have an actor come on and say to the audience 'beach' and in some way it appears, it's very strange and brilliant, but if you do that in the Lyttelton you've got to somehow have a projection of waves or something of the kind. John Dove, the director of *Anne Boleyn*, said 'the fewer the props the better', so only King James sat down, there were a couple of benches right at the edge, briefly used. We have a scene in an orchard, they came on with two lanterns and we cut the lanterns. We were debating whether a character could actually eat an apple or not: the sense of purity over whether or not to cut the apple!

CM: Could you talk a little about your more recent plays that seem to me to attend to a crisis of belief – religious, ideological – in the contemporary context.

HB: It wasn't that so much as I thought, 'How can I write about the Islamic problem?' The dangers of militant Islam were, of course, incredibly apparent after 9/11 and I thought, 'How can I possibly write about Islamic faith, an Islamic Jed?' There was no way I could do it, I mean I can't get there. Shakespeare could write about Macbeth, a homicidal sociopath, and I could get to that, but it's just impossible. Then I thought, but I know about religion inside out in my own culture because my father was a Methodist minister and because of being a Sartrean, which is about disabusing yourself of faith and inventing a faith in the ability to free-fall in some way. That's there in Sartre. I then thought of Saint Paul. *Paul* was an attempt to say: 'This is what fundamentalist faith is, this is psychologically how it works, how you can believe two things at once, and this is what happens to someone when it hits them, and this is why they can cut through social obstacles, obstacles of organisation, how they can attract followers. Because they've gone through a certain barrier.' That's what I believe historically happened with Paul and how he was virtually able to found the Christian religion. I tried to dramatise that. Similarly, with *Anne Boleyn*, I was interested in the way Protestantism was a revolutionary force. That was another aspect of faith, really.

I've written a new play, *55 Days*, which is about Oliver Cromwell. What started with the English Reformation finally explodes just over a hundred years later in the English Civil War. James I saw the danger, that the monarchy would be threatened by the extreme Protestant position because, if God disappears, 'I and my God' becomes 'I and the World', it's individualism, it's shopping, it's democracy, royalty's done for. Somehow James, I think, did sense that and that's why he launched the Hampton Conference but he failed, he couldn't put the lid on it, and it exploded in 1642 with, later, the execution of his son. Of course, Cromwell was trying to find his way. I concentrate on the few days, the fifty days or so before Charles's execution and how the Parliamentary leadership got their heads around putting the King on trial and executing him. They were riven, the internal debate was agonised, they couldn't get their heads around it and Cromwell was waiting for Providence, can you imagine? Cromwell would open the Bible, like John Wesley, and point at a passage and say, 'Is there policy in this?' I've now finished these three plays – *Paul, Anne Boleyn, 55 Days* – or four with *In Extremis*. There is a theme that I've always had which is the future breaking out before its time, a kind of optimistic thing, which Abelard and Eloise had and which in some way the Protestants in the 1530s had.

CM: I want to conclude with the current political context of coalition government and escalating concerns about recession, terrorism, the environment, energy. Would you say all this is quite redolent of the 1970s?

HB: I think it's quite different now from the 1970s and certainly different from the 1980s, in that, in the 1980s, the people in power certainly did know what they wanted to do and so you were in opposition to that. In many ways, our most fertile decade was when Thatcher was in power: me, David Hare, Caryl Churchill, David Edgar did some of our best work in the 1980s. The 1970s were when you were still trying to live the kind of hope of new form but, nowadays, what I sense is that we don't know what we're living. We don't know whether we're in the middle of a huge crisis or whether there has been a financial crisis and it's passed, or whether we're looking at a huge wave that's about to break over us. We don't know. I don't think anyone knows and so there's a sort of short-term spirit about both on the street, where people are clearly drinking more and more, and in government: when negotiating about Greece, they talk about a month's time or a year's time, they don't have a grip on what is happening to us at any level.[10] The 1970s in England was a time of national crisis, a crisis of economic power, power waning, it was a long decline, the decline was getting to us, it was economic, but it was British. The world and finance wasn't as global as now. What we're living in now is a world crisis, or are we? Or how bad is it? In fifteen years from now, we'll be asked by our grandchildren: 'What was it like in 2011?' and say, 'Do you know, it sort of wasn't like anything.' It's a very odd time.

David Edgar

David Edgar gave the following interview to the author on 18 March 2011 in London.

CM: After graduating from university in 1969, you worked on the Bradford *Telegraph & Argus* newspaper. How did you become involved in theatre?

DE: I was born into a theatre family, so it was a matter of what branch of the theatre I was going into not whether I was going into the theatre. My dad was a television producer and my mum had been a radio announcer during the Second World War. They had both left the theatre and my mum gave it up to raise the family but my aunt was still administrator of the Birmingham Repertory Theatre, with a variety of titles: she was Barry Jackson's right-hand person for a long time. So I was brought up in that and wanted to be an actor, and then I directed and designed shows at school, and I wrote a play at university. I was at Manchester University from 1966–9, and became editor of the student newspaper and that was at the height of the student revolt in 1968–9. That led me to the idea that what I wanted to do was write and, because I couldn't set up shop immediately as a playwright, that I'd be a journalist and write plays in the evening. I'd chosen to go to Bradford; although I'd applied to a number of newspapers, the one that accepted me was the Pearson Group which owned the *Financial Times* and which also had a very wide range of local newspapers. They asked which one I would like and I said, 'Well, which is the biggest?' and they said Bradford was the biggest. They also had the *Oxford Times*, and I remember thinking that the *Oxford Times* would be interesting – you know, Oxford and everything – but it was an absolutely crucial decision in my life that I went for Bradford rather than Oxford. I assisted Ray Fitzwalter, who went on to run

World in Action, on the first story to expose the corrupt Yorkshire architect John Poulson. It's interesting that, in Dominic Sandbrook's book, he does quote Ray Fitzwalter but he promulgates the myth that *Private Eye* broke the Poulson story, which is not true as the Bradford *Telegraph & Argus* broke it.[11] In effect I was Bernstein to Fitzwalter's Woodward, in that I turned the piece into English. My other major contribution was interviewing Reginald Maudling on the phone – he was charming but said he didn't understand why this was important, which was an irony in terms of the fact that it went on to destroy his career.[12] So I was a crucial part of it, although it was very much Ray's thing. That was my biggest journalistic achievement, of which I'm very proud. I also covered Bradford University, which was an interesting place at the time.

In terms of useful training for my future career as a playwright, the Bradford *Telegraph & Argus* was much more important than reading Drama at Manchester. It wasn't the Drama department's fault, it was mainly because of everything else that was going on. I was really an absentee student for my second year, and quite a lot of my first and third years, because everything else was so thrilling – being active in the Union and the Socialist Society and all that – but Bradford gave me research skills and the wide variety of *stuff* you come across, the people you meet. *Destiny* [1976] came out of that. *Destiny* was inspired by a group called, first of all, the Yorkshire and then the British Campaign to Stop Immigration which eventually got folded into the National Front and was run by a guy called Jim Merrick. I got to know Merrick a bit, he always complained about the way that we treated his movement. He once said to me, 'You've always treated me with respect, Mr Edgar', which I wasn't quite sure was my intention and certainly I never wrote any piece that was in any sense anything other than hostile. But I got to know him and I attended the meeting which is the basis of the chaotic 'Patriotic League' meeting in *Destiny* – in fact, it wasn't that the microphones fed back (as happens in the play), it was that they were trying to show a film which kept breaking down. All of that was very important and I think *Destiny* certainly wouldn't have happened if I hadn't been at the Bradford *Telegraph*.

What then happened was that, in 1970, I met Chris Parr and

wrote plays for him. Chris was Fellow in Theatre at Bradford University, which was strange as there wasn't a Drama department, so in essence he was there to encourage dramatic activity by students. He had this idea of commissioning writers he knew to write plays for £50. They included Richard Crane, Howard Brenton and, subsequently, me and the actor John Grillo, and a number of others. Brenton's early plays such as *Gum and Goo* [1969] were written for Bradford. He wrote a play about Wesley for the Methodist Hall and a play about Scott of the Antarctic, in which I played God, which was done at the Ice Rink and was actually defeated in a way by the same things that defeated Scott – it was too large, too cold and there was too much ice. But it was a great thing to do. Jeff Nuttall designed the costumes and it was extraordinary.

CM: This was in the context of the Bradford Arts Festivals?

DE: Yes, in addition to Chris at the university, there was Albert Hunt at the Art College doing pieces that seem extraordinarily prescient now. The famous piece on the bombing of Dresden: the raid of Dresden lasted twenty-two minutes and they tore up cardboard boxes for twenty-two minutes, which was most extraordinary. For the Bradford Festival, he also did some big public things like the American presidential election with a live elephant in the streets of the city. John Fox's Welfare State was there at that time, based in Leeds but doing a lot of work in Bradford. John Bull's Puncture Repair Kit, too. The People Show were very regular visitors so there was all that counter-cultural stuff.

There was a wonderful occasion when the NUS Festival came. The idea was to have an opening ceremony that was jointly done between Chris Parr and Albert Hunt and they had to meet in neutral territory: the art college and the university were just over the road from each other but they went to a café to meet. I think I came up with the idea but certainly I ended up writing it. The then Vice-Chancellor of Bradford used honorary degrees as a way of creating theatrical events: Harold Wilson was the Chancellor so they offered an honorary degree to TUC General Secretary Vic Feather when there was lots of conflict between the two of them. But the big coup was getting Heath when he was prime minister and giving him an honorary degree because some great science building had just opened and that was at the height of the Common Market stuff, and then there was naturally a student occupation to protest against Heath getting a degree and there was lots of tension between Heath and Wilson. So we reproduced that degree ceremony and gave everybody from the NUS an honorary doctorate from the University of Bradford. I wrote the script because I'd been there as a journalist. So there were terrific, big-scale, site-specific events forty years before the Arts Council thought that it invented them. There was all of that going on.

Chris's principle was, as I said, to commission playwrights. I wrote a play about apartheid called *The White and White Springbok Show* which was inspired by the anti-Springbok protests, which he didn't like very much.[13] Another tradition which was to become common-place in the theatre – you write the first play, which people don't like, so they commission your next one! He asked me to write a play for two female students, so I wrote a play about two young women who share a flat, one of whom hero-worships Marilyn Monroe and the other of whom hero-worships Rosa Luxemburg. It was called *Two Kinds of Angel*. It was my first play for Chris and turned out to be my first professional production which opened at the Basement Theatre in Soho on Decimalisation Day, 15 February 1971.

I wrote several other plays for Chris, one of which was called *The National Interest* [1971] which led to the creation of the General Will, the small agitprop group I was involved with. There was this extraordinary counter-cultural mish-mash. One of my complaints about the 1970s books written by people who weren't there is this tendency to put everything in very particular boxes. Sandbrook says *Dixon of Dock Green* was so different from *Softly, Softly* and more people watched *Dixon of Dock Green*. Well, I watched both. I listened to the Searchers *and* I listened to progressive rock. I was a student revolutionary *and* I watched *Dad's Army*. In the late 1960s, both here and in America, there was an increasing ideological division between the hippie-left, which you could call the pre-figurative left, people who believed that you should act out the revolution in the here and now, and the

Marxist left, for whom that was an unserious delusion. On the other hand, it didn't mean that, if you were in the Marxist left, you couldn't wear flowers or smoke dope and do hippie-ish things and, indeed, the Angry Brigade, which was a kind of militarised version of the hippie-left, attempted to blow up Robert Carr, who'd piloted the Industrial Relations Act.[14] They were concerned with the harder-edged metallic industrial issues that would be seen as a more appropriate concern for the Marxist left. So there was lots of cross-fertilisation and the Bradford Festivals were a sort of classic example of that. The General Will and Red Ladder were performing there as well as all these performance art groups, as well as mounting these large-scale spectaculars based at colleges and universities.

CM: Your first engagement as a full-time writer was *England's Ireland*?

DE: Yes, as a professional playwright. That was very important for me. It was the follow-up to the group-written *Lay By* [1971] and I wasn't involved with *Lay By* but I was asked to be part of *England's Ireland* because I knew Howard Brenton, who'd been one of the *Lay By* writers. It was in spring 1972. I left journalism on the Thursday and on the Friday I drove down to Pembrokeshire to this funny little house over the road from a pub that David Hare had rented for a week claiming we were a walking party – seven unhealthy-looking writers and, it being the early 1970s, a female typist. We spent a week writing the play that became *England's Ireland*. It was extraordinary. I was sitting there writing about internment with Howard Brenton – what an apprenticeship! We wrote it in twos and threes, we didn't sit in a big circle, but we didn't write anything on our own either. That was very important, and *England's Ireland* was agitprop and cartoonish in a way, it certainly wasn't realist, but working with Hare and Snoo Wilson contributed to an expansion beyond the very cartoon agitprop that I was doing with the General Will.

CM: In 1978, David Hare gave his lecture at Cambridge University called 'The Play is in the Air', and makes his break with Marxist theatre. That year, you also published (in the *Socialist Review*) an article that then goes into *Theatre Quarterly* the following year, 'Ten Years of Political Theatre', which marks your own turn-away from agitprop. This disavowal of agitprop in theatre takes place in 1978 but its roots are deeper. For Hare, there was something very interesting around the time of *Fanshen* in 1975 when he discovers that he can no longer write plays where he already knows the answers before he starts. The result is *Plenty*. You've traced your own disillusionment to around 1975 because of a range of things including Kampuchea and the failure of the left over Europe. By mid-decade, you've also produced a body of work and there's a desire to push oneself as a playwright, to write more complexly about the world. The result is *Destiny*. Is this a fair summary?

DE: It is. I delivered 'Ten Years of Political Theatre' to the same Cambridge conference that David spoke at.

The political activism of the second half of the decade which came out of *Destiny* was on a very different track to the sense, in the early part of the decade, of one-hundred-flowers-blooming. There were huge arguments about feminism and its importance or lack of importance, and gay rights, but the crucial thing for me was the General Will falling apart, which resulted from a conflict between the heterosexual men in the group and the one gay man in the group, Noël Greig. That was the moment when I realised that a kind of fragile unity had been broken. You could see the great historical division, in theatre terms, between art-college-based, visual, non-cerebral, performance art and the political, university-based, verbal, cerebral theatre. That sort of stuff was happening in the middle of the decade. It's at that point that Pip Simmons and John Bull's Puncture Repair Kit and Welfare State start feeling like a different thing. They formed their own circuits with their own devotees – a lot of them abroad in the case of Pip Simmons. And then there was also the division between those of us who went into the mainstream, I think partly for careerist reasons, but also partly for the reasons I'll try to outline.

In all of these things one tends to (a) impose a retrospective but (b) you forget to talk about institutions. In other words, the reason that David and I and Howard Brenton went into the institutions was not because we got up one fine morning and decided that we were now going to write our next play for the Lyttelton. It was a bit more of a two-way street than that. It relied on the Lyttelton wanting to take the play, and I think in the same way that George Devine didn't *have* to do John Osborne or Arnold Wesker – he could perfectly well have done (as he did a bit) continental Absurdism and the occasional sprinkling of N. F. Simpson or early Harold Pinter – there was no reason he *had* to take up those plays. Similarly, bless their hearts, Trevor Nunn and Peter Hall decided to do the work of that generation at a point when the Royal Court wasn't doing that generation very much. Hare and Brenton fought their way on to the main stage of the Court in the early seventies but it wasn't easy, it was still an aesthetic dominated by David Storey really. The fact that *Destiny* goes on at the Aldwych, the fact that *Plenty* [1978] and *Weapons of Happiness* [1976] go on at the Lyttelton, was not inevitable. It was partly that we were providing plays and we were shouting and saying, 'Look at Nottingham!', but also that those directors were open for that, and they didn't have to be. I think there was an opportunity and, if it hadn't been for that, then things might have been quite different.

While the General Will still existed, to a certain extent things weren't in one's hands and I was commissioned to do my anti-Common Market panto spoof *Tedderella* and that was done by the Bush [1973]. Then they said do a thing about Nixon and I did *Dick Deterred* (based on *Richard III* [1974]). I don't think any playwright career involves 'I write this play', it goes on, it gets reviews and, 'Now I will decide where the next will be.' I think regarding *Destiny* as a hinge to move away from agitprop towards realism is absolutely right, even though there's a period of overlap.

I started writing *Destiny* in 1973 so I'd still got a number of agitprop plays to go, though the great agitprop explosion was 1972 in terms of my own work. I'd written *Excuses, Excuses* for the Coventry Belgrade Theatre [1972], I'd written *Death Story* for the Birmingham Rep [1972], so I'd written plays that were not agitprop: I saw it as two parallel strands. Around this time, the General Will falls apart and is taken over first on a banner of gay rights and then I think there's a conflict between the male gays and the lesbian members of the group and eventually it collapses. I no longer had an outlet for that work and actually *Dunkirk Spirit* [1974], which was a two-act agitprop play, a history of Western capitalism since the war, probably was stretching the bounds of the medium beyond a scale that it could take. I did the big spoof shows *Tedderella* and *Dick Deterred*, so I was spreading in various different directions. But there is no question that *Destiny* is a self-conscious effort to break away: it's the first play that says, 'This is the sort of play I now want to write, which is the large-scale realist drama.'

I haven't re-read 'Ten Years of Political Theatre' for a long time but I think I was headed in the direction of Lukácsian realism. *Destiny* developed over time, there were various drafts of it, but it was intended to say to the liberal intelligentsia – people like Peter Jenkins of the *Guardian* with whom I had a spat back and forth – that the National Front was important, it was a Nazi front, which was a very unfashionable idea at the time because that was seen as being the far left self-aggrandising: if the National Front was a Nazi party, and if it was growing in strength, then we were back in the 1930s when the left was much more important. This view reasserted a Trotskyite vocabulary, it was a reassertion of the old battle-lines, and I think people like Jenkins felt that was self-aggrandising and self-importance on the left. For him, the National Front was an anti-immigration group that wasn't very important but was expressing something that probably ordinary people felt. To the far left, or to the left that I felt a part of, the play was saying, however, that just to treat people who supported the National Front as jack-booted thugs is to misunderstand that they're addressing a very real sense of loss.

CM: You connect that to the recognition that you're talking to a particular audience that had perhaps not been addressed before in theatre, or had been ignored?

DE: I'm addressing the liberal left intelligentsia and also the public sector, the people who were actually coming to left-wing shows. I've often said that in taking stuff around with the General Will, even to working men's clubs, what was happening was that the local polytechnic and local government left were actually coming to see the show and only three or four real workers were standing at the bar at the back. That's an exaggeration: we got some working-class audiences, Red Ladder did and obviously 7:84 particularly in Scotland did, so it wasn't a *total* failure. But I did come to the view that between 1965, which was the founding of CAST, and the fall of the Heath government, there could not be a more propitious time for socialist theatre to be toured to working-class audiences. You had a combination of the cultural upsurge, which obviously touched the working classes as much as it touched everyone else in the late 1960s, followed by the industrial upsurge of the early 1970s. There could have been no better time – and it didn't happen. We didn't gain that mass audience and, therefore, you had to look, not at the audience that we *weren't* getting, but at the audience we *were* getting and that audience was important. And of course it became increasingly important, the white-collar public sector came to be very influential in the trade union movement in the 1970s. It was really *that* audience – the audience you could satirise as the polytechnic left – which I think we were increasingly addressing. You could address that audience at the National and the RSC because they came to those places as well as provincial theatres. So that was a pretty self-conscious move and that was built around *Destiny*.

With regard to the wider polity, I think 1975 was important because it was the year that we realised that the miners hadn't gone on strike to bring down the government, but had brought down the government in order to win their strike, and that the militancy had been exaggerated or we had thought it to be more revolutionary than it was. There was a sense with the victory of the National Liberation Front in Vietnam, and even more the victory of the Khmer Rouge, that we were now going to enter a more politically complicated period. The anti-imperial struggle, which was 100 per cent supported by the left, became more politically complicated when those regimes took over. The third factor: in this country, women's liberation proverbially starts at the Ruskin Conference in 1970, and the disruption of 'Miss World', but there's no doubt that feminism was delayed by the industrial upsurge and by the fact that a lot of people, including me shamefully, were saying that the miners were on strike, the Vietnam War is raging, this is not a time to talk about different sorts of orgasm . . . and so I think feminism and anti-racism became important later than they did elsewhere because we had this extraordinary apparent confirmation of what Marx had said – that was the vital thing. My only real criticism of Beckett's book is that he concentrates so over-whelmingly on the 1972 and 1974 miners' strikes.[15] By not dealing at all, or only in passing, with the shipbuilders' and postmen's strike, and the electricity workers' strikes which were the first set of black-outs, with the 1973 rail strike, with the dock strike, he doesn't make the point that it *wasn't* just the miners, it was everybody, and it did seem that Marx was right. To that extent the hippies were wrong: a traditional industrial upsurge seemed to be happening and really there were only two places where it did happen – here and in Italy – and so that delayed the full emergence of identity politics. There were agit-prop feminist plays, and very good ones, but identity politics was much more susceptible to the full range of the armoury of theatre and certainly should be treated in a style that went far beyond cartoon theatre.

CM: Could you talk about how *Destiny* became part of a broader base of campaigning on race politics at the time?

DE: While I was researching it I met people who I then got involved with politically and I think the starting point was that I became involved with *Searchlight* magazine which started in 1975. I became involved in the anti-racist struggle and the Institute of Race Relations who I researched the play with. I wrote a pamphlet called *Racism, Fascism and the Politics of the National Front* in 1977. When *Destiny* went on I became a bit more of an anti-fascist celebrity, and therefore was invited to meetings as the author of *Destiny*. I did a lot of speaking, particularly in the 1976–8 period. I was probably doing a meeting a week for quite a long period and also got heavily involved with the Anti-Nazi League when that started, and there was also a big campaign against racism and fascism meeting which I was involved with as well.

There were some complaints about *Destiny*. John McGrath criticised it for not wearing its politics on its sleeve. The way I put it, and I think this is right, was that I was working on a twin track: I was a political polemic-maker at meetings and campaigning, and I'd also written a play that was attempting to see psychologically into the minds of supporters of such a movement. That was a different approach but they were complementary and not oppositional.

CM: You talk about *The Jail Diary of Albie Sachs* [1978] as a history play for South Africa but you also say the play is about the present in Britain. There's a dialogue between *Destiny* and *Albie*, not least in the preoccupations that you're addressing about fascism or about violence and state violence in relation to the extreme right.

DE: Yes, the first act of *Destiny* is the collapse of Conservatism which is one of the wrong predictions of the play; the second act is about the far right, and the third act is about the left response. I think the liberal left had a dilemma which is partly what *Albie Sachs* is also about.

CM: What recollections do you have of the working culture of the RSC at that time?

DE: It was a thrilling season because it featured a whole new generation of young actors like Roger Rees and Richard Griffiths, and Paul Moriarty, Paul Shelley, John Nettles, Greg Hicks, Bob Peck, Ian McDiarmid and Cherie Lunghi, who were all in *Destiny*; it was a golden season of young actors. It also had one of the greatest productions ever by the RSC, which was Trevor Nunn's production of *Macbeth*. It had a rather extraordinary season in the main house as well which tends to be forgotten about: Donald Sinden's *Lear*, a musical version of *The Comedy of Errors*. It was a very golden and wonderful season to be a part of. The only problem, which indirectly led to the foundation of the Theatre Writers' Union and the rest is history, was how miserably you were paid as a writer. I was paid for attending rehearsals, which was unusual then. I was paid for attending five weeks of rehearsal the cost of one pair of boots for *The Winter's*

Tale; I was paid for the play one week of Ian McKellen's salary, which was about £250. It was very exciting actually and you really did feel part of the company. Trevor became very excited about the play because it had been rejected by the RSC, it had been rejected by everybody.

CM: And I believe it was rejected by Birmingham as well?

DE: The story is that it was written for Nottingham. The first draft, which was an awful baggy thing, was turned down by Richard Eyre which he's always been very embarrassed about, although I think if one re-read the first draft one would see it was quite bad. Then I was commissioned to do another draft for Birmingham and the board instructed Michael Simpson not to do it, I think the only time the board of Birmingham Repertory Theatre has ever done that. We then hawked it around, and it was rejected partly on the grounds of its politics and partly on the grounds that it was very expensive and very large and it was felt that it was going to empty the theatre. (I was obviously very delighted when it eventually played to nearly 80 per cent at the Aldwych.) It was turned down by Ronald Bryden who was then the RSC Literary Manager, it was turned down by the National, it was turned down by pretty much everybody. Then Ron Daniels, who was a junior director at the RSC, read it and he took it to Trevor, who said, 'Let's do it in the Other Place', and I didn't really want it done there as it was written to be done in a large-scale provincial theatre with a large immigrant population, not in a tin hut in rural Warwickshire, but beggars couldn't be choosers. It was very well reviewed and, in the funny way that things happen, it would have gone into the Warehouse – because the next year was the first year of the Warehouse – but for the fact that the RSC was doing the *Henry VI* plays the next year and they couldn't cast them partly because Terry Hands, who was directing them, was directing something at the Comédie Française. There were problems with the phone in the rehearsal room. Eventually it got beyond the point where their schedule was going to work so they did one production of *A Midsummer Night's Dream* in Stratford by the preceding year's

Stratford company, and at the same time they decided to run the Donald Sinden *King Lear* at the Aldwych in repertoire with something else. Trevor said, 'Why don't we do *Destiny?*' We were sort of inside the *King Lear* set and it was a great and bold decision, but my career is sort of attributable to the inadequacies of the French telephone system.

It was on during the Silver Jubilee and we were the only two shows that didn't dip during Jubilee week: one of our shows was about a mad king going crazy and provoking a civil war and the destruction of his kingdom, and the other was suggesting that we were about to be taken over by the Nazis. The patriotic bunting on the Aldwych was echoed but also contradicted by the patriotic but ironical stuff on our posters. Indeed we got attacked but it wasn't by the National Front – it was by the National Party, which was an off-shoot that actually got the only two councillors in the 1970s.

CM: Your final plays of the 1970s explore a key preoccupation in your work from this point on: that individual personality *matters* on the left and that you neglect it at your peril.

DE: *Teendreams* [1979] and *Mary Barnes* [1978] are both plays about the failure of liberal dreams and that's a tradition that goes back to Wesker's *I'm Talking About Jerusalem* and certainly it's the subject of both Brenton's *Magnificence* and his *Weapons of Happiness*.

Mary Barnes is a better play than *Teendreams*. *Teendreams* has an odd sort of structure, which is flashback. The idea is that you start in the despair of the central character, the teacher who has encouraged her students through feminist ideals to have a greater view of their lives and that has ended up in catastrophe. You then flash back to her history and go up through the history of her being a teacher and get to that point again, with three extra scenes at the end. The audience is invited to believe that this is a destruction-of-liberal-ideals play, but in fact we then see that the young women had gone on to do other interesting things. I did another version of it for Bristol University, which made that a bit clearer by making the end much shorter. Part of the problem with that is that, when you've got to the end of the flashback, you think this is the end of the play, when in fact there are three more scenes, so it's quite difficult for the audience to take. Some of the scenes are very good and some of the scenes aren't very good but it was absolutely about the conflict between political ideals and the realities of human nature, as was *Mary Barnes*. Both end with a suggestion which I hope is realistic but also has an element of hope about the future. I think the meat of both those plays was an idea that political movements have to go through a period of extremes, a period of madness and lunacy, in order to get the revolutionaries to create good reforms later.

CM: The darker the night, the closer the dawn.

DE: Yes, absolutely. There are all sorts of paradoxes and problems: it's great if you're twenty in a revolutionary era, it's not so great if you're twenty in a reformist era. Looking at Islamicism, I think you can see that pattern and you can certainly see it in feminism and gay rights. The slogan is that there wouldn't have been *Queer as Folk* without the Stonewall riots, certainly the Cameron 'A-list' wouldn't have happened without revolutionary feminists in dungarees.[16] I think both *Teendreams* and *Mary Barnes* are about the extremity and the apparent 'looniness' that you need to go though, the ultimate questions and the extreme questions that you have to raise, in order to get to a point where people are cracked out of their presumptions. *Mary Barnes* is set in a therapeutic community set up by the anti-psychiatrist R. D. Laing and I think I'm probably responsible for the Laing bit in Dominic Sandbrook's book about the early 1970s because one of my criticisms of his 1960s book *White Heat* was that there was a long chapter on *Play Power* by Richard Neville, which seems to me not a very important book in terms of understanding the late 1960s, and nothing at all on R. D. Laing, who seems to me very, very important. So there's a very big attack on Laing in the new book.[17] You *can* attack Laing but there's absolutely no question that challenging conventional psychiatry was hugely important. There were some bad consequences, like people being thrown out of mental hospitals on to the streets under Margaret Thatcher. But the critique of conventional treatment was very powerful and his idea that the mad were saying something – later on it becomes that the mad are saner than the sane, and a lot of dangerous nonsense results from that – that critique was really important.

I think probably the big subject is how you come to terms with the moment when the revolutionary energy recedes and therefore things that seemed eminently sensible start seeming lunatic or ridiculous or risible. How you hang on to the good stuff when the tide goes out, and obviously *Maydays* [1983] – which I think is the culmination of the 1970s plays – is absolutely about 'How do you avoid ending up moving to the right?' The RSC are doing a series of readings for their fiftieth anniversary and they were going to do *Destiny* but actually said, 'Would you read *Maydays* instead?' so in a way it's more interesting now. *Destiny* predicted various things about the far right, including Nick Griffin, but *Maydays* predicted Christopher Hitchens, David Aaronovitch, Nick Cohen, the sort of muscular liberal defector group. I think *Maydays* arises directly out of *Teendreams* and *Mary Barnes*.

David Gant

The actor David Gant played the role of Simon in the original production of Edgar's Mary Barnes *(1978).*

For me, it was the most rewarding and exciting time working on the production both at Birmingham Rep and then at the Royal Court in London from the beginning of rehearsals in Birmingham to ultimately meeting Simon Barnes, Mary's brother, in a café in Camden during the run at the Court. I went with Mary and the actress who played her, Patti Love. I asked Mary what I could take Simon as a gift. The answer – a bag of satsumas!

[Email to the author, 12 July 2011]

Tim Hardy

*The actor Tim Hardy played the role of Douglas in the original produc-
tion of Edgar's* Mary Barnes *(1978).*

Long before we transferred to the Royal Court, I think it was clear to
all of us that this was an exceptional text, that as well as saying something so important at the time, it was also in no way a polemic, but
wonderful theatre.

Towards the end of our extended run at the Court, by which time
we had, of course, lived with our characters for some time, my mind
went back to a quite heated discussion the company had entered into
in – I think – the very first weeks of rehearsals in Birmingham.
Remembering the different viewpoints from which we had each
argued, I realised how amazingly well cast we were! We all, quite naturally it seemed, spoke for the point of view we would each come to
adopt on behalf of our characters. As a case in point, I very much
espoused what you might call the liberal, centrist standpoint, which I
think I very quickly realised put me well in the minority. I entirely
subscribed to the ideas behind the experiment that was the subject of
the play, but could not agree with the seemingly total freedom within
the establishment that was being suggested. Indeed, my character had
a line that summed up what I felt perfectly. [Douglas] said: 'Rule
One. There are no rules.'[18] Indeed, one of the principal talking points
with those who saw the play was the issue of Mary Barnes's wellbeing
as opposed to the other patients: that while her very strong personality
thrived under the lack of rules, others did not.

My other memory is that those of us playing the psychiatrists
noticed that in conversations in the pub after the show, on several
occasions, people would soon start to talk to us as though we were
psychiatrists, and would share things, and ask our opinion, in a way
which would never have normally been the case. I actually think this
is indicative of the extraordinary effect the play had on so many
people, of the quality of the text, and how those responsible sought to
realise it. I believe that when theatre really works, people don't bother
talking so much about whether he or she was good in it, if it was well

directed, written, and so on. Those things become almost invisible, as they should, while what remains centre-stage, as the focus of the audience's attention, is the play.

[Letter to the author, 31 May 2011]

Barry Kyle

The director Barry Kyle, Honorary Associate Director of the RSC, staged the RSC revival of Brenton's The Churchill Play *at the Other Place, Stratford, in 1978.*

What was the reason for the RSC to remount this play, only four years after it was premiered at the Nottingham Playhouse?

Firstly, it was becoming clear that too many good plays were being mothballed after their premiere, due to no longer being 'new plays'. The chase for the 'new' became mad (and got worse). Secondly, this period was the countdown to the 'Orwell moment' – 1984. There was a tendency for the left to need to address that prophecy, and Howard's play did it. There's no doubt that left-wing sensibility became uppermost in how contemporary play policy developed then at the RSC. Admittedly, 'left-wing sensibility' seems a horribly woolly term now, but most people knew then what it was. Another reason the play appealed was because it batted deep down the cast list. With so many Shakespeare seasons at Stratford (particularly history-play seasons) requiring thirty-strong male actors, *The Churchill Play* was attractive, containing a large cast of fully realised characters. It was like reading a Ben Jonson play. This meant that it strongly contributed to offering interesting Stratford seasons to a large group. The cast included David Bradley, Malcolm Storry, John Nettles, Juliet Stevenson (just out of RADA), Hilton McRae and a cast of good, tough, 'regional' actors whose personalities were gradually changing the way the RSC cast its Shakespeare work too. This year (1978) was the year I recall Ian Charleson coming to audition for the season, and being asked if he would retry his Hamlet audition, without his Edinburgh accent. 'No,' he replied, 'but I'll sing you "My Love is Like a Red Red Rose" by

Robbie Burns.' He was brilliant, and got in. The 'Stratford voice' was changing slowly, and it made casting *The Churchill Play* easier, or perhaps the influence went a little the other way round too.

While we were rehearsing, the Lib–Lab pact came to an end (coalitions unglue in Britain), the Yorkshire Ripper was on the loose and the IRA was involved in a shoot-out with the British Army (21 June). A minority Labour government under Jim Callaghan was trying to rule, and there was a feeling that the left was badly split and something very different might be around the corner. That was Margaret Thatcher, who was elected in 1979. I think our revival sensed the chill that was coming and was, indeed, a little prophetic. The play actually describes a Guantánamo, twenty-five years before it came into being. 'Camp Churchill', the setting of the play, is an internment camp somewhere in England, where 'political' prisoners – Irish republicans, Marxists, journalists and trade unionists – are held without trial by a reluctant British Army. The politicians, particularly on the left, are portrayed as worried to death by this, and so encourage a drama club and a more civilised regime, to reconcile it with British democracy. In other words, how might a democratic society, possibly led by a left-of-centre government, set aside *habeas corpus* and the judicial system, to run a secret isolation unit where 'terrorists' can disappear? Just the dilemma the Obama administration is facing now with Guantánamo, and it can seem the best of several worse options, that's the problem.

Some critics, and not only journalists, found the play a typically leftish overstatement. I remember that Jonathan Pryce was in that same season at Stratford. He had played Mike McCulloch in Richard Eyre's production at Nottingham, and would sit in the Green Room and openly share his dislike of the play with others! But everybody involved with the production was strongly committed to it. We were in the Other Place, which meant that the play with its large cast had an enhanced sense of urgency and a visceral power. At the end, when the political delegation watching the play is taken hostage, and the unhinged Jimmy Umpleby (Mal Storry) runs amok with a machine gun, the terror of terrorism erupted in that small space. The IRA was very active in 1978. In that same year the European Court of Human

Rights found the British government guilty of mistreating prisoners in Northern Ireland. One of the characters in the play – a small role, George Lamacraft – is reserved for special measures by the soldiers, and it becomes clear that he is beaten to death by them. You could feel at that time how impossible it was to get anyone in the British government to consider the Irish question more deeply than as a terrorism matter. Indeed, some involved with the production believed MI5 was keeping an eye on the RSC mounting this play. How striking, in hindsight, that the Good Friday Agreement, exactly two decades later, in spring 1998, was driven by two Labour politicians, Mo Mowlam and Tony Blair, who in 1978 may have shared some of this play's point of view. I knew Mo Mowlam personally, and she saw the play when we took it to Newcastle. I think Howard views Churchill with a surprising sympathy in the play, particularly for his tenacity, and the personal struggle with his 'black dog' – depression. Although the play was pitiless about 'Churchillism' – I think that Raymond Westwell, our excellent Joby Peake/Churchill, found so much in the role because Howard had written it from a personal corner of himself.

At the start of the fourth act, a giant Union Jack serves for the curtain of the prisoners' play-within-a-play. The act – particularly to actors doing Shakespeare the next night – seemed to be like *Pyramus and Thisbe* with machine guns. I recall overhearing a critic, sitting in front of me at the press night, muttering to a companion: 'Here we go. The RSC abuses the flag again.' And yet it seemed then that another Churchill was not really likely to emerge. In 1978, Margaret Thatcher was not elected, and Boris Johnson was fourteen and still at Eton. No, at that time, the piece was a biting satiric work in the line of Swift's *Modest Proposal.* A warning, a *faux* prophecy, a 'never in England', as the officer Captain Thompson puts it.[19] Ten years later, in 1988, I directed a revival of the play at the Barbican with Colin Welland, Phil Daniels and James Fleet. After a decade of Thatcherism, it seemed even more important to consider the play's proposition. In that year, the SAS shot dead three IRA Provisionals in Gibraltar, and Lockerbie happened; it seemed right. But the era of the issue play was coming to an end. The British stage was becoming preoccupied with musical theatre, postmodern design and star acting, and the wide open spaces of the Barbican Theatre, plus high ticket prices, muted the play's impact. It seemed its time was past. Gorbachev was implementing *perestroika* in the Soviet Union, and I think the left was holding its breath.

[Letter to the author, 16 May 2011]

Peter McEnery

Peter McEnery, a leading actor with the RSC, played the title role in the original production of Edgar's The Jail Diary of Albie Sachs *(1978). He gave the following interview to the author on 15 March 2011 in London.*

CM: How did you become involved in the RSC?

PM: I was a founder member in 1961 when it was granted the Royal Charter and I was with the company with Peter Hall for five, six years in the 1960s. Then I left to do movies in England and France and then went back.

CM: Famously, you did the film *Entertaining Mr Sloane* [1970] in that period.

PM: I did, yes, it was a good picture – still holds up actually. I went back to the RSC in 1977 and we did a wonderful programme of the three parts of *Henry VI* as part of the previous season's *Richard II* and the *Henry IVs*. Then we did the three parts of *Henry VI* and *Richard III* and then, the following year, we took all that into the Aldwych – the good old days!

CM: The *Henry VI* was a defining moment for the RSC in the seventies.

PM: You're right. The most important part of it was that actually only a company like the RSC or the National could even attempt to do something on that scale. They'd only ever been done as a trilogy, I think they'd been done in the 1950s at the Vic, but greatly edited. The RSC did them in 1963 but that was part of John Barton's compilation of *The Wars of the Roses* but, in terms of the original versions, there were certain parts of *Henry VI, Part I* particularly that hadn't been done in its entirety since it was written, so we were dealing with a lot of virgin stuff, which was wonderful. Terry Hands put them on and it was a massive undertaking because we would get scene numbers and whatever scene was being rehearsed would be wheeled in front of Terry, who was whey-faced with fatigue as you can imagine, and we would then do this scene and there was no time for any fine tuning. Then the next scene would be wheeled in and he then assembled this massive programme and worked on it and put it into a viewable shape. It was a hell of an undertaking and had to be done with very broad strokes, so he had to have pretty experienced people in the cast. Actors had to be equipped vocally and in terms of technique because there wasn't time to actually spend on 'bringing somebody on' in that sense. That then led to going to the Aldwych. Then Howard Davies had been asked to do *Albie Sachs*.

CM: What attracted you to the play?

PM: What attracts me to most plays is that I love the demonstration of theatricality. I like the fact that you get a group of people who will come on and say, 'Now, look, there's nothing up our sleeves and we're going to make you say "how do you do it?"', like a circus acrobat. I think that's really exciting. What David did with *Albie Sachs*, he took this subject about which I knew nothing at all and turned it into a very theatrical piece: the leading actor has to be onstage the whole time, so there's no going off for any reason whatsoever, and he has to maintain that through-line and learn it all as a demonstration of the art of theatre. Equally he has to do that with a subject that is based on real events and turn it into a theatrical piece. The television version is not a 'theatrical' piece because we recorded it, we stopped, we went back. It's worth seeing but there is a difference: the audience came to see how you're going to convey, in this tiny space, the events surrounding this man who bravely stood up against the authorities and said, 'I'll take solitary confinement, see what else you can throw at me', and he capitulates, he gives in.

CM: One of the striking things about the play is that Albie starts out with an innocent outlook: he's alert to the terrible situation in South Africa but none the less there's a kind of innocence.

PM: Yes, and I never questioned why. This was Howard Davies's first major production for the RSC and it was never a question of bringing any kind of realistic or documentary evidence to it. The usual question is, 'Do you look like Albie Sachs?' I don't look anything like Albie Sachs – I'm not Jewish, I'm not South African – but the point is that it's the essence of the piece that David had written and I was entrusted to put that over. So it never worried me that I didn't try and make myself look like Albie Sachs. However, I think that if you were doing it for television in a more documentary, 'fly-on-the-wall' sense you would probably need somebody who resembled Albie Sachs. I met Albie on several occasions. We had the luxury of rehearsing for eight weeks, which is unusual in the theatre because of scheduling and other people's commitments, and it was a wonderful way of being able to digest the material: there was a hell of a lot to learn, and once you're on stage there's no way out, that's it.

CM: There's a very interesting moment at the end of Act One where Albie steps out and imagines an actor playing him in some future time, and speculates how an audience can experience the unendurable isolation of being in prison. As the actor you have to hold the silence for what seems to be two or three minutes, and I wondered if you had recollections of preparing for that.

PM: Yes I do remember, and there's no way you can rehearse for that in the rehearsal room, the effect has to be on the audience. Anyone who's in the rehearsal room – the director and the designer maybe, or one or two other actors who are waiting to rehearse – they've seen it, you've done it, you've had a read-through of it, you've done that passage and you can't do a three-minute silence in a read-through and there's no point doing all of that every time you rehearse it. So that was something that was never rehearsed. So I had to find a way of putting a sense of timing to it, and you had to feel the audience – I didn't know how they were going to be, but he does say, 'I want you, just for once, to see what it's like, just for two or three minutes, see what solitary confinement is like'. I lay on the bed and then I'd start internally counting for say about half a minute, and then I'd turn over and say another half a minute. But the point is stillness, not move-ment or anything to break that. And the audience would, without fail, just focus; it was quite, quite extraordinary.

CM: And I guess that the only time the audience experiences that silence for a minute or two is during things like Remembrance Day, a time of mourning, a ritual coming-together to mark a moment of grief, so it chimes into those sorts of preoccupations.

PM: Exactly. They are there thinking: 'How is he going to do it?' They don't cough, they don't move, every single performance. It was quite extraordinary how they accepted it, how they took it, and then they would talk about it afterwards and say how marvellous it was. Of course, you can't do that on telly.

The play was done to my knowledge at Lancaster but there haven't been many productions of it.[20] Then there was a benefit performance at the Young Vic in 1988. It was a benefit for Albie who was going to be in London and David asked if I'd play the doctor, which is a tiny part, who comes on and says, 'What's the matter with you? There's nothing wrong with you at all.' Then I introduced Albie to the audi-ence at the end of the performance and by then he'd lost an arm and his eye in another bomb blast in Mozambique when his car was bombed. But he was without any kind of self-pity. We said, 'Well, how do we come down the stairs of the Young Vic on to the stage?' But he came down unaided and spoke fluently and easily about certain things.

CM: Edgar himself had written *Destiny* a couple of years before *Jail Diary*. There's an interesting dialogue between the two plays: clearly, he's still pursuing a set of preoccupations about racism and its social and personal costs. I just wonder if you recollect any way in which this piece articulated with those wider political concerns in Britain at the time?

PM: No, I'm not really a political animal at all and I didn't know about Albie Sachs – not a lot of people did, though everyone knew about racism and apartheid at the time. It was just a wonderful part with a wonderful director and I'd wanted to work with Howard, who is really good – so simple and decisive. So really those are my main reasons for doing it. I was a member of the RSC and this was a wonderful part.

CM: Do you have any recollections of the rehearsal process?

PM: The way Howard envisaged it with the designer [Chris Dyer] was to keep it to that small space in the Warehouse but to delineate the prison. He was in different cells, he was moved about quite a lot, with those pipes and conduits of lighting cable, plumbing pipes and all that, so you got a sense of a small space. Obviously you have to keep a very minimal set except for a very big practical double-door so this door could slam and then the second door could slam and the noise of locks and keys being used was very important. Apart from that there was the bed, a table, very limited furniture. All the props if there were any had to be brought on – books, etc. – and he wins his battle about getting writing paper. One of the most difficult things was the word games: he started playing word games, and remembering all the states of America clockwise and then going from the outside all the way down and then alphabetically – I had to remember all that, so I cheated on that, I used to write them all down on this paper that I'd got so I could refer to it.

CM: During the performance?

PM: Oh yes, the paper was there and he talks about one of the great inventions – paper and pencil, secret communication – and he's doing 'the quick brown fox jumped over the lazy dog' stuff and I was able to write on this, as a sort of 'aide memoire', the names of certain states of the USA that I couldn't remember so I could just do a quick glance. Sometimes I wrote things on the floor, things that I had a bit of a problem with, that I could never remember. Just pencil on the floor when I knew I was going to be near it, just like a little nudge. And then you get fairly short scenes where the interrogators come and you think, 'Which scene is this, which interrogation is this?' out of the three that I have. I must say all the other actors were terrific, very supportive.

CM: It's almost as if the playing of the role conjures just a tiny fraction of the disorientation that Albie himself experiences as a prisoner, without doing any injustice to the scale of that experience.

PM: I remember when Albie came to see it fairly early on. I was asked if I'd like to meet him and I said I'd rather meet him after the show, because by then I had an idea of what he looked like. He resembled very closely Simon Callow and I met him and apparently one of the things he said was, 'Peter puts his hands in his pockets quite a lot. I don't think I put my hands in my pockets quite so much.' I got this little note from Albie and I thought, 'OK, fair enough.' Only a personal view of his, which was helpful, but didn't make much difference to the piece. It's part of his discipline: Albie's battle against authority was to make sure that he was always polite and always clean and presented himself as best as he could, and always be respectful so, therefore, he wouldn't have put his hands in his pockets. Quite right.

It's very interesting now in the light of the emphasis on torture and all those various methods of 'extraordinary rendition' and the fact of how much of that would be allowed now. He hung out there for ninety days, three months, on his own and then they said, 'You're free to go.' 'You mean I can go? Can I call my mother?' 'Yeah.' And then they arrest him immediately again. But the important thing about the play, and Howard's direction, is that any violence in the play is something that Albie hears. He hears the blacks being beaten and verbal abuse is directed towards them. It's quite important that Albie doesn't receive any brutal treatment at all, and yet he is completely broken down by this insidious solitary confinement and the effect it has on him.

CM: You went on, after *Albie*, to do *Pericles* for the RSC at the end of the decade.

PM: That's right. I did *Pericles* in 1979. When you read it you think that the play doesn't quite work, it grates in as much as you realise that it obviously isn't all Shakespeare and then, in the last movement of the play, you can feel you're back on the muscularity of his later writing. By all accounts it was co-written with somebody else, and you can tell. We did that at the Other Place and Ron Daniels directed and he just did it very simply, which you have to do in that space, and it was wonderful, wonderful storytelling which is what the play requires. I found it very difficult to do and didn't really enjoy doing it that much; I wasn't drawn to it entirely but we had a big success with it.

CM: It had been a very full decade of work for you. If I asked you to look back on that decade and reflect on it, what are the sorts of things that strike you?

PM: The early part of the 1970s was taken up with [the ITV series] *Clayhanger*. I did twenty-six episodes of the Arnold Bennett adaptation which was absolutely fantastic, and that was a long haul. I was in my prime, you need a lot of energy for this kind of stuff and you need to be like an Olympic athlete doing a repertoire at Stratford. I was able to take on all that workload: good stuff, adventurous stuff under Trevor Nunn, greatly enhanced by the opening of the small spaces both in Stratford and London enabling these other smaller pieces of work to be shown. It was an important time of my career because I'd been with the RSC for quite a long time, but *Jail Diary* was such a terrific piece to do. David is such a vibrant writer. With the *Henry VIs* and that kind of storytelling, it probably laid the foundations for David's *Nicholas Nickleby* [1980], a great, great piece of theatre which has influenced many modern productions that you now see at our big theatres, national theatres, subsidised theatres. Peter Hall had always wanted to get an ensemble company together: a group of actors that worked together for a long time and therefore are familiar with each other and work in a kind of easy way together. I mean the word 'ensemble' when I first started was a foreign word. 'Berliner Ensemble' – we didn't know what it meant to get together an ensemble company, and that's really the norm now, to get an integrated company of actors together.

Ian McNeice

The actor Ian McNeice appeared in the original production of Edgar's The Jail Diary of Albie Sachs *(1978).*

I played Rossouw, one of the S.A. policemen responsible for repeatedly interrogating Albie Sachs. During rehearsals, just as a bit of fun, I asked the director, Howard Davies, if we could have a water cooler in the scene, so that when things got a bit stressful, we could scrunch up the paper cups, and dramatically (!) throw them in the trash bin. He berated me – saying: 'McNeice, you've seen too many Hollywood movies and we will definitely NOT be having a water cooler.' *Jail Diary* turned out to be one of the highlights of my career – not least, when all the cast received a letter of thanks from Albie Sachs himself. It was an exciting time working at the Other Place theatre – a basic shack – on a play that seemed so important and relevant. Both the play and production went on to win excellent reviews.

[Email to the author, 15 March 2011]

Ann Mitchell

The actress Ann Mitchell played the role of Brenda in the original production of Edgar's Mary Barnes *(1978).*

On train to Birmingham. Feeling sad and apprehensive. Hate leaving my children but I must work. Knowing my friend Simon [Callow] will be playing [the renowned psychotherapist] Joseph Berke helps. And that Patti [Love] will be playing Mary. The rest of the actors I don't know personally but admire.

Digs OK. Rehearsals begin. Good actors. Good people. All committed to telling this story. We're a little tentative with each other but soon everyone's passion for the piece takes over.

Heated discussion. It's clear this is a cast utterly committed to the work. Peter Farrago [the director] has the foresight and courage to let us talk and argue for a very long time. We're getting to know each other and what each will bring to the table. This company want and need to honour the very soul of this piece – we all have a personal connection of some kind with the material and soon we start to 'become' our characters. I'm playing the only female therapist in the play, which means I end up doing a lot of mothering on and off the stage as does Si. The actors playing the therapists begin to become powerful and competitive and the actors playing the 'patients' eye us warily!

Joe Berke comes to some rehearsals. He is funny, irreverent, insightful, kind and wise. Listens to a barrage of questions patiently and answers them with clarity and startling honesty.

Suddenly we're on our feet. Patti embodies the very soul of Mary. Heated discussions go on long after rehearsals finish – over that age-old actors' comfort food: egg and chips.

These are British actors doing 'the Method' to the manner born.

First night a triumph. Patti giving a truly wonderful performance – every one of us there – in the moment – living, breathing this play. It pays off. We're transferring to the Royal Court. We are a company and a special one – we look out for each other and respect each other. David [Edgar], Peter, Joe – everyone over the moon – we're bringing it home to London!

On the night some of the therapists who had worked at Kingsley Hall came to the Court to see the play, I was asked if I had ever thought of becoming a therapist.[21] I'd had a lifelong interest in analysis and had devoured Freud, Jung, Adler – you name it – since the age of seventeen – and R.D. Laing and Joe Berke. To my amazement I was invited to become a student of Joe's at Arbours and eventually his boss when I was asked years later to become a trustee of Arbours![22]

Simon continues to be one of my best friends and Joe and his family have become close friends. My children blossomed and took their place in the world. It was a great experience and I look back on it with tremendous affection.

[Email to the author, 9 July 2011]

Di Seymour

Di Seymour designed many seminal theatre productions of the 1970s including Churchill's Owners *(1972),* Hare's Fanshen *(1975) and Edgar's* Destiny *(1976).*

The 1970s marked the start of my career and covered its most exciting period. I had won an Arts Council bursary and, within three days of finishing my studies, started at the Royal Court designing Howard Barker's first professional production, *Cheek*, which was reviewed by the national press.[23] Happily inexperienced and ignorant, I was terrified and thrilled by turns. The design was very Pop Art – vulgar and highly coloured – a radical departure for the director Bill Gaskill, who usually favoured Brechtian restraint and a subtle palette. I realised he regarded my work as innovative – very much 'new blood' – and this gave me confidence. My youth and fresh outlook were in my favour.

Caryl Churchill's first professional production, *Owners*, was quite challenging as both director and writer had very little idea about how they wanted the design to work. I had to go it alone to some extent and covered the walls of the Theatre Upstairs with a collage of faces and pieces of meat culled from advertising hoardings. I think it caught the wonderful wildness of the play. Deciding to work on the collage alone, I spent all night on it, helped by a couple of spliffs and cups of coffee.

Due to the extreme limits of our budget, I gingerly approached [the actress] Jill Bennett to ask her to use her own clothes for Marion, the property developer. Often a prickly and haughty woman, fortunately she loved the idea. She regarded the experience of working in the 'Fringe' as amusing 'slumming', although she came to rehearsals in a leopard-skin coat. I was invited to her house and sat on her bed as she opened an impressively large wardrobe of Yves St Laurent outfits. I then had the odd job of making *haute couture* look *nouveau riche* smart but rather flash and tasteless. Buttons, belts and other fittings were removed by nervous wardrobe staff and replaced by nasty trim from Woolworths with cheap scarves. We had made Yves St Laurent look like a butcher's wife.

It was a wonderful experience to be in at the beginning of the careers of such two radical and striking playwrights. I had struck lucky being at the Court that year, when the theatre was making waves and attracting lively and young audiences and a wide and interesting group of performers, directors and technicians. All this energy and innovation found the perfect outlet in the 'Come Together' festival [1970], for which I painted the façade of the theatre with a rainbow sunburst, assisted by two mates and two passing American bikers. Health & Safety notwithstanding . . .

All this was not happening in a vacuum, but was a reflection of the dynamic atmosphere in the arts at that time. You really felt you could gather a group, hire a van, get a grant and just do it. How and where theatre was created was up for grabs and, during these years, I designed many new plays in an ex-synagogue, pubs, school and student halls, churches, an ex-morgue, demonstrations and festivals – one strange piece by Edward Bond featured Bob Hoskins as Buddha, a crucified pig and the Hell's Angels who decided to give us kindly protection from the crowds.[24]

In 1974 I won a travelling bursary to China, then at the end of the Cultural Revolution. A few days before I was due to fly out, I bumped into Max Stafford-Clark who was planning Joint Stock's *Fanshen*. I was able to research the play as I travelled, visiting theatres, rural homes and farms. During rehearsals, I became a group member with the cast, doing Tai Chi every morning, taking part in improvisations and then going home to paint miles of red silk banners in my flat at night. Despite our ignorance of the horrors going on in China, and our naivety, the project was bold – trying to present rural, revolutionary life in China on stage was daunting. We were haunted by 'The *Mikado* syndrome' of crass impersonation – the story was dramatic and violent. Our work was thoughtful and exact – design, directors, writer and performers. Its subsequent success and the televised version on BBC2 were something of a surprise but very gratifying.

At this time, the Other Place seemed to be where the most exciting and innovative work was being done at the RSC. 'It's the tail wagging the dog' was one observation. It was an innovation for the RSC to stage David Edgar's *Destiny* – a contemporary writer and setting, and very current and controversial issues presented. A play about a Midlands by-election? Where were the frocks and poetry? With its many scenes and different settings, the play was a challenge to design. We also had a large cast and the building was pushed to the limit. One hapless punter, caught short, had the alarming experience of a group of Nazi supporters in black shirts and swastikas tramping through the gent's loo to access the stage.

More than any other play I have designed, *Destiny* brought the theatre and the outside world into the closest proximity – very important for me. I recall David [Edgar] hurrying into rehearsal with a changed scene to reblock and relearn because of some political development that had occurred overnight. The play was in the news, questions were asked in the House and its troubling issues were debated.

When the play transferred to the Aldwych, my rather conventional parents came to see it. Their daughter had finally gone 'legit' – the RSC, the West End – something to tell their friends. Sadly, on the night of their visit a National Front and Anti-Nazi demonstration took place outside the front of the theatre, and I had to usher them out of the stage door into a taxi. Legit maybe, but our work was at the heart of life, having something important to say. Just where the theatre should be.

[Letter to the author, 3 June 2011]

Mary Sheen

The actress Mary Sheen appeared in the premiere of Brenton's The Churchill Play *at Nottingham Playhouse in 1974.*

I was lucky enough to be one of the ensemble company of actors working at the Nottingham Playhouse in 1974. This was a spanking new play – an imaginative and challenging take on what could happen in an England controlled by anti-democratic and repressive forces (or neo-cons as we know them now). Freedom had been curtailed and internment camps set up for anyone who opposed the state. The play was set in a men's internment camp and had a male-dominated cast so I only had a small part, but the action was dramatic and emotional and I enjoyed the challenge performing it. I can only remember two other female characters in it: they were played by Louise Breslin (who became a great friend but sadly died some years ago) and Jane Wymark, both excellent actors.

I played Mrs Glenda Ball, the Colonel's wife. With her husband, she welcomes the visiting dignitaries who have come to inspect the camp, during which time the inmates perform 'The Churchill Play'. They attempt to break out of the camp and it all ends in mayhem. I had difficulty at first creating Glenda – I had very little knowledge of the military world, particularly the high-ranking officer class. I remember moaning on about this to an actor in the company (he's a star now!) and to shut me up he memorably said, 'Well, that means you'll do it better, doesn't it?' Actually he was right – because that meant I couldn't unthinkingly fall back on playing the usual stereotype but had to create and inhabit a genuine and unique character, which is always much more interesting.

Plus, I was intrigued to find that Howard had peppered all Glenda's lines in the newly typed script with the most bizarre punctuation. He had put commas and stops in the most unlikely and unnecessary places, sometimes before and after single words, thus fracturing her sentences. Instead of ignoring it, I made the punctuation part of her character and played her as a basically decent, frightened, neurotic woman teetering on the verge of a nervous breakdown. Having to live with the brutal, tense and potentially violent atmosphere of a concentration camp, she's desperately trying to hang on to some class of normality. I must say it has always amused and delighted me over the years that I based a whole performance on bad punctuation and/or typos. I don't know if that's what Howard wanted, but I do know he was manically typing the play up to the first day of rehearsal.

I have always enjoyed performing new and original writing and Howard Brenton at that time was one of a group of up-and-coming, innovative playwrights creating experimental, contemporary and political work. The few times I encountered Howard, he was kind, thoughtful and supportive – a gentle giant of a man. I called him the Hulk, but then I'd discovered the humour and graphic art of Marvel Comics – nuff said!

At Nottingham, we performed more plays in one season than most rep theatres now put on in a year. Miserably these days, there are very few theatres left producing whole seasons of in-house productions with ensemble companies and new writing. Looking back on those two exciting seasons performing at the Nottingham Playhouse in the 1970s, during which I was able to develop and learn so much, I do solemnly swear that I have never worked with a more creative, intelligent, hilarious and fun bunch of actors, directors, writers, designers and stage management since then.

[Letter to the author, 12 May 2011]

Kit Surrey

Kit Surrey designed Brenton's The Churchill Play *for the RSC at the Other Place (1978), his third production after* Dingo *by Charles Wood for the director Barry Kyle (1976) and* Captain Swing *by Peter Whelan for Bill Alexander (1978).*

The legacy of Buzz Goodbody was still palpable, in the building itself and in the intense commitment and dedication of the staff, people like the indefatigable administrator, Jean Moore, the head of lighting,

Leo Leibovici and Andrew Tansley, the production manager. In *Other Spaces: New Theatre and the RSC*, Colin Chambers describes Goodbody's ethos as 'hard-headed radical realism' hand in hand with the concept of the 'empty space' with the minimal of set design.[25] Most of this, of course, was dictated by very restricted budgets, yet one must not forget that designers, in theory, had the impressive resources of the RSC available to them, with some caveats. The main house productions did sometimes still seem to take precedence when it came to the amount of time allocated from scenic, wardrobe and prop departments.

One huge advantage to being part of the RSC structure was the six- or seven-week rehearsal period which allowed detailed research from both cast and designer. With *The Churchill Play* I can recall the unnerving trip to a local army camp for the cast, director and designer to handle and fire Sterling sub-machine guns and the weekly sessions led by a scary drill sergeant to try and instil a credible military discipline in the cast.

By 1976 the permanent auditorium was in place which had been designed by Chris Dyer and John Napier. This arrangement was four-sided with an upper gallery level and a maximum seating capacity of 180. Plays could be staged 'in the round', or as was more often the case, with the audience on three sides allowing the back wall and its gallery as an acting/design focus. Ron Daniels, who had become artistic director in December 1976, argues that a 'policy of giving playwrights a second or third production of a play that might otherwise not be produced for reasons of taste, box office, or resources – such as *The Churchill Play* or *Dingo* – is as important a service to writers as is the Warehouse policy of staging their new work'.[26] My main impression of this 'tin hut down the road' (from the Royal Shakespeare Theatre) was the intensity of the place, its lack of any pretension, its small size and yet perhaps just large enough for epic qualities to be realised. Just what I felt *The Churchill Play* needed. I felt that we had to work *with* the space, not against it. As always with small theatre spaces, attention to detail is imperative because of the proximity of the audience and, together with the need to point up the central image in the text of the 'play within the play', we decided to make Churchill's catafalque for his lying in state at Westminster Hall as realistic as it could be. It was designed to dominate and oppress the intimate space with dim atmospheric lighting and a huge, glowing, backlit stained-glass window. We hoped to trick the audience into perhaps believing that this was where the play was genuinely set. This impressive image then suffers the abrupt intrusion of neon strip lights being switched on and armed military guards destroying the inmates' lovingly built props – this was deliberately shocking and calculated to emphasise the shift from the lying in state of Churchill in 1965 to the stark and brutal reality of a disused aircraft hangar that had become the twenty-eighth internment camp in contemporary Britain.

The floor of the Other Place acting area became desperately important. The existing bare wooden boards that had worked so well for *Captain Swing*, which I had designed two months earlier for Bill Alexander, were simply not a harsh enough statement for the environment of *The Churchill Play*. I designed a rough 'concrete' oil-stained hangar floor which was built in sections that could be laid quickly for the changeovers in the repertoire and utilised the existing corrugated-iron back wall and its upper gallery level with additional sections of corrugated-iron walling. This, plus a few empty oil barrels and a makeshift stage erected for the second performance of the play within the play, was all there was. I hoped in many ways that the audience would feel that there was in fact no 'designed' set and that they were occupying the same bleak space as the protagonists.

I still remember feeling that the work being presented at the Other Place was a crucial and integral part of the RSC's artistic policy with only the occasional concern that the main house took precedence in the order of things, that it was down to the dedication, ingenuity and belief of all of us who worked 'down the road' that everything got done on budget and on time. In later years there did grow a feeling that the Other Place became its own 'establishment' and perhaps less radical. As budgets grew, designs grew more complex, there were worries that perhaps there was a possible loss of the initial integrity that had been dictated by necessity. There always has been a lively debate over the effect on design imposed by low budgets – whether they help engineer creativity out of need or whether they restrict the designer's imagination. Of course, in all of this, what is crucial is that the design serves the text and not the designer's ego.

[Letter to the author, 24 March 2011]

A final word . . .

The following article by Howard Brenton was first published as 'Howard Brenton on The Churchill Play*' (RSC Warehouse Writers – A Series, No. 3) to accompany the RSC production in 1978.*

I wrote *The Churchill Play* in 1974, with a mind wonderfully concentrated by the fun of the three-day week and Edward Heath's lukewarm rehashes of wartime rhetoric. A critic called the play a plum piece of 'the theatre of paranoia'. It was meant as an insult but I rather like it. It certainly is a play about worst fears coming true. (At least, about the worst fears of a lot of us coming true. It's scary to realise that the play's 'worst fears' are some people's fondest wishes.)

The play's themes are to do with a future we might have to face foretold from how the Second World War was fought and won and the nature of the peace that followed and in which we still live. But it's not a prophecy, it's a satire for the present – though a satire which aspires to the heavy-mob tradition of Swift and Orwell, not the debased satire of silly walks and literary send-ups that passes today.

Some years ago I had a job on a traffic survey. An old man drove me up and down a mile of road outside Portsmouth. We had to park now and again to count the passing cars. After a day we gave up, cooked the figures and spent the time talking. Perhaps irritated by the callow child of the peace he was stuck with, the old man handed out, day after day, the memories he had of Portsmouth during the war (I was a 'blitz baby' born in that city). He spoke of the panic, the looting, the hatred for police and wardens, the universal anger, the 'trekkers' who walked out of the city on to the Downs where they camped for weeks (the same thing happened in Glasgow). He was not describing defeatism or cowardice. They occurred but so did the kindness of neighbour to neighbour, the legendary 'dawn cups of tea after the raid'. What was extraordinary and overwhelming was that the torrent of stories, impressions and comments was nothing less than a detailed account from personal experience of the beginning of a popular uprising, a people's revolt that was on the boil in a bombed English city thirty-five years ago. It was a glimpse of a history other than that in the books, in the television documentaries and the war films.

In Portsmouth the heavy bombing died away, the authorities got a grip, the weariness of the last three years of the war dampened down the city. Minds closed to the memories of the blitz. Just as a state like Russia cannot tolerate in its collective memory the truth of what happened in the 1920s and 1930s, so individuals cannot live with certain personal memories, which must be forgotten or changed into funny and heroic stories ('The night Grandma's house went') to tell the children. Real history is very dangerous. In a state if it gets widely known it can make political legitimacy impossible. For an individual it can make a lie of day-to-day existence.

The old man had committed a shocking indiscretion. Playwrights depend on such encounters. *The Churchill Play* was fuelled by them. Real history is very unofficial. Its only authenticity is the human voice, gleaned as it is from a chance meeting with a drunken Army Officer in a provincial hotel who turns out to be on forty-eight hours' leave from guard duty at Long Kesh (now the Maze Prison) and sick to his soul with his job, from the stories and remarks of old men and women told bitterly and furtively, as if something huge and dead and intimidating overshadows their memories.

The play, then, is written in the belief that the real history of the war the people won is not the official history reflected today in the mythic, though musty, figure of Winston Spencer Churchill – huge, dead and intimidating. Writing him I thought a lot of an engraving that is often printed in Hobbes's *Leviathan*. A king stands astride a country. His body is made up of thousands of tiny figures, 'the people'. The leader becomes the people, the people become the leader. That's how the official history of 'The Nation' and 'Churchill the War Leader' looks. But to live it, to be one of the toes, or a speck in the armpit of that giant? Of course no one actually lived the official history of the war – not Annie, bombed in Peckham in the play, not

Churchill himself. The official past has nothing to do with real history, it has everything to do with the present.

Writing a play together recently, Trevor Griffiths and I had a motto, pinched from Gramsci, for playwrights trying to detonate and crack the mould of the official view of the world that holds us in thrall.[27] It was 'Pessimism of the intellect: Optimism of the will'. It does very well too for how I tried to write *The Churchill Play*. Anything but 'intellectual pessimism' would be dishonest and trivial trying to write straight, serious plays today. But the optimism? Well, I think that some day, in a sane and granted a probably very distant Britain, the answer to the question 'What was the most important outcome of the Second World War?' will not be 'Hitler was defeated' but 'The chance to build a free socialist Britain was lost'. But then those British citizens of the future good will shrug and say 'But that was just a defeat along the way. They wrote plays about that, around then.'

NOTES

Introduction: Living in the 1970s

1. Some of the factual information in this introduction is sourced from the excellent 'Books on the 1970s' listed in the Select Bibliography. Plus: Martin Bright, 'Look Back in Anger', *Guardian*, 3 February 2002; Derek Gillard, 'Education in England: a Brief History', www.educationengland.org.uk/history/chapter07.html (accessed 17 March 2011); Michael McCarthy, '1970 vs 2010: 40 Years when We Got Older, Richer and Fatter', *Independent*, 3 July 2010; Office for National Statistics, www.statistics.gov.uk/ (accessed 17 March 2011).

1 Theatre in the 1970s

1. Francis Wheen, *Strange Days Indeed: The Golden Age of Paranoia* (London: Fourth Estate, 2009), p. 309.
2. These books are listed in the Select Bibliography.
3. Andy Beckett, *When the Lights Went Out: What Really Happened to Britain in the Seventies* (London: Faber and Faber, 2009), p. 521.
4. Anthea Gerrie, 'Fondue: It's a Cheesy Seventies Revival', *Independent*, 20 October 2010.
5. Alwyn W. Turner, *Crisis? What Crisis? Britain in the 1970s* (London: Aurum Press, 2008), p. 42.
6. Beckett, op. cit., p. 5.
7. Simon Callow, '"This is my playground"', *Guardian*, 8 January 2003.
8. Thanks to Dan Rebellato and John Marshall for the observation about the Transit van.
9. Quoted in Susan Painter, *Edgar the Playwright* (London: Methuen Drama, 1996), p. 18.
10. John McGrath, 'The Theory and Practice of Political Theatre', *Theatre Quarterly*, Vol. 9, No. 35 (Autumn 1979), p. 45.
11. This chapter explores some of the major alternative theatre companies of the 1970s with the exception of Portable Theatre, which is discussed in Chapter 2, and Joint Stock, which is discussed in Chapter 3.
12. Tony Bicât, 'Portable Theatre: "fine detail, rough theatre". A Personal Memoir', in

Richard Boon (ed.), *The Cambridge Companion to David Hare* (Cambridge: Cambridge University Press, 2007), p. 18.

13. J. W. Lambert, *Drama in Britain: 1964–1973* (Essex: Longman, 1974), p. 43.

14. Catherine Itzin, *Stages in the Revolution: Political Theatre in Britain Since 1968* (London: Eyre Methuen, 1980), p. 9.

15. See http://www.unfinishedhistories.com/interviews/interviewees/noel-greig/ (accessed 13 March 2011).

16. Quoted in Catherine Itzin and Simon Trussler, 'Petrol Bombs through the Proscenium Arch', *Theatre Quarterly*, Vol. 5, No. 17 (1975), p. 7. The interview itself was given in the previous year.

17. Quoted in ibid., p. 53.

18. Sandy Craig, 'Reflexes of the Future', in Sandy Craig (ed.), *Dreams and Deconstructions: Alternative Theatre in Britain* (Ambergate: Amber Lane Press, 1980), p. 23.

19. Quoted in Itzin, op. cit., p. 51.

20. Quoted in Turner, op. cit., p. 199.

21. Theatre programme for David Edgar's *Rent or Caught in the Act*, the General Will: 1972, n.p.

22. For further commentary about his early work in Bradford, see the author's interview with David Edgar in Chapter 4 of this book.

23. Quoted in Itzin, op. cit., p. 140.

24. From the author's interview with David Edgar in Chapter 4 of this book.

25. John McGrath, *A Good Night Out – Popular Theatre: Audience, Class and Form* (London: Methuen, 1981), pp. 103–4.

26. David Edgar, 'Ten Years of Political Theatre, 1968–78', *Theatre Quarterly*, Vol. 8, No. 32 (Winter 1979), p. 25.

27. Nadine Holdsworth, 'Introduction', in John McGrath, *Naked Thoughts that Roam About: Reflections on Theatre*, ed. Nadine Holdsworth (London: Nick Hern, 2002), p. xvi.

28. Quoted in Turner, op. cit., p. 234.

29. Anonymous, 'Theatre Survey No. 1: Guide to Underground Theatre', *Theatre Quarterly*, Vol. 1, No. 1 (January–March 1971), p. 64.

30. There is an affectionate pastiche of feminist agitprop in scene two of Howard Brenton's *Greenland* (1988) when a three-person '*street theatre troupe*' perform the crucifixion of a 'housewife' Christ outside a polling station during the 1987 general election. See Howard Brenton, *Greenland* in *Plays: Two* (London: Methuen Drama, 1989), p. 317.

31. Quoted in Michelene Wandor, *Carry On Understudies* (London and New York: Routledge & Kegan Paul, 1986 [1981]), p. 40.

32. Press release quoted in ibid., p. 51.

33. Ann McFerran, 'The Theatre's (Somewhat) Angry Young Women', *Time Out* (28 October–3 November 1977), pp. 13–15.

34. Quoted in Wandor, op. cit., p. 161.

35. Gillian Hanna, 'Waiting for Spring to Come Again: Feminist Theatre, 1978 and 1989', interview with Lizbeth Goodman, *New Theatre Quarterly*, Vol. 6, No. 21 (February 1990), p. 44.

36. Michelene Wandor, 'The Fifth Column: Feminism and Theatre', *Drama – The Quarterly Theatre Review*, Vol. 2, No. 152 (Summer 1984), p. 5.

37. See Wandor, *Carry On . . .*, op. cit., pp. 122–3.

38. Clare Venables, 'The Woman Director in the Theatre', *Theatre Quarterly*, Vol. 10, No. 38 (Summer 1980), p. 3.

39. Hanna, op. cit., p. 56.

40. Alan Sinfield, *Out on Stage: Lesbian and Gay Theatre in the Twentieth Century* (New Haven, CT and London: Yale University Press, 1999), p. 304.

41. See www.unfinishedhistories.com/interviews/interviewees/noel-greig/ (accessed 13 March 2011).

42. Rupert Smith, 'Straight Theatre Is All Fake', *Guardian*, 5 December 2005.

43. Dominic Shellard, *British Theatre Since the War* (New Haven, CT and London: Yale University Press, 1999), p. 155.

44. Colin Chambers, *Black and Asian Theatre in Britain: A History* (Abingdon: Routledge, 2011), p. 140. Chapter 6 of this excellent book focuses on the 1970s and I am grateful to Chambers for allowing me to see an advance copy before its publication.

45. Ibid., p. 156.

46. Ibid., p. 155.

47. David Edgar, 'Towards a Theatre of Dynamic Ambiguities', interviewed by Clive Barker and Simon Trussler, *Theatre Quarterly*, Vol. 9, No. 33 (Spring 1979), p. 13.

48. Edgar, 'Ten Years . . .', op. cit., pp. 25–33.

49. Quoted in Maria DiCenzo, *The Politics of Alternative Theatre in Britain, 1968–1990* (Cambridge: Cambridge University Press, 1996), p. 48.

50. Edgar, 'Ten Years . . .', op. cit., p. 28.

51. Ibid., p. 26.

52. See the author's interview with David Edgar in Chapter 4 of this book.

53. Clive Barker, 'Alternative Theatre/Political Theatre', in Holderness, Graham (ed.), *The Politics of Theatre and Drama* (Basingstoke: Macmillan, 1992), p. 31.

54. Howard Barker, *Howard Barker Interviews 1980–2010: Conversations in Catastrophe*, ed. Mark Brown (London: Oberon Books, 2011), p. 197.

55. Trevor Griffiths, 'A Play Postscript', interview with Nigel Andrews, *Plays and Players* (April 1972), p. 83. Italics in original.

56. McGrath, 'Theory and Practice . . .', op. cit., pp. 43–54; McGrath, *Good Night Out*, op. cit.

57. McGrath, 'Theory and Practice . . .', op. cit., p. 54.

58. McGrath, *A Good Night Out*, op. cit., p. 34.

59. John McGrath, 'Better a Bad Night in Bootle . . .', *Theatre Quarterly*, Vol. 5, No. 19 (September–November 1975), pp. 45–6. See also McGrath, *Good Night Out*, op. cit., pp. 110–17.

60. Edgar, 'Towards a Theatre . . .', op. cit., p. 15. Italics in original.

61. Quoted in Itzin, op. cit., p. 187.

62. Peter Ansorge, *Disrupting the Spectacle: Five Years of Experimental and Fringe Theatre in Britain* (London: Pitman, 1975), p. 80.

63. See the author's interview with David Edgar in Chapter 4 of this book.

64. Itzin, op. cit., p. 139.

65. See Steve Grant, 'Voicing the Protest' in Craig, op. cit., p. 117.

66. Ansorge, op. cit., p. 81.

67. See Chapter 3 for a detailed examination of two major state of the nation plays: David Edgar's *Destiny* (1976) and David Hare's *Plenty* (1978).

68. Anthony Everitt, 'David Edgar', programme note for *Destiny*, RSC: 1976, n.p.

69. Howard Brenton, 'Preface', *Plays: One* (London: Methuen Drama, 1986), n.p. See also the author's interview with Brenton in Chapter 4 of this book.

70. For further discussion, see the author's interview with Howard Barker in Chapter 4 of this book.

71. John Calder, 'Political Theatre in Britain Today', *Gambit*, Vol. 8, No. 31 (1977), p. 7, p. 11.

72. Quoted in DiCenzo, op. cit., p.28.

73. Wandor, *Carry On . . .*, op. cit., p. 80.

74. DiCenzo, op. cit., p. 63.

75. Ibid., p. 74.

76. Clive Barker, op. cit., p. 33; Marowitz quoted in Itzin, op. cit., p. 158; McGrath, *Good Night Out*, op. cit., p. 104.

77. Itzin, op. cit., p. 158.

78. Baz Kershaw, *The Politics of Performance: Radical Theatre as Cultural Intervention* (London: Routledge, 1992), p. 137.

79. Bicât, op. cit., p. 29.

80. Itzin, op. cit., p. 159.

81. Ibid.

82. Quoted in Sandy Craig, 'The Bitten Hand', in Craig, op. cit., p. 182.

83. Itzin, op. cit., p. 156.

84. Quoted in ibid., p. 157.

85. DiCenzo, op. cit., p. 67.

86. Itzin, op. cit., p. 33; William Gaskill, *A Sense of Direction: Life at The Royal Court* (London: Faber and Faber, 1988), p. 138.

87. Colin Chambers, *Other Spaces: New Theatre and the RSC* (London: Eyre Methuen, 1980), p. 46.

88. Shellard, op. cit., p. 185.

89. Ibid., p. 159; Turner, op. cit., p. 106.

90. Peter Hall paraphrasing Mishcon, quoted in Wheen, op. cit., p. 54.

91. Quoted in Turner, op. cit., p. 160.

92. Trevor Griffiths, 'Transforming the Husk of Capitalism', interview by Catherine Itzin and Simon Trussler, *Theatre Quarterly*, Vol. 6, No. 22 (Summer 1976), p. 40.

93. Turner, op. cit., p. 106.

94. Quoted in Wandor, *Carry On . . .*, op. cit., p. 83.

95. Gaskill, op. cit., p. 95.

96. Philip Roberts, *The Royal Court and the Modern Stage* (Cambridge: Cambridge University Press, 1999), p. 137.

97. Terry Browne, *Playwrights' Theatre: The English Stage Company at the Royal Court* (London: Pitman, 1975), p. 94.

98. See Di Seymour's contribution to Chapter 4 of this book.

99. Gaskill, op. cit., pp. 117–8.

100. Ibid., p. 118.

101. Quoted in Browne, op. cit., p. 88.

102. Gaskill, op. cit., p. 129.

103. Quoted in Roland Rees, *Fringe First: Pioneers of Fringe Theatre on Record* (London: Oberon, 1992), p. 204.

104. Quoted in Duncan Wu, *Making Plays: Interviews with Contemporary British Dramatists and Their Directors* (Basingstoke: Macmillan, 2000), p. 25.

105. Gaskill, op. cit., pp. 122–3.

106. Gresdna A. Doty, and Billy J. Harbin (eds), *Inside the Royal Court, 1956–1981: Artists Talk* (Baton Rouge and London: Louisiana State University Press, 1990), p. 57.

107. Gaskill, op. cit., p. 106.

108. Doty and Harbin, op. cit., p. 61.

109. Quoted in ibid., p. 65.

110. Shellard, 1999, p. 163.

111. Quoted in ibid., p. 164.

112. Ansorge, op. cit., p. 80.

113. Anon, *Sunday Telegraph*, 23 September 1973.

114. McGrath, 'Better a Bad . . .', op. cit., p. 50.

115. David Wiles, *A Short History of Western Performance Space* (Cambridge: Cambridge University Press, 2003), p. 248.

116. Lambert, op. cit., p. 43.

117. Gaskill, op. cit., p. 117.

118. See also Lambert, op. cit., p.45.

119. Ibid., p. 43.

120. Howard Brenton, 'For Mickery with Love' in *Hot Irons: Diaries, Essays, Journalism* (London: Methuen, 1995), p. 53. Italics in original.

121. Itzin, op. cit., p. 337.

122. John Calder, 'Editorial: Political Theatre in 1980', *Gambit*, Vol. 9, No. 36 (1980), p. 3.

123. David Edgar, 'Public Theatre in a Private Age', in *The Second Time as Farce: Reflections on the Drama of Mean Times* (London: Lawrence & Wishart, 1988), p. 165.

2 Introducing the Playwrights

1. John Russell Taylor, *The Second Wave: British Drama of the Sixties* (London: Eyre Methuen, 1971).
2. Ibid., pp. 7–15.
3. See also Chapter 4 of this book, where both Brenton and Edgar discuss their early careers in their respective interviews with the author.
4. Philip Roberts, *About Churchill: the Playwright & the Work* (London: Faber and Faber, 2008), p. 44.
5. Ibid., p. 58. Roberts's analysis of Churchill's unpublished radio plays is detailed and illuminating.
6. Geraldine Cousin, *Churchill the Playwright* (London: Methuen, 1989), p. 80.
7. Quoted in Linda Fitzsimmons (ed.), *File on Churchill* (London: Methuen, 1989), p. 85.
8. Caryl Churchill, 'Introduction', *Plays: One* (London: Methuen, 1985), p. xi.
9. Caryl Churchill, 'The Common Imagination and the Individual Voice', interviewed by Geraldine Cousin, *New Theatre Quarterly*, Vol. 4, No. 13 (February 1988), p. 5.
10. Churchill, 'Introduction', op. cit., p. 130.
11. Tony Bicât, 'Portable Theatre: "fine detail, rough theatre". A personal memoir' in Richard Boon (ed.), *The Cambridge Companion to David Hare* (Cambridge: Cambridge University Press, 2007), p. 22. Bicât's memoir in this collection offers an entertaining and evocative insight into Portable's work.
12. Richard Boon, *Brenton the Playwright* (London: Methuen Drama, 1991), p. 58.
13. J.W. Lambert, *Drama in Britain: 1964–1973* (Harlow: Longman, 1974), p. 45.
14. Peter Ansorge, *Disrupting the Spectacle: Five Years of Experimental and Fringe Theatre in Britain* (London: Pitman, 1975), p. 20.
15. Bicât, op. cit., p. 26.
16. Ibid., p. 27.
17. Quoted in Catherine Itzin and Simon Trussler, 'David Hare: From Portable Theatre to Joint Stock ... via Shaftesbury Avenue', *New Theatre Quarterly*, Vol. 5, No. 20 (1975–6), p. 111.
18. Howard Brenton, *Hot Irons: Diaries, Essays, Journalism* (London: Methuen, 1995), p. 3.
19. Quoted in Steve Grant, 'Voicing the Protest: The New Writers' in Sandy Craig (ed.), *Dreams and Deconstructions: Alternative Theatre in Britain* (Ambergate: Amber Lane Press, 1980), p. 122.
20. Howard Brenton, 'Petrol Bombs Through the Proscenium Arch', interviewed by Catherine Itzin and Simon Trussler, *Theatre Quarterly*, Vol. 5, No. 17 (March–May 1975), p. 20.
21. David Hare, 'Raymond Williams', in *Obedience, Struggle and Revolt: Lectures on Theatre* (London: Faber and Faber, 2005), p. 161.
22. Quoted in Duncan Wu, *Making Plays: Interviews with Contemporary British Dramatists and Their Directors* (Basingstoke: Macmillan, 2000), p. 20.

23. Brenton, 'Petrol Bombs . . .', op. cit., p. 8.

24. Bicât, op. cit., p. 21.

25. Quoted in John Bull, *New British Political Dramatists* (London: Macmillan, 1984), p. 41.

26. Howard Brenton, *Fruit*, 1970, unpublished manuscript.

27. Brenton's 1989 essay 'The Spaceman Amongst the Tower Blocks', published in his autobiographical collection *Hot Irons*, extols the Situationist influence at length. See Brenton, *Hot Irons*, op. cit., pp. 38–43, and also my interview with Brenton in Chapter 4 of this book.

28. Howard Brenton, *Epsom Downs* in *Plays: One* (London: Methuen Drama, 1986), p. 305.

29. Brenton, *Hot Irons*, op. cit., pp. 42–3.

30. Quoted in Wu, op. cit., p. 25.

31. Brenton, 'Petrol Bombs . . .', op. cit., p. 12.

32. David Edgar, 'Towards a Theatre of Dynamic Ambiguities', interviewed by Clive Barker and Simon Trussler, *Theatre Quarterly*, Vol. 9, No. 33 (Spring 1979), p. 4.

33. See also my interview with Edgar in Chapter 4 of this book.

34. Edgar, 'Towards a Theatre . . .', op. cit., p. 9.

35. David Edgar, 'Public Theatre in a Private Age', in *The Second Time as Farce – Reflections on the Drama of Mean Times* (London: Lawrence & Wishart, 1988), p. 171.

3 Playwrights and Plays: Caryl Churchill

1. Caryl Churchill, 'Not Ordinary, Not Safe: A Direction for Drama?', *The Twentieth Century* (November 1960), p. 450.

2. Churchill quoted in Kathleen Betsko, Rachel Koenig and Emily Mann, 'Caryl Churchill', in Kathleen Betsko, and Rachel Koenig (eds), *Interviews with Contemporary Women Playwrights* (New York: Beech Tree Books, 1987), p. 78.

3. Philip Roberts, *About Churchill: The Playwright and the Work* (London: Faber and Faber, 2008), p. xxvi. Roberts's book offers useful analysis of Churchill's work, including her early writing for theatre and radio prior to the 1970s.

4. Christian W. Thomsen, 'Three Socialist Playwrights: John McGrath, Caryl Churchill, Trevor Griffiths', in Christopher W. E. Bigsby (ed.), *Contemporary English Drama* (London: Edward Arnold, 1981), p. 166. Feminist critics also tend to analyse *Owners* as formative.

5. Jane Thomas, 'The Plays of Caryl Churchill: Essays in Refusal', in Adrian Page (ed.), *The Death of the Playwright? Modern British Drama and Literary Theory* (Basingstoke: Palgrave Macmillan, 1992), pp. 160, 162.

6. Daniel Jernigan, '*Traps, Softcops, Blue Heart,* and *This is a Chair*: Tracking Epistemological Upheaval in Caryl Churchill's Shorter Plays', *Modern Drama*, Vol. 47, No. 1 (2004), p. 40.

7. Harry Derbyshire, 'Churchill's 21st Century Poetics', paper presented at International Symposium 'Churchill Now: 21st Century Caryl Churchill', University of Lincoln, 16 April 2011.

8. Dan Rebellato, 'On Churchill's Influences', in Elaine Aston and Elin Diamond (eds), *The Cambridge Companion to Caryl Churchill* (Cambridge: Cambridge University Press, 2009), p. 169.

9. Caryl Churchill, *Owners*, *Vinegar Tom* and *Cloud Nine* in *Plays: One* (London: Methuen Drama, 1985). Subsequent quotations from the plays and their introductions are from this edition.

10. Janelle Reinelt, 'On Feminist and Sexual Politics', in Aston and Diamond (eds), op. cit., p. 18.

11. Michelene Wandor, *Post-War British Drama: Looking Back in Gender* (London: Routledge, 2001), pp. 143, 144, 145.

12. Margot Canaday, 'Promising Alliances: The Critical Feminist Theory of Nancy Fraser and Seyla Benhabib', *Feminist Review*, No. 74 (2003), p. 51. The 'Critical Theory' denomination comes from the Frankfurt School's (neo-Marxist) tradition of thought.

13. Nancy Fraser, *Justice Interruptus: Critical Reflections on the 'Postsocialist' Condition* (London: Routledge, 1997), p. 186, p. 187, p. 31.

14. Peggy Ramsay, letter to Caryl Churchill (1 August 1973), quoted in Roberts, op. cit., p. 45.

15. Churchill, interviewed by Steve Gooch, 'Caryl Churchill', *Plays and Players*, No. 20 (January 1973), p. 40.

16. John Elsom, review of *Owners*, *The Listener*, 21 December 1972; B. A. Young, review of *Owners*, *Financial Times*, 13 December 1972; Robert Brustein, 'Subjects of Scandal and Concern', *Observer*, 17 December 1972. Selected reviews and interviews, up to 1988, are collated in Linda Fitzsimmons (ed.), *File on Churchill* (London: Methuen, 1989). I have made use of this excellent resource in my research for this essay.

17. Churchill admits that re-reading Joe Orton's *Entertaining Mr Sloane* (1964) might have influenced the style of the play. See her introduction to *Owners* in *Plays: One*, op. cit., p. 4. Churchill's comment about characters is quoted in Roberts, op. cit., p. 49.

18. John Vidal, review of *Owners*, *Guardian*, 9 April 1987.

19. Michael Billington, review of *Owners*, *Guardian*, 13 December 1972.

20. Churchill, interviewed by Gooch, op. cit., p. 40.

21. Jean E. Howard, 'On Owning and Owing: Caryl Churchill and the Nightmare of Capital', in Aston and Diamond (eds), op. cit., p. 36.

22. Mark Thacker Brown, '"Constantly Coming Back": Eastern Thought and the Plays of Caryl Churchill', in Phyllis R. Randall (ed.), *Caryl Churchill: A Casebook* (New York and London: Garland, 1988), pp. 25, 45.

23. Churchill, interviewed by John Hall, 'Close Up', *Guardian*, 12 December 1972, my emphasis.

24. Brown, op. cit., pp. 26, 28.

25. See R. Darren Gobert, 'On Performance and Selfhood in Caryl Churchill', in Aston

and Diamond (eds), op. cit., pp. 105–25. Gobert emphasises the 'patrilineal logic' of the anxieties about identity presented in *A Number* (2002), an all-male play about father and son/s (p. 119). Clegg in *Owners*, who wants to keep Lisa's baby in order to continue his 'Clegg and son' business, is an early representative of this 'patrilinear' obsession.

26. Elaine Aston, *Caryl Churchill*, 2nd edn (Plymouth: Northcote House, 2001 [1997]), p. 19.

27. Helen Keyssar, 'Doing Dangerous History: Caryl Churchill and *A Mouthful of Birds*', in Randall (ed.), op. cit., p. 132.

28. Lisa Merrill, 'Monsters and Heroines: Caryl Churchill's Women', in Randall (ed.), op. cit., p. 86, p. 82.

29. Rebellato, op. cit., pp. 167–9.

30. Amelia Howe Kritzer, *The Plays of Caryl Churchill: Theatre of Empowerment* (Basingstoke: Macmillan, 1991), p. 62.

31. Seyla Benhabib, 'The Debate Over Women and Moral Theory Revisited', in Johanna Meehan (ed.), *Feminists Read Habermas: Gendering the Subject of Discourse* (London: Routledge, 1995), pp. 181–203.

32. Michelene Wandor, *Understudies: Theatre and Sexual Politics* (London: Methuen, 1981), p. 36.

33. Elin Diamond, 'Closing No Gaps: Aphra Behn, Caryl Churchill, and Empire', in Randall (ed.), op. cit., p. 169.

34. Siân Adiseshiah, *Churchill's Socialism: Political Resistance in the Plays of Caryl Churchill* (Newcastle upon Tyne: Cambridge Scholars, 2009), pp. 60–1.

35. Arthur Miller, *The Crucible*, in *Collected Plays* (London: Secker & Warburg, 1967).

36. Janelle Reinelt, 'Beyond Brecht: Britain's New Feminist Drama', in Sue-Ellen Case (ed.), *Performing Feminisms: Feminist Critical Theory and Theatre* (London: Johns Hopkins University Press, 1990), pp. 150–9.

37. Michael Coveney, review of *Vinegar Tom*, *Financial Times*, 15 December 1976; David Zane Mairowitz, 'God and the Devil', *Plays and Players* (February 1977), p. 24.

38. Aston, op. cit., p. 26.

39. Arthur Miller, 'Introduction to the Collected Plays', in Miller, op. cit., pp. 42, 43.

40. D. Keith Peacock, *Radical Stages: Alternative History in Modern British Drama* (London: Greenwood, 1991), p. 68.

41. Adiseshiah, op. cit., p. 95.

42. Wandor, *Understudies*, op. cit., p. 37. See also Reinelt, 'On Feminist and Sexual Politics', op. cit., p. 20.

43. Richard H. Palmer, *The Contemporary British History Play* (Westport, CT: Greenwood, 1998), pp. 12–13.

44. Mark Berninger, 'Variations of a Genre: The British History Play in the Nineties', in Bernhard Reitz and Mark Berninger (eds), 'British Drama of the 1990s', *Anglistik & Englischunterricht*, No. 64 (2002), pp. 39–40. The 'alternative', in Berninger's definition, could be seen in terms of form or content; in this case, it is both.

45. Sue-Ellen Case, *Feminism and Theatre* (Basingstoke: Macmillan, 1988), p. 74.

46. Churchill, quoted in Catherine Itzin, *Stages in the Revolution: Political Theatre in Britain Since 1968* (London: Methuen, 1980), p. 285.

47. Adiseshiah, op. cit., p. 124. Adiseshiah quotes from Barbara Ehrenreich, and Deidre English, *Witches, Midwives and Nurses: A History of Women Healers* (London: Writers and Readers Publishing Cooperative, 1976), p. 33.

48. Kritzer, op. cit., p. 91.

49. Gillian Hanna, 'Feminism and Theatre', *Theatre Papers*, Second Series, No. 8 (1978), pp. 9–10.

50. Antony Sher in Rob Ritchie (ed.), *The Joint Stock Book: The Making of a Theatre Collective* (London, Methuen, 1987), p. 139.

51. Churchill, interviewed by John Simon, 'Sex, Politics and Other Play Things', *Vogue* (August 1983), p. 126; Churchill, interviewed by Lynne Truss, 'A Fair Cop', *Plays and Players* (January 1984), p. 10.

52. Aston, op. cit., pp. 32–4. See also Susan Carlson, 'Comic Collisions: Convention, Rage, and Order', *New Theatre Quarterly*, Vol. 3, No. 12 (1987), pp. 303–16.

53. Frances Gray, 'Mirrors of Utopia: Caryl Churchill and Joint Stock', in James Acheson (ed.), *British and Irish Drama Since 1960* (Basingstoke: Macmillan, 1993), p. 53. See also Elin Diamond, 'Refusing the Romanticism of Identity: Narrative Interventions in Churchill, Benmussa, Duras', in Sue-Ellen Case (ed.), op. cit., pp. 92–105. Following French psychoanalytic theory, Diamond reads Betty's invisibility in terms of women's absence from the symbolic order and criticises Churchill for presenting a 'reassembled female identity', in the second act.

54. Rhonda Blair, '"Not ... but"/"Not-Not-Me": Musings on Cross-Gender Performance', in Ellen Donkin and Susan Clement (eds), *Upstaging Big Daddy: Directing Theatre as if Gender and Race Matter* (Ann Arbor: Michigan University Press, 1993), pp. 295, 292. Blair quotes from Judith Butler's seminal chapter 'Performative Acts and Gender Constitution: An Essay in Phenomenology and Feminist Theory', in Sue-Ellen Case (ed.), op. cit., pp. 270–82.

55. Blair, op. cit., p. 296.

56. Kritzer, op. cit., p. 115. For a detailed analysis of Churchill's 'ghosts' see Ann Wilson, 'Hauntings: Ghosts and the Limits of Realism in *Cloud Nine* and *Fen* by Caryl Churchill', in Nicole Boireau (ed.), *Drama on Drama: Dimensions of Theatricality on the Contemporary British Stage* (Basingstoke: Macmillan, 1997), pp. 152–67.

57. John Clum, '"The Work of Culture": *Cloud Nine* and Sex/Gender Theory', in Randall (ed.), op. cit., p. 108.

58. Reinelt, 'On Feminist and Sexual Politics', op. cit., p. 28.

59. Churchill in Betsko and Koenig (eds), op. cit., p. 83.

60. Apollo Amoko, 'Casting Aside Colonial Occupation: Intersections of Race, Sex, and Gender in *Cloud Nine* and *Cloud Nine* Criticism', *Modern Drama*, Vol. 42, No. 1 (1999), p. 45.

61. James M. Harding, 'Cloud Cover: (Re)Dressing Desire and Comfortable Subversions in Caryl Churchill's *Cloud Nine*', *PMLA*, Vol. 113, No. 2 (1998), pp. 260, 261, 270.

62. Marc Silverstein, '"Make Us the Women We Can't Be:" *Cloud Nine* and The Female Imaginary', *Journal of Dramatic Theory and Criticism*, Vol. 8, No. 2 (1994), p. 19.

63. Susan Bennett, 'Growing Up on *Cloud Nine*: Gender, Sexuality, and Farce', in Sheila Rabillard (ed.), *Essays on Caryl Churchill: Contemporary Representations* (Winnipeg: Blizzard, 1998), pp. 31, 30.

64. Charles Spencer, 'Cross-Dressing "Classic" is Really Just a Drag', *Daily Telegraph*, 29 March 1997.

65. Benedict Nightingale, review of *Cloud Nine*, *The Times*, 2 November 2007; Patrick Marmion, review of *Cloud Nine*, *Daily Mail*, 2 November 2007.

3 Playwrights and Plays: David Hare

1. David Hare, 'Introduction', *Writing Left-Handed* (London: Faber and Faber, 1991), p. xiii.

2. David Hare, 'Introduction', *Plays One* (London: Faber and Faber, 1996), p. viii. Subsequent quotations from the introduction and the play are from this edition.

3. See Terry Browne, *Playwrights' Theatre: The English Stage Company at the Royal Court* (London: Pitman, 1975), p. 127.

4. Peter Ansorge, *Disrupting the Spectacle: Five Years of Experimental and Fringe Theatre in Britain* (London: Pitman, 1975), p. 11; Richard Boon, 'Keeping Turning Up: Hare's Early Career', in Richard Boon (ed.), *The Cambridge Companion to David Hare* (Cambridge: Cambridge University Press, 2007), pp. 37–8.

5. Catherine Itzin and Simon Trussler, 'David Hare: From Portable Theatre to Joint Stock . . . via Shaftesbury Avenue', *Theatre Quarterly*, Vol. 5, No. 20 (1975–6), p. 110.

6. Georg Gaston, 'Interview: David Hare', *Theatre Journal*, Vol. 45, No. 2 (May 1993), p. 216. This interview was conducted in 1990.

7. See also author's interview with Howard Barker in Chapter 4 of this book, in which Barker discusses his 'state of England' plays.

8. *If . . . .*, directed by Lindsay Anderson (Paramount Pictures, 1968).

9. Itzin and Trussler, op. cit., p. 110.

10. Michelene Wandor, *Carry On, Understudies: Theatre and Sexual Politics*, revised edn (London and New York: Routledge & Kegan Paul, 1986 [1981]), p. 155.

11. Itzin and Trussler, op. cit., p. 114.

12. Quoted by William Gaskill, *A Sense of Direction: Life at the Royal Court* (London: Faber and Faber, 1988), p. 136.

13. David Hare, 'Introduction', *Plays Two* (London: Faber and Faber, 1997), p. viii. Subsequent quotations from the introduction and the play are from this edition.

14. David Bradby, Louis James and Bernard Sharratt (eds), *Performance and Politics in Popular Drama: Aspects of Popular Entertainment in Theatre, Film and Television 1800–1976* (Cambridge: Cambridge University Press, 1980), p. 299.

15. See Rob Ritchie (ed.), *The Joint Stock Book: The Making of a Theatre Collective* (London: Methuen, 1987) and Philip Roberts, and Max Stafford-Clark, *Taking Stock: The Theatre of Max Stafford-Clark* (London: Nick Hern, 2007) for illuminating analyses of Joint Stock's work. See also the designer Di Seymour's contribution to Chapter 4 of this book, in which she discusses her work on *Fanshen*.

16. Boon, op. cit., p. 40.

17. See Paul Freeman's comments in Bradby et al., op. cit., p. 301.

18. Cathy Turner, 'Hare in Collaboration: Writing Dialogues', in Boon (ed.), op. cit., p. 116.

19. See Bradby et al., op. cit., pp. 302–3.

20. Gaskill, op. cit., p. 136.

21. Christopher Innes, *Modern British Drama 1890–1990* (Cambridge: Cambridge University Press, 1992), p. 209.

22. Bradby et al., op. cit., p. 304.

23. Ibid., p. 302.

24. Hare, 'The Awkward Squad' [1986], in *Writing Left-Handed*, op. cit., p. 70. *The Mousetrap* is of course the world's longest-running theatre production.

25. Itzin and Trussler, op. cit., p. 112.

26. Gaston, op. cit., p. 214.

27. Jonathan Hammond, 'Messages First: An Interview with Howard Brenton', *Gambit*, Vol. 6, No. 23 (1973), p. 27.

28. David Hare, 'Time of Unease' [1981], in *Writing Left-Handed*, op. cit., p. 63.

29. Ibid.

30. Randall Craig, 'Plays in Performance – Experimental', *Drama: TQTR*, No. 105 (Summer 1972), p. 38.

31. Itzin and Trussler, op. cit., pp. 111, 114.

32. David Hare, 'I Have a Go, Lady, I Have a Go' [2002] in *Obedience, Struggle and Revolt: Lectures on Theatre* (London: Faber and Faber, 2005), p. 43.

33. See Chapter 1 of this book for further discussion about this conference, including Edgar's and McGrath's contributions.

34. David Hare, 'A Lecture', in *Licking Hitler* (London: Faber and Faber, 1978), pp. 57–71; Hare, 'The Play is in the Air – On Political Theatre', in *Writing Left-Handed*, op. cit., pp. 24–36; David Hare, 'On Political Theatre', in *The Early Plays* (London: Faber and Faber, 1992), pp. 1–11; Hare, 'The Play Is in the Air', in *Obedience . . .*, op. cit., pp. 111–26. Subsequent quotations are from the version published in *Obedience, Struggle and Revolt*.

35. Catherine Itzin, *Stages in the Revolution: Political Theatre in Britain Since 1968* (London: Eyre Methuen, 1980), p. 330.

36. Richard Eyre, 'Directing Hare', in Boon (ed.), op. cit., p. 139.

37. Hare, *Plenty*, in *Plays One*, op. cit., p. 380. Subsequent quotations from the play are from this edition.

38. Lib Taylor, 'In opposition: Hare's response to Thatcherism', in Boon (ed.), op. cit., p. 51.

39. The painting can be viewed on the Foreign and Commonwealth Office (FCO) website: http://collections.europarchive.org/tna/20080205132101/fco.gov.uk/files/kfile/distantlands.jpg (accessed 26 July 2011).

40. Steve Nicholson, '"To ask how things might have been otherwise . . .": History and Memory in the Work of David Hare', in Boon (ed.), op. cit., p. 189; John J. Su, 'Nostalgic Rapture: Interpreting Moral Commitments in David Hare's Drama', *Modern Drama*, Vol. 40, No. 1 (Spring 1997), p. 23.

41. Innes, op. cit., pp. 205, 208.

42. Janelle Reinelt, 'Performing histories: *Plenty* and *A Map of the World*', in Boon (ed.), op. cit., pp. 204, 209.

43. Hare quoted in Richard Boon, *About Hare: The Playwright & the Work* (London: Faber and Faber, 2006), p. 92.

44. Innes, op. cit., p. 208.

45. Hare, 'Obedience, Struggle & Revolt' [2004] in *Obedience . . .*, op. cit., p. 12.

46. Duncan Wu, *Making Plays: Interviews with Contemporary British Dramatists and Their Directors* (Basingstoke: Macmillan, 2000), p. 172. This interview was conducted in 1997.

47. David Hare, 'Mere Fact, Mere Fiction', *Guardian Review*, 17 April 2010.

3 Playwrights and Plays: Howard Brenton

1. Jonathan Miles, third-year drama student, University of Hull, November 2010.

2. 'The Plays of Howard Brenton', PhD thesis (University of Sheffield, 1986); *Brenton the Playwright* (London: Methuen Drama, 1991).

3. Quoted in Richard Boon, *About Hare: the Playwright and the Work* (London: Faber and Faber, 2003), p. 224.

4. Les Wade, 'Hare's Trilogy at the National: Private Moralities and the Common Good', in Richard Boon (ed.), *The Cambridge Companion to David Hare* (Cambridge: Cambridge University Press, 2007), pp. 64–5. The quotation by Ravenhill is taken from Peter Buse, 'Mark Ravenhill', British Council, www.contemporarywriters.com, p. 1 (originally accessed 19 April 2006); the one from *Shopping and Fucking* from Mark Ravenhill, *Plays: One* (London: Methuen Drama, 2002), p. 63.

5. *Daily Express*, 18 October 1980; Milton Shulman, letter to the *Guardian*, 12 November 1980. Had Shulman never read *Timon of Athens* or *Oedipus*?

6. For a full account of the *Romans* furore, see Boon, *Brenton the Playwright*, op. cit., pp. 173–80.

7. Hans-Thies Lehmann, *Postdramatic Theatre*, trans Karen Jürs-Munby (London: Routledge, 2006; first published in German in 1999).

8. See Janelle Reinelt, 'The "Rehabilitation" of Howard Brenton', *TDR*, Vol. 51, No. 3 (2007; T195), pp. 167–74.

9. The titles of published plays are placed in italics, those of unpublished plays in inverted commas. A fuller list of Brenton's output in the 1970s is to be found in Boon, *Brenton the Playwright*, op. cit., pp. xi–xv.

10. From an unpublished interview with Malcolm Hay and Philip Roberts, London, 14 January 1978.

11. Quoted in Jonathan Hammond, 'Messages First: An Interview with Howard Brenton', *Gambit*, Vol. 6, No. 23 (1973), p. 31.

12. Quoted in Catherine Itzin and Simon Trussler, 'Petrol Bombs through the Proscenium Arch', *Theatre Quarterly*, Vol. 5, No. 17 (1975), pp. 10–11. The interview itself was given in the previous year.

13. Quoted in Hammond, op. cit.

14. B. A. Young, '*Magnificence*', *Financial Times*, 29 June 1973.

15. *Sunday Telegraph*, 1 July 1973.

16. Howard Brenton, *Magnificence*, in *Plays: One* (London: Methuen Drama, 1986), p. 84. Subsequent quotations from the play are from this edition.

17. Boon, *Brenton the Playwright*, op. cit., pp. 54–5.

18. Quoted in Itzin and Trussler, op. cit., p. 13.

19. Quoted in R. B. Marriott, 'Howard Brenton, a brick-thrower to the Left', *Stage*, 19 July 1973. The paper's editorial on the same day offers wholehearted endorsement of Brenton and what he stood for, suggesting 'brick-throwers' in the theatre always are and will continue to be 'the shapers of the future'.

20. John M. East, 'New Writer's Play at the Royal Court', notice for South London News Group, 13 July 1973; Kenneth Hurren, 'Review of the Arts', *Spectator*, 7 July 1973; J. C. Trewin, 'New Plays', *Lady*, 12 July 1973; Jonathan Marriott, '*Magnificence*', *Plays and Players*, August 1973, pp. 42–3.

21. For a full account of *Magnificence*'s difficult passage at the Royal Court, see Philip Roberts, *The Royal Court Theatre, 1965–1972* (London: Routledge, 1986).

22. The younger cast included such still familiar names as Michael Kitchen, Kenneth Cranham and the late Pete Postlethwaite.

23. Arthur Thirkell, 'Magnificent Bore', *Daily Mirror*, 29 June 1973.

24. Steve Grant, 'Political Drama Poses a Question', *Morning Star*, 30 June 1973. The line quoted from the play is from the Rolling Stones' 'Street Fighting Man'.

25. *Sunday Telegraph*, op. cit.

26. Unsigned, 'Sardonic protest all too strident', *Yorkshire Post*, 2 July 1973.

27. David Gow, 'Brenton's Naïve Politics', *Scotsman*, 2 July 1973.

28. John Elsom, 'Squatters', *Listener*, 5 July 1973.

29. Unsigned, *Amateur Stage*, Vol. 28, No. 8, August 1973.

30. Ibid.; J. C. Trewin, '*Magnificence*', *Birmingham Post*, 30 June 1973 and 'New Plays', *Lady*, 12 July 1973; Felix Barker, '*Magnificence*', *Evening News*, 29 June 1973; John Barber, 'Play with Message Lacks Dramatic Fire', *Daily Telegraph*, 29 June 1973; David Nathan, 'Backwards with the Bomb', *Jewish Chronicle*, 6 July 1973; East, op. cit.; R. B. Marriott, 'Idealism and Violence in *Magnificence*', *Stage*, 5 July 1973.

31. John Russell Taylor, 'British Dramatists: The New Arrivals. The Dark Fantastic', *Plays and Players*, Vol. 18, No. 5, (February 1971), pp. 24–7.

32. Michael Billington, *State of the Nation: British Theatre Since 1945* (London: Faber and Faber, 2007), p. 220.

33. David Hare, 'Time of Unease', in Findlater, Richard (ed.), *At the Royal Court: 25 Years of the English Stage Company* (Ambergate: Amber Lane Press, 1981), p. 141.

34. See Boon, *Brenton the Playwright*, op. cit., pp. 81–2.

35. Quoted in Itzin and Trussler, op. cit., p. 8.

36. Ibid.

37. Marriott, 'Howard Brenton, a Brick-thrower to the Left', op. cit.

38. Ibid.

39. See Richard Boon, 'Keeping Turning Up: Hare's Early Career', in Boon (ed.), *Cambridge Companion*, op. cit., pp. 31–48.

40. Brenton means the late Minnie Riperton, whose 1975 single 'Lovin' You' reached number two in the UK charts. Sung at a characteristically very high pitch, and with birdsong included, the very particular dynamic the song lends the scene is best judged by listening to it. It is easily accessible on the internet.

41. Howard Brenton, *Weapons of Happiness* in *Plays: One*, op. cit., pp. 229–30.

42. See James Aubrey's letter to Philip Roberts in Chapter 4 of this book.

43. Quoted in Catherine Itzin, *Stages in the Revolution: Political Theatre in Britain Since 1968* (London: Eyre Methuen, 1980), p. 192.

44. Charles Marowitz, '*Weapons of Happiness*' in *Plays and Players*, Vol. 23, No. 2 (September 1976), pp. 18–9.

45. Itzin, op. cit., p. 196.

46. See Boon, *Brenton the Playwright*, op. cit., p. 210.

3 Playwrights and Plays: David Edgar

1. Dominic Sandbrook, *State of Emergency: The Way We Were: Britain, 1970–1974* (London: Allen Lane, 2010), p. 10; Beckett, Andy, *When the Lights Went Out: What Really Happened to Britain in the Seventies* (London: Faber and Faber, 2010), p. 209.

2. See Chris Megson's interview with David Edgar in Chapter 4 of this book. The Searchers were a 1960s group from Liverpool, coming to prominence about the same time as the Beatles, and perhaps best known for their version of 'Needles and Pins'. *Dad's Army* was a British TV sitcom about the Home Guard during the Second World War.

3. David Edgar, 'Public Theatre in a Private Age', in *The Second Time as Farce* (London: Lawrence & Wishart, 1988), p. 161.

4. Megson, op. cit.

5. Michael Oakeshott, *Rationalism in Politics and Other Essays* (London: Basic Books, 1962), p. 112.

6. David Edgar, *Wreckers* (London: Methuen, 1977), p. 23. Subsequent quotations from the play are from this edition.

7. Portions of the descriptions of *Destiny, Mary Barnes* and *The Jail Diary of Albie Sachs* have been adapted from Janelle Reinelt, and Gerald Hewitt, *The Political Theatre of David Edgar: Negotiation and Retrieval* (Cambridge: Cambridge University Press, 2011). See Chapters 4 and 5 of this book for more detailed analyses of the plays.

8. Tony Judt, *Postwar: A History of Europe Since 1945* (Harmondsworth: Penguin, 2006), p. 336.

9. Ibid.

10. Beckett, op. cit., p. 445.

11. Quoted in ibid., p. 446.

12. David Edgar, *Destiny* (London: Methuen Drama, 2005), p. x. Subsequent quotations from the introduction and the play are from this edition.

13. Quoted in Beckett, op. cit., p. 448.

14. David Edgar, 'The National Front *is* a Nazi Front', *Socialist Challenge*, 21 July 1977, pp. 113–14.

15. Susan Painter, *Edgar the Playwright* (London: Methuen, 1996), p. 35.

16. David Edgar, *The Jail Diary of Albie Sachs*, in *Plays: One* (London: Methuen Drama, 1994), p. 85. Subsequent quotations from the play are from this edition.

17. See Chris Megson's interview with Peter McEnery in Chapter 4 of this book.

18. Ibid.

19. Ibid.

20. Albie Sachs, *Running to Maputo* (New York: HarperCollins, 1990), p. 198.

21. The exhibition took place at Space Gallery, November 2010. Paul Pieroni curated a collection of Mary Barnes's art works including paintings, sketches and some photographs and videotapes. To see some of her art and other information about her life, visit http://mary-barnes.net/ (accessed 11 July 2011).

22. R. D. Laing, *The Politics of Experience* (New York: Ballantine, 1967), p. 58.

23. Kingsley Hall was the first of a number of 'community households' where similar therapies were practised. Laing founded the Philadelphia Association in 1965 as the umbrella organisation. It still exists and does some similar work. See www.philadelphia-association.co.uk/ (accessed 10 July 2011).

24. Simon Callow, *Being an Actor* (Harmondsworth: Penguin, 1985), pp. 90–1.

25. David Edgar, *Mary Barnes*, in *Plays: One*, op. cit., p. 114. Subsequent quotations from the play are from this edition.

26. See Ann Mitchell's contribution to Chapter 4 of this book.

27. David Edgar, 'The King James Bible Reconsidered', *Guardian*, 19 February 2011.

4 Documents

1. In respect of playwrights, this chapter includes new interviews with Howard Brenton and David Edgar conducted by the author, as well as an hitherto unpublished interview with Howard Barker that focuses on his important plays of the period. For first-hand reflections from Caryl Churchill (who has not given an interview since 1997) and David Hare on their work, readers are referred to the wide range of existing publications in the Select Bibliography. Hare, in particular, has published two stimulating collections of theatre-related articles and lectures, *Writing Left-Handed* (1991) and *Obedience, Struggle and Revolt* (2005).

2. Howard Barker, 'Energy – and the Small Discovery of Dignity', interviewed by Malcolm Hay and Simon Trussler, *Theatre Quarterly*, Vol. 10, No. 40 (Autumn–Winter, 1981), pp. 3–15.

3. Heinrich Kramer and James Sprenger are the authors of *Malleus Maleficarum* (*The Hammer of Witches*), a treatise on witches written in 1486, which was a key source for Churchill. They appear in the final scene of *Vinegar Tom*, played by women.

4. Caryl Churchill, *Vinegar Tom*, in *Plays: One* (London: Methuen Drama, 1985), p. 135. This is the opening line of the play.

5. Jean-Paul Sartre, *Existentialism and Humanism* (London: Methuen, 2007).

6. Raoul Vaneigem, *The Totality for Kids*, trans. Chris Gray and Philippe Vissac (London: Situationist International, 1966 [1962–3]).

7. See Bertolt Brecht, 'Der Messingkauf: An Editorial Note', in *Brecht on Theatre*, ed. and trans. John Willett (London: Methuen, 1964), p. 174.

8. At the time of the interview, Ibsen's *Emperor and Galilean*, directed by Jonathan Kent, was in production on the Olivier stage of the National Theatre.

9. This revival opened in February 2008, directed by Nathan Curry.

10. At the time of the interview, the enforced 'bail-out' of Greece by the International Monetary Fund (IMF) prompted huge protests in the country.

11. Dominic Sandbrook, *State of Emergency: The Way We Were: Britain 1970–74* (London: Allen Lane, 2010).

12. Reginald Maudling was a Conservative politician and, in 1972, Home Secretary when he was forced to resign after becoming ensnared in the Poulson scandal.

13. There was a controversial tour of Britain and Ireland by South Africa's rugby team, the Springboks, in 1969–70. It became a focus for anti-apartheid protests.

14. Robert Carr was Secretary of State for Employment in the Heath government. The Angry Brigade's attack on his house took place on 12 January 1971.

15. Andy Beckett, *When the Lights Went Out: What Really Happened to Britain in the Seventies* (London: Faber and Faber, 2009).

16. *Queer as Folk*, written by Russell T. Davies, was a TV drama series for Channel 4 about the lives of three gay men in Manchester's gay village; broadcast in 1999, it caused a furore for its explicit treatment of sex. The Cameron 'A-list' was drawn up in 2006 by the then Leader of the Opposition, David Cameron, in an attempt to make the

Conservative Party more electable: it was a list of priority candidates for the forth-coming general election and included many women.

17. Dominic Sandbrook, Dominic, *White Heat: A History of Britain in the Swinging Sixties* (London: Abacus, 2006); Richard Neville, *Play Power* (London: Cape, 1970); Sandbrook, *State of Emergency*, op. cit.

18. David Edgar, *Mary Barnes*, in *Plays: One* (London: Methuen Drama, 1987), p. 130.

19. Howard Brenton, *The Churchill Play*, in *Plays: One* (London: Methuen Drama, 1986), p. 149.

20. The play was performed at Duke's Theatre, Lancaster, in May 1981.

21. Kingsley Hall, in east London, is where R. D. Laing established an experimental residential community in 1965 to develop a more emancipatory model of treatment for psychosis and schizophrenia. Joseph Berke was a resident psychiatrist and Mary Barnes one of the residents.

22. Arbours is a crisis centre for psychotherapeutic care in London, co-founded by Joseph Berke in 1973.

23. Howard Barker's *Cheek*, directed by Bill Gaskill, was first performed at the Royal Court Theatre Upstairs in September 1970.

24. This is Edward Bond's *Passion – A Play for CND* performed by the Royal Court Theatre at the Alexandra Park Racecourse, for the CND Festival of Life, on Easter Sunday, 11 April 1971. The performance, directed by Bill Bryden, also featured Penelope Wilton as the Queen and Nigel Hawthorne as the Prime Minister. See Edward Bond, *Plays: Two* (London: Eyre Methuen, 1978), pp. 237–53.

25. Colin Chambers, *Other Spaces: New Theatre and the RSC* (London: Eyre Methuen, 1980), p. 13.

26. Ibid., pp. 45–6.

27. Brenton is likely referring to *Deeds*, co-written with Ken Campbell, David Hare and Trevor Griffiths for the Nottingham Playhouse (1978).

SELECT BIBLIOGRAPHY

1. Books on the 1970s

Beckett, Andy, *When the Lights Went Out: What Really Happened to Britain in the Seventies* (London: Faber and Faber, 2009). A witty and detailed account of the decade focused on the British political scene: a good place to start research.

DeGroot, Gerard, *The Seventies Unplugged: A Kaleidoscopic Look at a Violent Decade* (London: Macmillan, 2010). International in scope, DeGroot examines a series of seminal events in the decade with an overarching theme of violence.

Ferguson, Niall, Charles S. Maier, Erez Manela and Daniel J. Sargent (eds), *The Shock of the Global: The 1970s in Perspective* (Cambridge, MA: Belknap Press, 2010). A rigorous and scholarly book for the more specialist reader that sets out international and global perspectives.

Sandbrook, Dominic, *Mad as Hell: The Crisis of the 1970s and the Rise of the Populist Right* (New York: Knopf, 2011). Focuses on the emergence of right-wing groups and ideologies in the US during the 1970s.

——, *State of Emergency: The Way We Were: Britain 1970–74* (London: Allen Lane, 2010). A forensic and provocative look at the tumultuous Heath government.

Sounes, Howard, *Seventies: The Sights, Sounds, Ideas of a Brilliant Decade* (London: Pocket Books, 2007). From film to comedy, art to architecture, Sounes is passionate, personal and persuasive in his assessment of 1970s culture.

Turner, Alwyn W., *Crisis? What Crisis? Britain in the 1970s* (London: Aurum Press, 2008). Highly recommended: one of the first, and arguably the best, of the spate of recent books about the British 1970s. Detailed and thought-provoking.

Wheen, Francis, *Strange Days Indeed: The Golden Age of Paranoia* (London: Fourth Estate, 2009). Characteristically entertaining and humorous, Wheen recollects the 1970s as an era of deep and often absurd paranoia.

2. Key books on British theatre in the 1970s

The following books, most of them written during or in the immediate aftermath of the 1970s, focus in detail on British theatre of that decade and are very useful sources of first-hand information.

Ansorge, Peter, *Disrupting the Spectacle: Five Years of Experimental and Fringe Theatre in Britain* (London: Pitman, 1975).

Browne, Terry W., *Playwrights' Theatre: The English Stage Company at the Royal Court Theatre* (London: Pitman, 1975).

Bull, John, *New British Political Dramatists* (London: Macmillan, 1984).

Chambers, Colin, *Other Spaces: New Theatre and the RSC* (London: Eyre Methuen, 1980).

Cornish, Roger, and Violet Ketels (eds), *Landmarks of Modern British Drama: The Plays of the Seventies* (London: Methuen, 1986).

Craig, Sandy (ed.), *Dreams and Deconstructions: Alternative Theatre in Britain* (Ambergate: Amber Lane Press, 1980).

DiCenzo, Maria, *The Politics of Alternative Theatre in Britain, 1968–1990: The Case of 7:84 (Scotland)* (Cambridge: Cambridge University Press, 1996).

Itzin, Catherine, *Stages in the Revolution: Political Theatre in Britain Since 1968* (London: Eyre Methuen, 1980).

Lambert, J. W., *Drama in Britain: 1964–1973* (Essex: Longman, 1974).

Rees, Roland, *Fringe First: Pioneers of Fringe Theatre on Record* (London: Oberon, 1992).

Schiele, Jinnie, *Off-Centre Stages: Fringe Theatre at the Open Space and the Round House, 1968–1983* (Hatfield: Hertfordshire University Press, 2005).

Trussler, Simon (ed.), *New Theatre Voices of the Seventies: Sixteen Interviews from Theatre Quarterly 1970–1980* (London: Eyre Methuen, 1981).

Wandor, Michelene, *Carry On, Understudies: Theatre and Sexual Politics*, revised edn (London and New York: Routledge & Kegan Paul, 1986 [1981]).

3. Recommended books on post-war British theatre

The following books offer broader coverage but include insightful material pertaining to 1970s theatre.

Acheson, James (ed.), *British and Irish Drama Since 1960* (Basingstoke: Macmillan, 1993).

Aston, Elaine, and Janelle Reinelt (eds), *The Cambridge Companion to Modern British Women Playwrights* (Cambridge: Cambridge University Press, 2000).

Barker, Howard, *Arguments for a Theatre*, 3rd edn (Manchester and New York: Manchester University Press, 1997 [1989]).

——, *Howard Barker Interviews 1980–2010: Conversations in Catastrophe*, ed. Mark Brown (London: Oberon, 2011).

Berkoff, Steven, *Free Association: An Autobiography* (London: Faber and Faber, 1996).

Betsko, Kathleen and Rachel Koenig (eds), *Interviews with Contemporary Women Playwrights* (New York: Beech Tree Books, 1987).

Bigsby, Christopher W. E. (ed.), *Contemporary English Drama* (London: Edward Arnold, 1981).

Billington, Michael, *State of the Nation: British Theatre Since 1945* (London: Faber and Faber, 2007).

Bradby, David, Louis James and Bernard Sharratt (eds), *Performance and Politics in Popular*

Drama: Aspects of Popular Entertainment in Theatre, Film and Television 1800–1976 (Cambridge: Cambridge University Press, 1980).

Callow, Simon, *Being an Actor* (Harmondsworth: Penguin, 1985).

Cave, Richard Allen, *New British Drama in Performance on the London Stage, 1970 to 1985* (Gerrards Cross: Colin Smythe, 1987).

Chambers, Colin, *Black and Asian Theatre in Britain: A History* (London: Routledge, 2011).

—— and Mike Prior, *Playwrights' Progress: Patterns of Postwar British Drama* (Oxford: Amber Lane Press, 1987).

Coveney, Michael, *Ken Campbell: The Great Caper* (London: Nick Hern, 2011).

Davies, Andrew, *Other Theatres: The Development of Alternative and Experimental Theatre in Britain* (London: Macmillan, 1987).

Devine, Harriet (ed.), *Looking Back: Playwrights at the Royal Court 1956–2006* (London: Faber and Faber, 2006).

Doty, Gresdna A. and Billy J. Harbin (eds), *Inside the Royal Court Theatre 1956–1981: Artists Talk* (Baton Rouge and London: Louisiana State University Press, 1990).

Eyre, Richard, *Talking Theatre: Interviews with Theatre People* (London: Nick Hern, 2009).

——, *Utopia and Other Places: Memoir of a Young Director* (London: Bloomsbury, 1993).

—— and Nicholas Wright, *Changing Stages: A View of British Theatre in the Twentieth Century* (London: Bloomsbury, 2000).

Findlater, Richard (ed.), *At the Royal Court: 25 Years of the English Stage Company* (Ambergate: Amber Lane Press, 1981).

Gaskill, William, *A Sense of Direction: Life at the Royal Court* (London: Faber and Faber, 1988).

Griffiths, Trevor R. and Margaret Llewellyn-Jones (eds), *British and Irish Women Dramatists Since 1958 – A Critical Handbook* (Buckingham: Open University Press, 1993).

Hall, Peter, *Peter Hall's Diaries: The Story of a Dramatic Battle*, ed. John Goodwin (London: Oberon, 2000).

Hanna, Gillian (ed.), *Monstrous Regiment: A Collective Celebration* (London: Nick Hern, 1991).

Holderness, Graham (ed.), *The Politics of Theatre and Drama* (Basingstoke: Macmillan, 1992).

Hunt, Albert, *Hopes for Great Happenings: Alternatives in Education and Theatre* (London: Eyre Methuen, 1976).

Innes, Christopher, *Modern British Drama 1890–1990* (Cambridge: Cambridge University Press, 1992).

Kershaw, Baz, *The Politics of Performance: Radical Theatre as Cultural Intervention* (London: Routledge, 1992).

Kustow, Michael, *theatre@risk* (London: Methuen Drama, 2000).

McGrath, John, *A Good Night Out – Popular Theatre: Audience, Class and Form* (London: Methuen, 1981).

———, *Naked Thoughts That Roam About: Reflections on Theatre*, ed. Nadine Holdsworth (London: Nick Hern, 2002).

Patterson, Michael, *Strategies of Political Theatre: Post-War British Playwrights* (Cambridge: Cambridge University Press, 2003).

Peacock, Keith D., *Radical Stages: Alternative History in Modern British Drama* (London: Greenwood Press, 1991).

Rabey, David Ian, *British and Irish Political Drama in the Twentieth Century: Implicating the Audience* (Basingstoke: Macmillan, 1986).

———, *English Drama Since 1940* (London: Longman, 2003).

Reinelt, Janelle, *After Brecht: British Epic Theater* (Ann Arbor: Michigan University Press, 1994).

Ritchie, Rob (ed.), *The Joint Stock Book: The Making of a Theatre Collective* (London: Methuen, 1987).

Roberts, Philip, *The Royal Court Theatre and the Modern Stage* (Cambridge: Cambridge University Press, 1999).

——— and Max Stafford-Clark, *Taking Stock: The Theatre of Max Stafford-Clark* (London: Nick Hern, 2007).

Shellard, Dominic, *British Theatre Since the War* (New Haven, CT and London: Yale University Press, 1999).

Shepherd, Simon, *The Cambridge Introduction to Modern British Theatre* (Cambridge: Cambridge University Press, 2009).

Sinfield, Alan, *Out on Stage: Lesbian and Gay Theatre in the Twentieth Century* (New Haven, CT and London: Yale University Press, 1999).

Taylor, John Russell, *The Second Wave: British Drama of the Sixties* (London: Eyre Methuen, 1971).

Wandor, Michelene, *Post-War British Drama: Looking Back in Gender* (London: Routledge, 2001).

Wu, Duncan, *Making Plays: Interviews with Contemporary British Dramatists and Their Directors* (Basingstoke: Macmillan, 2000).

———, *Six Contemporary Dramatists – Bennett, Potter, Gray, Brenton, Hare, Ayckbourn* (London: St Martin's, 1995).

4. The playwrights

For each of the four playwrights included in this volume, a key critical book is recommended along with selected further reading. The editions of plays are those cited in Chapter 3. Further published resources on the playwrights are cited in the notes for Chapter 3.

Caryl Churchill

Plays

Churchill, Caryl, *Plays: One* [includes *Owners*, *Vinegar Tom* and *Cloud Nine*] (London: Methuen Drama, 1985).

Key book

Aston, Elaine and Elin Diamond (eds), *The Cambridge Companion to Caryl Churchill* (Cambridge: Cambridge University Press, 2009).

Recommended books

Adiseshiah, Siân, *Churchill's Socialism: Political Resistance in the Plays of Caryl Churchill* (Newcastle upon Tyne: Cambridge Scholars, 2009).

Aston, Elaine, *Caryl Churchill*, 2nd edn (Plymouth: Northcote House, 2001 [1997]).

Cousin, Geraldine, *Churchill the Playwright* (London: Methuen, 1989).

Fitzsimmons, Linda (ed.), *File on Churchill* (London: Methuen, 1989).

Kritzer, Amelia Howe, *The Plays of Caryl Churchill: Theatre of Empowerment* (Basingstoke: Macmillan, 1991).

Rabillard, Sheila (ed.), *Essays on Caryl Churchill: Contemporary Representations* (Winnipeg: Blizzard, 1998).

Randall, Phyllis R. (ed.), *Caryl Churchill: A Casebook* (London and New York: Garland, 1988).

Roberts, Philip, *About Churchill: the Playwright and the Work* (London: Faber and Faber, 2008).

David Hare

Plays

Hare, David, *Plays One* [includes *Slag* and *Plenty*] (London: Faber and Faber, 1996).

——, *Plays Two* [includes *Fanshen*] (London: Faber and Faber, 1997).

Key book

Boon, Richard (ed.), *The Cambridge Companion to David Hare* (Cambridge: Cambridge University Press, 2007).

Recommended books

Boon, Richard, *About Hare: the Playwright and the Work* (London: Faber and Faber, 2006).

Hare, David, *Acting Up: A Diary*, London: Faber and Faber, 1999).

——, *Asking Around: Background to the David Hare Trilogy* (London: Faber and Faber, 1993).

——, *Obedience, Struggle and Revolt: Lectures on Theatre* (London: Faber and Faber, 2005).

——, *Writing Left-Handed* (London: Faber and Faber, 1991).

Homden, Carol, *The Plays of David Hare* (Cambridge: Cambridge University Press, 1995).

Howard Brenton

Plays

Brenton, Howard, *Plays: One* [includes *Magnificence, The Churchill Play* and *Weapons of Happiness*] (London: Methuen Drama, 1986).

Key book

Boon, Richard, *Brenton the Playwright* (London: Methuen Drama, 1991).

Recommended books

Brenton, Howard, *Hot Irons: Diaries, Essays, Journalism* (London: Methuen, 1995).
Mitchell, Tony (ed.), *File on Brenton* (London: Methuen, 1979).

David Edgar

Plays

Edgar, David, *Destiny* (London: Methuen Drama, 2005).
——, *Plays: One* [includes *Destiny, The Jail Diary of Albie Sachs* and *Mary Barnes*] (London: Methuen Drama, 1994).

Key book

Reinelt, Janelle and Gerald Hewitt, *The Political Theatre of David Edgar: Negotiation and Retrieval* (Cambridge: Cambridge University Press, 2011).

Recommended books

Edgar, David, *How Plays Work: A Practical Guide to Playwriting* (London: Nick Hern, 2009).
——, *The Second Time as Farce: Reflections on the Drama of Mean Times* (London: Lawrence & Wishart, 1988).
—— (ed.), *State of Play – Issue 1: Playwrights on Playwriting* (London: Faber and Faber, 1999).
Painter, Susan, *Edgar the Playwright* (London: Methuen, 1996).
Swain, Elizabeth, *David Edgar – Playwright and Politician* (New York: Peter Lang, 1986).

5. Web resources

TheatreVOICE: www.theatrevoice.com/
A terrific resource for audio content relating to British theatre, featuring interviews with playwrights and other practitioners, round-table discussions and reviews of productions. The site was established in 2003 by founding editor Dominic Cavendish and is now managed

by the Department of Theatre and Performance at the V&A and Rose Bruford College.

Unfinished Histories: www.unfinishedhistories.com/
A pioneering and unique archive on British alternative theatre from 1968 to 1988, established by Susan Croft and Jessica Higgs. It includes photographic material and interviews with a number of key theatre people featured in this book.

What's Welsh for Performance?: www.performance-wales.org/
A useful archival resource on performance art and alternative theatre in Wales from 1965 to 1979, led by Heike Roms of Aberystwyth University.

INDEX

Note: Play titles are entered in the index under authors' names, if known. Page references in **bold type** denote main references to topics.

Index

NOTES ON CONTRIBUTORS

Richard Boon is Professor of Drama at the University of Hull, UK. He is author of *Brenton the Playwright* (Methuen Drama, 1992) and *About Hare* and editor of *The Cambridge Companion to David Hare*.

Paola Botham lectures in Drama and Performance at the University of Worcester, UK. She has published on political theatre in the anthology *Political Performances: Theory and Practice* and in *Contemporary Theatre Review*, as well as on modernity, identity and 1950s drama in the Chilean journal *Cátedra de Artes*.

Janelle Reinelt is Professor of Theatre and Performance at the University of Warwick, UK, and was President of the International Federation for Theatre Research (2004–7). She was awarded the Distinguished Scholar Award for lifetime achievement from the American Society for Theatre Research (2010). Her most recent book is *The Political Theatre of David Edgar: Negotiation and Retrieval* (with Gerald Hewitt, 2011).